GRASSROOTS UFOs

GRASSROOTS UFOs

Case Reports from the Center for UFO Studies

Written and Illustrated by
Michael D. Swords

From Original Interviews Conducted by
John P. Timmerman

Anomalist Books
San Antonio * New York

Grassroots UFOs

ISBN: 193366553X

This book was originally produced by The Fund for UFO Research in cooperation with the J. Allen Hynek Center for UFO Studies, with assistance from Kathryn Diehl and Sharon Stayonovich.

Cover image: Ansen Seale

Book Design: Martin Timmerman

AnomalistBooks.com

Anomalist Books
5150 Broadway #108
San Antonio, TX 78209

Contents

This book is dedicated to the memory of J. Allen Hynek, Founder of the Center for UFO Studies, who, through years of research, and investigation, brought more focus and understanding to the science of Ufology.

Preface
Grass Roots UFOs

J. Allen Hynek and John P. Timmerman at the Center for UFO Studies in Chicago, Illinois. Early 1980s.

If you are curious and challenged by the UFO Phenomenon, welcome to this book. If you have ever spoken with or listened to a witness describe what might be regarded by some as an "Unexpected Farfetched Occurrence," you would have noticed in their voice the emotions often detected in others during my travels with the CUFOS UFO Photo Exhibit project from 1980 until 1992.

Why this project? It was born at about 2:20 p.m., Wednesday, April 9, 1980. When the phone rang in the office of the J. Allen Hynek Center for UFO Studies in Evanston, Illinois, it was from Dallas, Texas, and Estelle Postol, Dr. Hynek's secretary, told me that it was a call for "help."

The caller was Ms. Geri Lowry, marketing director of Prestonwood Town Center, at that time the largest mall in the Dallas area. She was very excited. She explained that they were opening a new five-screen cinema and were having the premier showing of *The Empire Strikes Back -- Star Wars II*. They had rented Dick Hobson's UFO display for the occasion for five days in May. But, due to errors in the engagement contracts, he had to cancel.

Why call us? She had contacted John Williams of the St. Marks Observatory in Dallas, and he had suggested that they contact Dr. Hynek, offering to set up anything we would provide. When she told me how much they had agreed to pay Dick Hobson, we told her "for that price, we guarantee to be at your Mall on time and will present a UFO exhibit."

Our Board of Directors immediately agreed and Dr. Hynek said anything he had, such as photography, letters, charts, and drawings about UFOs, would be made available. While assembling the material and purchasing a display system, we saw possibilities for high public visibility and an exhibit to put on the road. We made it happen on time, and the exhibit was in place for the estimated 50,000 people going through that center daily in Dallas.

How did we get from Dallas to this book? It was a fascinating journey and it involved four improvements and enlargements of the original exhibit.

With the talent and help of our graphic artist son, Martin, it became two identical exhibits that appeared on display in 92 malls, schools, universities, banks, and even in an automobile agency in South Dakota over the next twelve years. Those interesting engagements ranged from Halifax, Nova Scotia, to the Island of Guam in the South Pacific and from Orillia, Ontario, to San Juan, Puerto Rico. It became a series of experiences this writer would never forget and would finally inspire this book.

In Dallas while presenting the exhibit, conversations developed with people who were willing to describe their unexplainable experiences. Written notes, names, and addresses began to pile up. A tape recorder and cassettes were used on the second engagement, which was in Grand Island, Nebraska, and always thereafter a recorder was at hand. It was thus that this amazing mass of unexplained experiences quickly began to accumulate. By the time for the final engagement at Sterling, Illinois, in 1992, the taped interviews had grown to nearly 1,200.

In San Juan, a radio interview in English and Spanish and many reports were taped. In Puerto Rico, many UFO experiences had been reported to local sighting investigators. The mall was immense and a very large crowd attended the exhibit. A government official of the Dominican Republic traveled to San Juan to see the exhibit and discuss the subject. He was very positive about the reality of UFOs.

The exhibit won repeat engagements in following years at several locations. In the Southcenter Shopping Center in Seattle, the Mall Director said that over 250,000 people passed through the mall during each week the exhibit was there. Some contracts were for a full week and some for only two days. The mall in Guam was not large, but paid over $6,000 in expenses and a fee to have the exhibit flown there by way of Tokyo for a three-day display. Engagements surged during the late 1980s.

The exhibit marketed many of the best publications. The panels displayed many of the most interesting images of objects to examine and books on the tables to buy. We later added a panel representing the positions of skeptics for those still undecided to consider and a panel on astronomy for those unfamiliar with the immensity of the Universe and the distance of nearby stars.

The next job in creating this book was to transcribe the audio recordings of witness testimony to the typewritten pages that began to accumulate in three-ring binders on shelves at my home. This required time and patience I did not possess as the project gained speed. I was at that time employed as a vice-president at a Savings and Loan in Lima, Ohio, taking time off and with a family at home needing my attention. But, then we got lucky.

A good friend in Lima, Kathryn Diehl, who shared my deep interest in the UFO subject, in addition to how to teach reading in schools, learned of my need and offered to do the transcribing for me. She believed that having a chance to hear the voices of the witnesses interviewed would be exciting and we believed having the tapes transcribed reinforced the sense of honesty that seems to be very obvious in so many of the narratives. If copies of these recordings become available for purchase, they may become convincing testimony to modify the thinking of our skeptical friends. All other participants in this endeavor are greatly indebted to Kathryn for her many years of listening and typing for this project and for an equal number of other interviews still unrevealed in the Timmerman UFO Files.

Another member of the team was my volunteer secretary, Sharon Stayonovich. She had become a highly experienced secretary serving for many years in the offices of the City of Lima. It was my good luck to learn that she, too, was deeply interested in this subject and would be willing to handle my correspondence by mail, tape or telephone and type letters I composed in my distant motel rooms after my note-taking from witnesses. I am very grateful to Sharon for many years of loyal help in maintaining this witness contact and in typing this book for Dr. Swords and for its graphic designer, Martin Timmerman.

Michael D. Swords is author of this book. I am certain that his knowledge of and dedication to this subject, together with his wit, energy, artistic talents, and personal UFO sighting years ago, motivated his willingness and commitment to author this publication. He had just recently retired from teaching the history of science to thousands of students for many years at Western Michigan University. His recent retirement provided the time to undertake this project. He will describe his experience while examining, evaluating, categorizing, and condensing the extensive transcriptions he has prepared for you in the pages ahead. As author of this book, Mike deserves all of the credit for creating a fascinating story from this mass of raw witness testimony he has named *Grass Roots UFOs*.

Finally, my luck was to remain deeply curious and to meet and talk with tens of thousands of people, not all of whom agreed with me about what I was doing. I was not surprised, but was amused by the variety of reactions encountered. Many only glanced at me standing with the 40-foot series of plastic glass panels down the center of the mall corridors. Some would smile from a distance at the panels with UFO photos, sketches, and wording, then turn to their companion and, with a big grin on their faces, glance at me as if I were, well, you know what I thought. Having become accustomed to it over the years since my first public UFO interest in Lima in the early 1950s, I still had that urge to walk over and engage them in a spirited discussion.

Waiting for them at the panels, however, worked very well. First, I would hand them our brochure and remark "This will explain who we are and what we are doing." If they accepted it and smiled, my next line would be: "Have you or anyone you know ever seen what you believe was an unidentifiable object?" If they glanced around and started to smile, I would ask "when did it happen and where were you?" Then, they often would reply "well, yes, I did" and begin sharing their experience with me.

If, after a short chat, I became aware of a possibly valuable report, I would invite them to accompany me to a prearranged private location nearby. This more secluded location, without a stranger eavesdropping, always produced a more complete set of details for the experience they related.

When they didn't have time for a secluded interview, notes would be made of the event, including names, addresses, and phone numbers. But, the mailed responses did not always arrive and were not as complete, even with the form for reporting. Actually, some forms and envelopes were discarded into a trash barrel when they thought they were out of my sight. How many good cases thus disappeared and were lost forever? We will never know. Was yours one of them? Will you now share it with us for confidential evaluation?

This suggests a request for your assistance. There is a slight possibility that one of the events described in this book may have happened to you or to someone you know. If so, please bring this book to their attention. Also, you will note, as you read through Mike's excellent summaries of these reports, that I (John) failed to ask an important question or the tape recorder stalled, or I ran out of tape and other pertinent information may have been omitted. If YOU happen to be the one I was speaking with at that moment or if YOU did not speak with me while at the exhibit, I would very much appreciate receiving your assistance. By correcting, completing, or adding your experience to our resources for study by comparison with cases now on file, yours may become the additional witness needed to verify or explain another report.

The mailing address is: CUFOS, P.O. Box 31335, Chicago , IL 60631, and thank you very much.

But the people who fascinated me most were those who were concerned about my mentality. There were more than a few who said I was "doing Satan's work" or that I was a demoniac. Once, I approached a man, who was in a formal business suit, staring at a panel. He turned to me and remarked, "You people will believe anything." Before I could engage him in conversation, he turned and walked away. Years later, at a mall at Ft. Saskatchewan, Alberta, Canada, a pastor of a church many miles south of the city drove up to meet me and to determine if I could be helped to understand that UFOs were evidences of God's presence among us, referring to many Biblical accounts. In a mall in Amherst, Nova Scotia, a mother and young son came by one morning to examine the exhibit. She returned later to stand there with me in the mall reading religious poetry in an effort to save my soul. I was gracious, listened, and thanked her very much for her kindness. What else could I do? Also, what does this say about why most world governments remain silent about UFOs?

On a few of my journeys, my Swiss-born wife, Margaretha, traveled with me and helped with the distribution of brochures. Besides the San Juan trip, she was with me on ten other exhibit engagements, including the eastern Canada trip, Guam, Houston, and Phoenix. She was a great help to me and was an excellent traveling companion. Yes, we have been in Switzerland many times. I recall a chat with the husband of a close friend there who told me that he had asked his superior Swiss military officer what he knew about the UFO phenomenon. The officer replied, "we don't talk about that." Are you surprised about the silence and denial from our own government? But, that's another long story that others have explored in great detail.

The CUFOS UFO Photo Exhibit Project neared its end when one of our exhibits was purchased by the International UFO Museum in Roswell, New Mexico, where it became a part of their display. That coincided with the trend away from the kind of event we represented to a different marketing strategy by malls. The requests for our engagements had begun to diminish, so the search began for a buyer for the second exhibit. An opportunity came with a call from the town of St. Paul, Alberta, in western Canada, to rent the second exhibit for a month as an attraction to tourists traveling in the region. We discussed their needs and ours and concluded that they should purchase the exhibit as a permanent display to attract travelers to their town. They did so two months later and constructed a small UFO exhibition building in which to have it on permanent display. Visit it in St. Paul, Alberta. You will be amazed at what you learn by examining it carefully.

Our main purpose in creating this book has been to capture some firsthand testimony for the ages, if not the hard evidence Carl Sagan once told me was needed for useful scientific analysis. I call it "the raw material of ufology." These may not be the types of completely accurate narrative, multiple-witness cases with photographic and or physical evidence demanded for high scientific credibility. But, they have for me the lingering taste of truth that has kept me curious for my many years of live testimony from firsthand witnesses to the yet unknown source of it all. The following is still my position statement after more than 57 years of curiosity.

> The UFO Phenomenon is still far more complex than originally thought to be by most researchers. The proper study of the subject will require consideration of the complex nature of human mental processes as well as a better understanding of the physical nature of our planet and of the universe using our best scientists and technologies. Anecdotal information will remain our major public source for study until a way is found to share the realities now held secretly by most of the governments in the world regarding the UFO Phenomenon.

Again, I want to state my deep appreciation to Michael Swords. He has devoted a year of his life to that mass of raw material I gave him, condensing it here for you to read in this book. But, in reading it, we must remember that this is only one small wave in an ocean of information that may never in our lifetimes be condensed into such a readable and understandable presentation as you have before you in this book of micro-ufology.

At this writing, CUFOS has more than 140,000 reports on file, and there must be tens of thousands of other reports in most languages throughout the world that you and I will never examine. The immensity of this old and ongoing phenomenon may never be fully known because of the reluctance of most witnesses to tell of their experiences.

I am not a scientist, though I wish I had been. I have never seen what I thought might have been a UFO, though I hope that someday I will. I can only guess what the experiences described in this book may be proven to represent. They appear to me to have been happening before and during my lifetime and yours and I believe that they may continue to occur during many if not all generations to come while humanity exists on Earth. We need the serious attention by scientists of the world to the valid testimony and visual evidence of unidentified objects apparently studying our planet.

I relish the fact that modern science can imagine a universe in which other life forms may have discovered how to arrive at a location near where I am writing these words. In fact, I have recorded conversations with two very credible women able to describe their amazing experience in 1958 about eight miles from where I happened to be on the evening that it occurred. The following is quoted directly from my first recorded telephone conversation with one of the two women and later separately agreed to completely by the other.

> ...and this object came in across the field. We saw this thing coming and it just squared off along their side of the road and came down... It was sort of like the shape of a boxcar. When it stopped...it's hard to say. I can't remember them turning the lights on, but there was a green halo over the thing. It put me in the mind of sheer curtains and (a) light was behind it and they had objects that they were standing in...these..these..peop..er..I don't know that they were people. I don't know what you call them. But, they were persons. They had to be. They had long arms, extremely long arms. They were not too tall in stature and there was one man standing in the front er...person. I don't know what you call them...and I thought like he was the one that operated it...and then there (were) two to the back and they had...it put me in the mind of school desks... that it was in the manipulating of them...we were shook up. Now, you can imagine...Evidently, they looked us over. They were on the one side of the road and we were on the other. They were right along the edge of the road...and then they just raised up, turned out the light and glided off to the southwest. They came in from the northwest and went off to the southwest...and that was it. We were shook up...and when we came home we didn't tell anyone about it...but now and then we would say we had seen one. We did. There is no doubt in my mind about what we saw.

Sometime later, Dr. Hynek came with me to hear and record their words. He and I were convinced that these two women were telling us the truth. The many thousands of experiences we have recorded convince me that "we are not alone" in our universe. I believe that reading this book will help convince you, as well.

Another pleasure in my life has been composing piano music. My lyric in one of my songs expresses what I hope for the future of mankind on our planet. If you or a friend might enjoy a copy of this music written for piano and voice, send a self-addressed stamped envelope to the Lima address mentioned above asking for a copy of "Some Fine Day" by John P. Timmerman. There will be no charge. If you are inclined to believe that what this book suggests is really happening, I believe you will find the lyrics in this song appropriate for what all humanity should do to prepare for that revelation. Please read the many good books on this subject recommended by Michael Swords. Learn basic astronomy. Inform yourself about science. Then, with wisdom, expand the thinking of others and share this book with all of your interested friends. If you do, thank you very much.

This book results from the Photo Exhibit Project undertaken by the J. Allen Hynek Center for UFO Studies and with the financial assistance of the Fund for UFO Research. Both are not-for-profit 501(c)(3) organizations created and maintained by volunteers and many contributors from throughout the world. I encourage you to support these and other serious organizations carefully revealing the truth.

Besides the outstanding talent, time and effort of retired History of Science Professor and writer, Dr. Michael D. Swords, volunteer transcriber Kathryn Diehl and volunteer secretary Sharon Stayonovich, I am deeply grateful to Dr. Mark Rodeghier, CUFOS Scientific Director, for technical and editorial guidance and to Rob and Susan Swiatek, representing the Fund for UFO Research for editorial and technical advice.

I thank my wife, Margaretha, and our children for forgiving my absence from part of their lives. I thank Michelle Baumeister and Georgia Porter for managing the CUFOS office in Lima, Ohio, for several years during my absence.

I am very grateful to the many hundreds of personal friends who have accepted with courtesy my many years of deep interest in this subject; and to all other persons and many organizations who have assisted me at home and at the 92 exhibit locations and many lectures. Finally, I thank again the thousands of witnesses with the courage to share with me details of those secret moments in their lives, some of which are included in this book. I hope that some of those with whom I spoke will read here and recognize their experiences. Without them, you would not be holding this book in your hands.

John P. Timmerman

Lakeview, Ohio June 2005

Section 1:
Introduction to the material
(what it is and what it is not)

Dear Reader: What you have in your hands is a collection of very interesting grass roots UFO stories from "just plain folks." I find these stories to be extremely exciting when read en masse, and to be validating of everything that veteran UFO researchers have believed to be real about the phenomenon. But there is good news and there is bad news.

Let's take the bad news first: as we read the condensed cases herein, remember where they came from. John Timmerman is standing around a fancy UFO exhibit in a mall somewhere and complete strangers wander up to him and begin telling him their UFO encounters. He flips on the tape recorder and they chat. If John remembers to ask all the right questions, then he does. But it's a dynamic and *natural* conversation (not an Investigator's Manual Checklist), and so some stuff gets left out. When John feels that the witness has run out of steam, he thanks them and clicks off the recorder. Now, 1180 *interviews* later we have *The Timmerman Files.*

So, what we *don't* have here are investigated cases. We don't have the time necessary to nail down every detail with as much precision as possible—this is particularly common with dates, the observer's guesses as to distance or at least apparent size, and things difficult to quickly describe (like shapes and positioning of lights, as well as many other details). Also, although many of the cases were multiwitnessed, as far as John-at-the-mall is concerned this is theoretical, as only one person (typically, though not always) is talking to him.

Having said all that, what we have here is still extremely valuable in my estimation. The reports (in vast majority) seem particularly *honest.* The speakers are almost happy to give John their names and addresses. They often thank him for being there to hear their story and not laugh at them. The stories are filled with sincere language, self-analysis with wondering about alternatives, vivid detail, often emotions. Even if the micro-details or side issues aren't clearly remembered, the core of the experience seems burnt into memory. And, we should keep in mind, the *stranger* the element of the experience the more it should imprint on our recall. Thus, when our reporter is having trouble remembering the date, or even how many people were around, the fact that the light beam from the craft came down in sawed-off columns like an elevator is probably just that: a fact.

Let us then take these condensed tales for what they are: stories told honestly between friends and associates, with all the good and bad elements that such exchanges bring.

Now, what do you do with audiotapes of 1180 mall stories to get to this volume? That, too, is a tortured tale, which you the reader should understand. Because: each stage of the handling of this material has in it choices and frailties of we who did the work. So, here is that odyssey.

1. *John got an angelic heroine to transcribe the tapes onto* paper. Wow. What a job. The quality of these hard copy transcriptions was excellent, amazing even. Still, there were two endemic flaws. Not all speakers have clear voices. Occasional lacunae, therefore, occur in the typing where they were mumbling, or whatever. Sometimes the word sounded clear, but didn't make sense. A question mark would be placed behind. (This person was an absolutely exceptional worker.)

   And, what some readers may grouse about but I wish they wouldn't, the transcriber had to guess about the person's name spelling as well as place names and locations. I'm not giving names, so that part is irrelevant to what we're doing here, but the reader may find place names, which seem invalid. I don't doubt it, but I have to go with the transcript, and, given what we're reporting here, this shouldn't be an obsessive concern. All I'd like to say is that the lady is a UFO saint.

2. John packed up all 22 three-ring notebooks worth of transcripts and drove them from Lima, Ohio, to Kalamazoo, Michigan, and we had a nice lunch. I don't believe that we lost any data precision in that step, but given this weird universe you never know.

3. I went through every *case*, coded it, highlighted what I felt were the salient points, and extracted them onto single extract sheets. This took over a year to do. The caveat here is that it was my choice as to what I thought was UFO important in any case to extract. I tried to understand exactly what the witness was saying and make an objective extract, but sometimes it was difficult to convince myself that one way of interpreting the words was obviously superior to another. I've given you my best shot. (Most of the time, by the way, there was not much difficulty in getting the hang of the case.)

4. Then it was time to count. Numbers of disks, triangles, close encounters, missing times, etc. A lot of that was straightforward, but some was not. See my comments in Sections 2 and 3, as to how seriously to take my numbers on this stuff.

5. The real fun of this business is the phenomenology. I've grouped handfuls of cases in forty sections devoted to different categories of UFO experiences. This is the main area where the reader can have a bone to pick with me. I chose which cases to group together. Sometimes that may be puzzling. Well, don't worry about it, just enjoy the stories. Use the case that you don't think fits as an opportunity for creative thought. Worse probably is my editing of the cases. I've condensed the transcripts to make the stories orderly and coherent, I hope. Did I do a good job of honestly keeping the true essence of the experience? All I can say is that I tried to do that as a number one priority. And lastly: the drawings. Almost no one gave John a drawing of their experience's *UFO*. Almost all of the simple line drawings in this document are made up out of my reading of the case. If they add anything to your enjoyment of the cases, that is what they were intended to do. If they bother you because they may be a source of error, then you know that you can ignore them. As with the honesty and tone of the story condensations, I tried to give as unembellished a line drawing as the words in the case allowed.

In summary of all this *flawed methodology*, I have a few suggestions for the reader: (A) Don't look at this as hard data or scientific; (B) don't sweat the small stuff, like misspellings, etc.; and (C) sit back and enjoy the ride. The phenomenology here is honest, vividly remembered, and mind-expanding. It was great fun for me to read these cases for John, and, with the exception of the domed disk that my brother Tom and I saw personally, has been the experience that has most strengthened my convictions in the reality of the UFO phenomenon.

Section 2: The Timmerman file cases as-a-whole

Rounding up bulk statistics is an academic necessity, I suppose, and that's what you'll get here. But, frankly, this is probably the least interesting part of this story. I can promise you, the reader, that you will be increasingly delighted by the long sequence of phenomenology sections (boiled down case reports) which are numbered 4 through 42. And, don't skip Section 3, either; John found something very interesting. And, even in Section 43, the so-called "Anti-climax," I believe that there are some things worth reading. But, we have to start with the statistics, so let's get to it.

John took 1179 reports all told. There were a few things that weren't ufological and a few that were obviously utter nonsense or so minimal that you couldn't make anything out of them, but 1179 (of about 1200) made enough sense to be called "UFO or UFO-related reports." Of these cases 781 were of shaped objects, 291 merely lights or objects of unseeable structures, 72 cases with no UFO at all, and a special section of about 35 classics, such as the Mantell case, et. al. The pie chart graph for these numbers is included.

1179: total cases

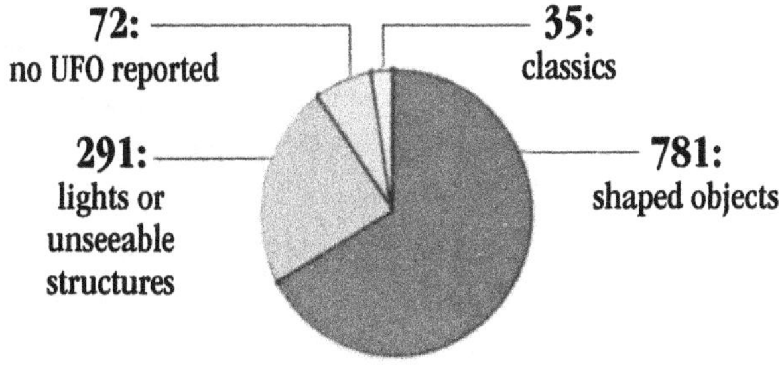

Concerning the shapes: I have initially broken them down into three categories: everything along the line of radial symmetry (disks to ovals to cigars, etc.), triangles and boomerangs, and everything else (the "odd" shapes). The overwhelming preponderance was in the "disk-to-cigar" category. There are doubtless lots of reasons for this. The public thinks that this is what a UFO is, and so will likely report those cases to a guy standing in a mall with pictures of disks on the panels. However, a lot of people are willing to report wildly different things, so that's not all of it. Another reason would be, surprise, that this is really what the UFO phenomenon

651: objects with radial symmetry

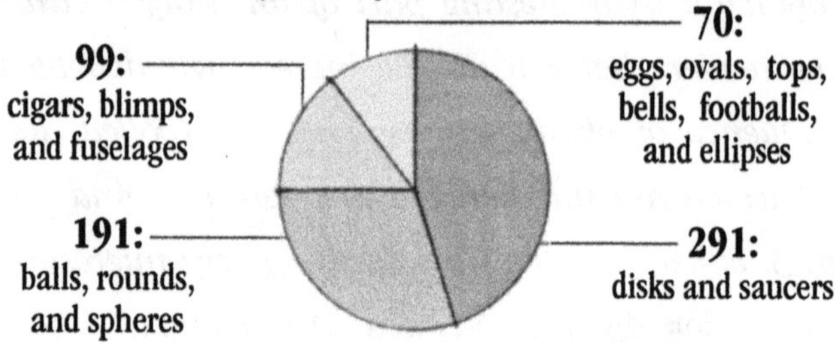

mainly consists of. (A shocking thought that we should actually credit the witnesses.) Some of the more distant sightings reported as disks or balls may not have been, of course. The human eye tends to round out marginal inputs, and the physics of light reflection will fool you into thinking that an irregular reflective material is round or oval. But all that aside, when the objects get close up they are mainly disks—clearly, positively stated by the witnesses. Why the other stuff is in there is anyone's guess. Why do our visitors do any of the weird things they do? All we can say is that the UFO phenomenon appears to be based on objects having radial symmetry (mainly) and augmented by a dose of triangular, boomerang, and odd shapes thrown in. Disks, et. al.: 651; Triangles and Boomerangs: 45; Odd balls: 85.

Considering the radial symmetry category of 651 objects: This was a bit of an arbitrary game to break down on my part. Example: when does a disk become an oval? When does an oval become a cigar? When is a ball just a fuzzy ball-of-light, versus a hard-edged object? Does that luminous ball belong in the radial symmetry object category, or just with the lights-in-the-sky? If it's a football, where is it on the spectrum? Is a top a disk? How tall can the top be before we quit calling it a disk? And on and on...

781: shaped objects

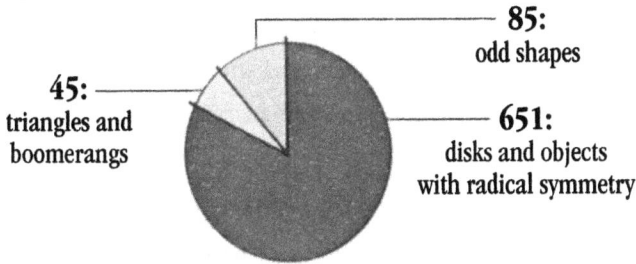

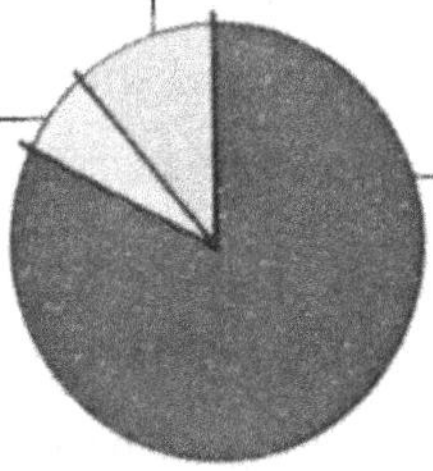

So I'm winging it. I'm giving you my best shot at taking individual experiences with all their differences of linguistic description, perceptual idiocyncracy and real, external object, and crudely creating lumps. I have no doubt that if you read the 651 cases, you'd break them down differently. I also believe that the impression that the two of us would end up with would be much the same.

For better or worse, then: 291 disks and saucers; 191 balls, rounds, and spheres; 99 cigars, blimps, and fuselages; and 70 eggs, ovals, tops, bells, footballs, and ellipses. Now, doesn't that make everyone feel better? My analysis, poor as it is on this, is that some of the rounds were meant to mean disks, and that this is probably true of the ovals and ellipses. Flattened tops and bells are precariously close to disks, as are thin footballs, eggs, etc. But suit yourself.

Concerning Close Encounters: There is also a bit of imagination in sorting this out. If you use Allen Hynek's arbitrary 500 foot (and less) distance for a CE I, then—surprise!— very few people tell you how far away the object was. So, you read their words carefully and make conservative guesses. On the CE IIs and CE IIIs, there is no distance required; just the phenomenology, so those were straightforward counts. The problem there is that witnesses reported CE IIs with no UFOs (usually traces), and CE III creatures with no UFOs. The column of numbers is my count of all cases with or without a UFO.

CE I: 185
CE II: 127
CE III: 71

But to give you a little better handle on the reports:

CE IIs involving vehicle interference: 14

CE IIs involving physiological effects: 14

CE IIs involving traces (with a UFO): 16

CE IIs involving traces (with no UFO): 18

CE IIIs involving entities (with a UFO): 36

CE IIIs involving entities (with no UFO): 35

Note: *for all you folks who obsessively count, the CE III figures doubtless gave you comfort because they added up to 71. The CE IIs, however, don't come anywhere near 127, which has given you great stress. Sorry. There are a lot of CE II effects which are not vehicle interference, health, or ground trace related. Read the stories/examples in Section 19.*

Concerning a few other categories of things:

* There were 18 cases involving radar.
* There were 8 cases of underwater activity.
* There were 38 cases of apparent missing time.
* There were 32 cases of plane pursuit or search.
* There were 28 triangles.
* There were 13 boomerangs. (Oops. You're counting again. The missing four cases were cones.)

Sounds: This, frankly, was one of the few bits that seemed interesting to me. The UFO phenomenon has, in its majority, been characterized by silently, hovering disks capable of rapid (impossible) changes of motion. All this was present aplenty in John's cases. But there was quite a bit more sound than I expected. Not loud sound, but sound nevertheless.

There were 93 cases involving sounds: Nine of these were idiosyncratic, one-time bangs, pops, etc., that were not associated with the object's general behavior. Still, that leaves 84 cases where the witness felt that the object was generally making a noise. In about 40 percent of these cases the sound was described as a hum or a low whir (a white noise emission at low frequency and low decibels). In one out of every six of the sound cases the sound was at the other end of the frequency spectrum (hiss or buzz). Sometimes such a high frequency sound was reported as shrill and loud (whistle or whine). Sometimes the low frequency sound was loud (thunder, rumble, roar). There were only three pulsing sounds, and three sounds like engine malfunction (moan or grind). Two cases had a multiplicity of sound. Still the low, slow hummers prevailed. Maybe UFOs aren't as silent as we thought.

Summary of what John found, so far: John rediscovered the whole phenomenon—its round theme, its impossible hovering and motions, its general silence. He found cases of multiple witnesses, military witnesses, expert witnesses. He found close encounters of every kind, and missing time and abductions (quite remarkable when you consider that this was standing around in malls). Most of his UFOs showed up at night, often at midnight or deep into the A.M. He found government cases, government interest, and government coverups. He even found Roswell.

And there is at least one other astonishing thing that he found (completely without knowing it), which I'd like to present to you in the next section.

Section 3: The temporal pattern of the cases

Before we get into the charting of the reports by date, let me tell you of an observation that I made while reading the transcripts, and then an idea that popped up, so you'll be able to decide for yourself whether this section (and my reasoning) is crazy or not.

First, the vast majority of John's malls were in the 1988 to 1991 period. I noticed that people were coming up to him and giving him lots of "recent" reports (especially for 1988 and 1989), many of which were of low quality, but lots of good-sounding stuff as well. It dawned on me that if you were standing on the street corner in any given year, your chances of getting case reports from that year should be better than for, say fifty years earlier. Most of the people passing you by weren't even born fifty years ago, some of them have forgotten about their experiences, some of them have rationalized that they're not important enough to mention, etc. The main point was: an investigator should expect that there is a "drop-off" function in the harvesting of case reports, with a maximum opportunity for high-percentage harvest sometime near the interview time, and going down to zero or a random odd report sometime well back in time.

So, I logged the dates of all John's cases. Often the witness gave a specific year. Often not. You had every kind of feeling about these dates. Some people sounded too sure. Some people sounded too conservative (ex. giving a date and then adding "or…" the next year as an afterthought). As a logger, you can't deal with that, so I just took them at their word, exactly as they said.

These numbers were plotted, cases versus years, on Graph One. You can see many peaks and valleys, and the expected diminishment of cases as you slip back far into the past. So, I thought, and please take this or leave it as it is a mere intuition on my part, "Can I make a simple assumption to

Graph 1

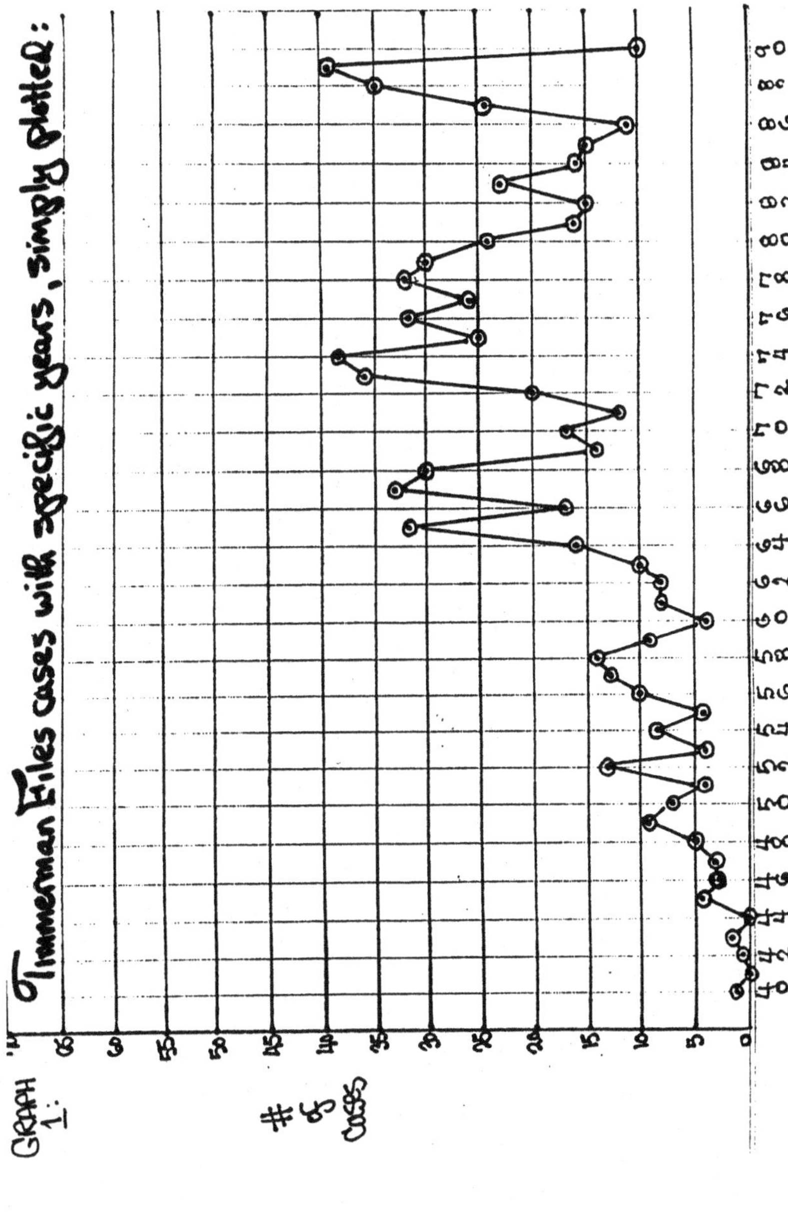
Timmerman Files cases with specific years, simply plotted:
GRAPH 1:
# of cases

try to get a handle on the real frequency and intensities of the data?" Could I imagine some kind of "fair" line-of-diminishment, over and under which might be expressed something more like the real ups and downs of the phenomenon?

Graph Two is my guess. I took 1988 and 1989 as years current to the reporting where there seemed to be a fair number of cases to report, and arbitrarily imagined them to be "average" UFO years (we didn't notice any flap particularly) and having an excellent chance of being harvested by John. For the other end of the drop-off line, I picked 1947, our alleged "beginning", and back when John's numbers showed that forty-some years had wreaked their toll. The method is too simple (agreed) and the anchor points too arbitrary (also agreed), but I believe that the intuition is essentially sound.

So, and again, take this as you will, I drew the line and looked. I was impressed with what I felt (still feel) that John had "rediscovered". If the graph makes sense at all, John has discovered the whole North American UFO wave phenomenon. Now this is more astonishing than that first sounds, I believe. What this says to me is this: here is a data set which is entirely independent of UFO media, literature, or even any leading/forcing by John. People literally came in off the street and verified the history of the UFO phenomenon. If they verified the temporal history of the UFO phenomenon in this multiply independent way (they certainly were, in bulk, independent of one another), *they verify that the phenomenon is real.* If there is no objective phenomenon that has gone on throughout all those years, sometimes with heavy cultural deprogramming to try to cancel it out, how can independent data sets (i.e., our own professional history versus John's "innocent" data) come up with the same gross pattern? Maybe someone has a better idea. All I can say is: reading John's transcripts is one way of assuring oneself that the phenomenon is real, and looking at his cases graphed is another.

Being a scientist-explorer at heart, I decided that the graph still had an obvious unfairness about it. Some people couldn't give a date (1967), but could give a spread (1966 or 1967) (or mid-'60s), etc. I decided that it would be legitimate to give years fractional credit for spreads, where the language of the spread made any sense at all. This has an upside and a downside. The adding up of fractions is a no-brainer (I dropped halves and lower in the sums), and a consequent graph is easy (see Graph Three).

Graph 2

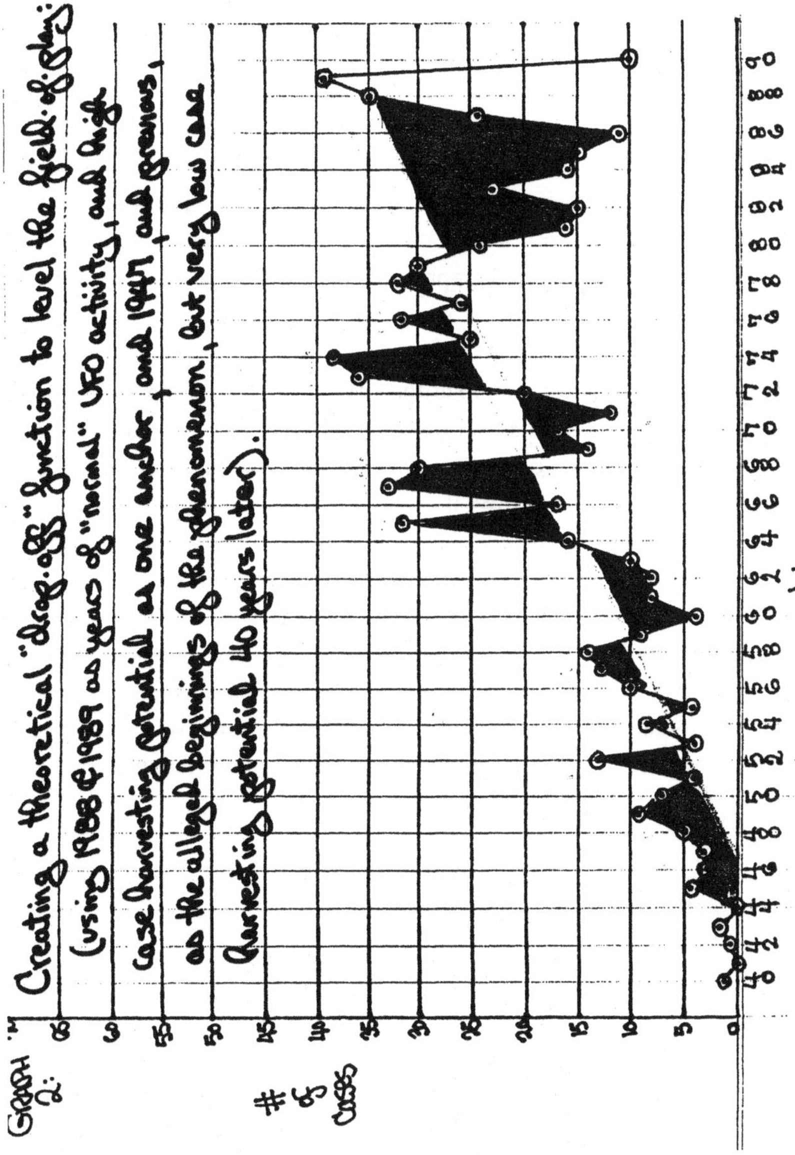
GRAPH 2:
Creating a theoretical "drop-off" function to level the field of play:
(using 1988 & 1989 as years of "normal" UFO activity, and high
case harvesting potential as one anchor, and 1947, and previous,
as the alleged beginnings of the phenomenon, but very low case
harvesting potential 40 years later).
# of cases
date-year

But the peaks and valleys will be a little "smeared" by the technique (i.e., valleys get equal credit, perhaps, with peaks for spread years... maybe justifiably and maybe not). Still, it does a better job leveling the field on a decade-by-decade basis. I then drew my old anchor line (Graph Four), and you can see the result.

This is when something else struck me. Our experience with UFO case reports does not indicate that 1988 and 1989 were particularly good years. What if the upper anchor should be well above them (indicating that they were, as we believe, somewhat less-than-average years)? Whereas, my earlier intuitions were honest in that I wasn't looking at results before I engineered the drop-off line, at this stage I was "dishonest" in that I was looking right at a completed graph and feeling that something wasn't quite right. So I'm guilty of post hoc reasoning at this stage—extra humility and caution all around. Although the general shape of the graph (with its waves and dips) was still there, some of the UFO lulls nearly disappeared. That is all a function of the slant of the drop-off line. If 1988 and 1989 were not average, as all our general information suggests, but were rather quite below average (as we believe), then a new line was in order.

So, I drew it in Graph Five. You can view it in all its warts and pimples, but I believe that it's the most honest (really) rendition of the data John found that I can present, given the vagueness of some of the dating. As I say, the final graph is a lot better in showing decade-by-decade case numbers, but as you go back in time, my procedure of giving several years in a smear-date equal shares will tend to lessen the contrast between peaks and valleys. Still, I believe, the history of our phenomenon, temporally, is there. Way to go, John!

Graph 3

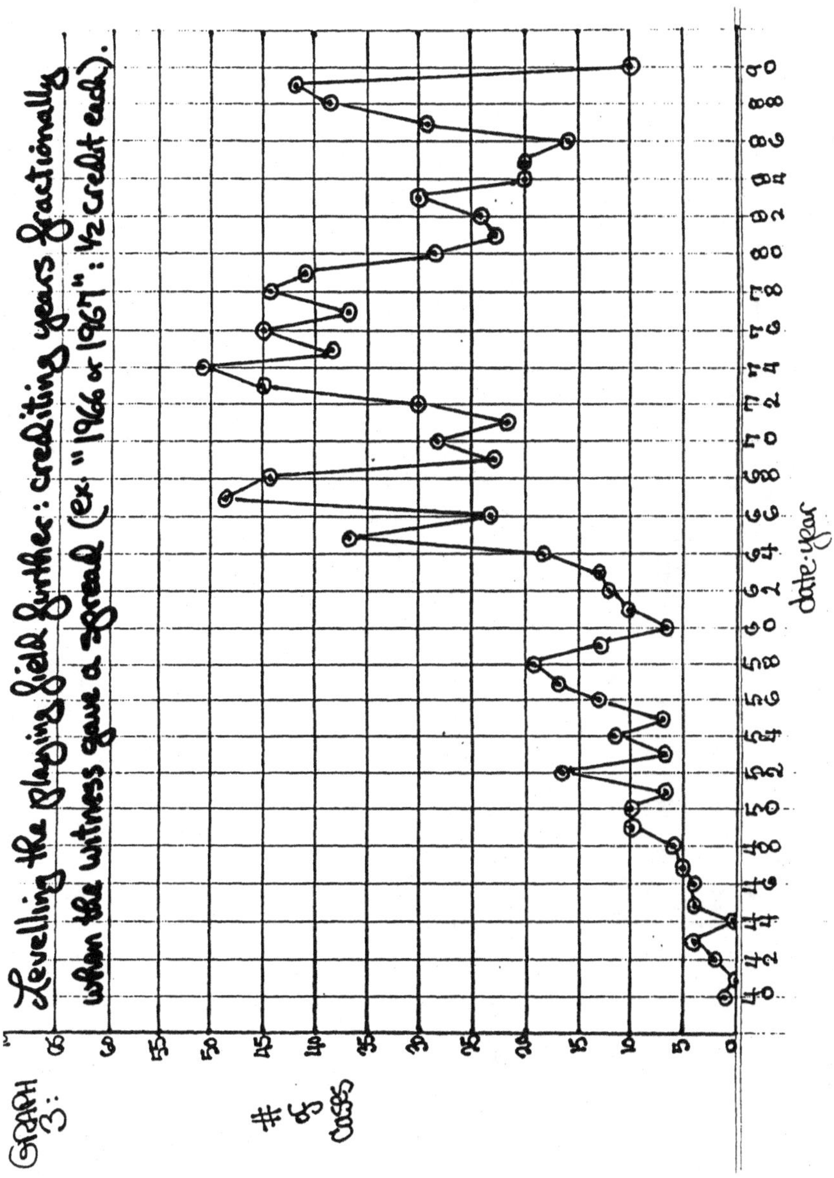
Levelling the playing field further: crediting years fractionally when the witness gave a spread (ex. "1966 or 1967": ½ credit each).
GRAPH 3:
# of cases
date-year
0
5
10
15
20
25
30
35
40
45
50
55
60
65
40
42
44
46
48
50
52
54
56
58
60
62
64
66
68
70
72
74
76
78
80
82
84
86
88
90

Graph 4

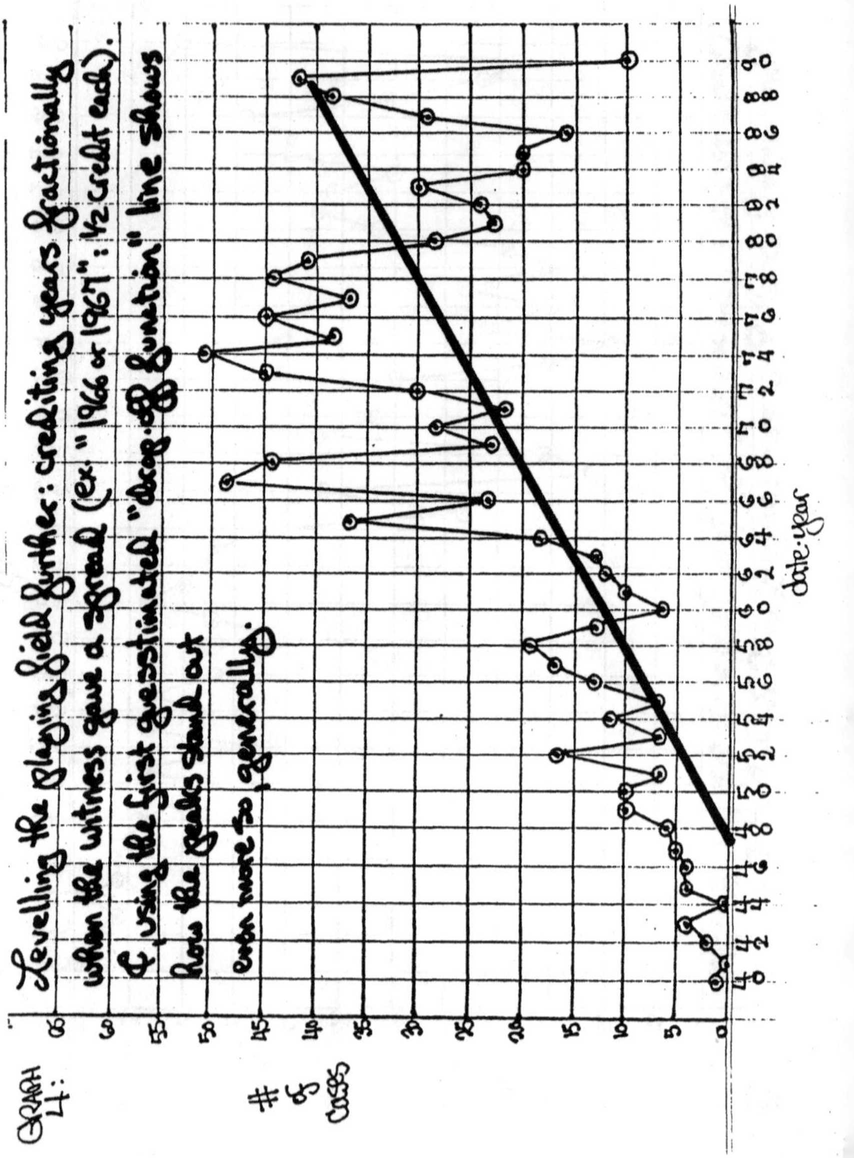
GRAPH 4:
Levelling the playing field further: crediting years fractionally
when the witness gave a "spread" (ex. "1966 or 1967": 1/2 credit each).
& using the first guesstimated "decay" function" line shows
how the peaks stand out
even more so, generally.
# of cases
date-year

Graph 5

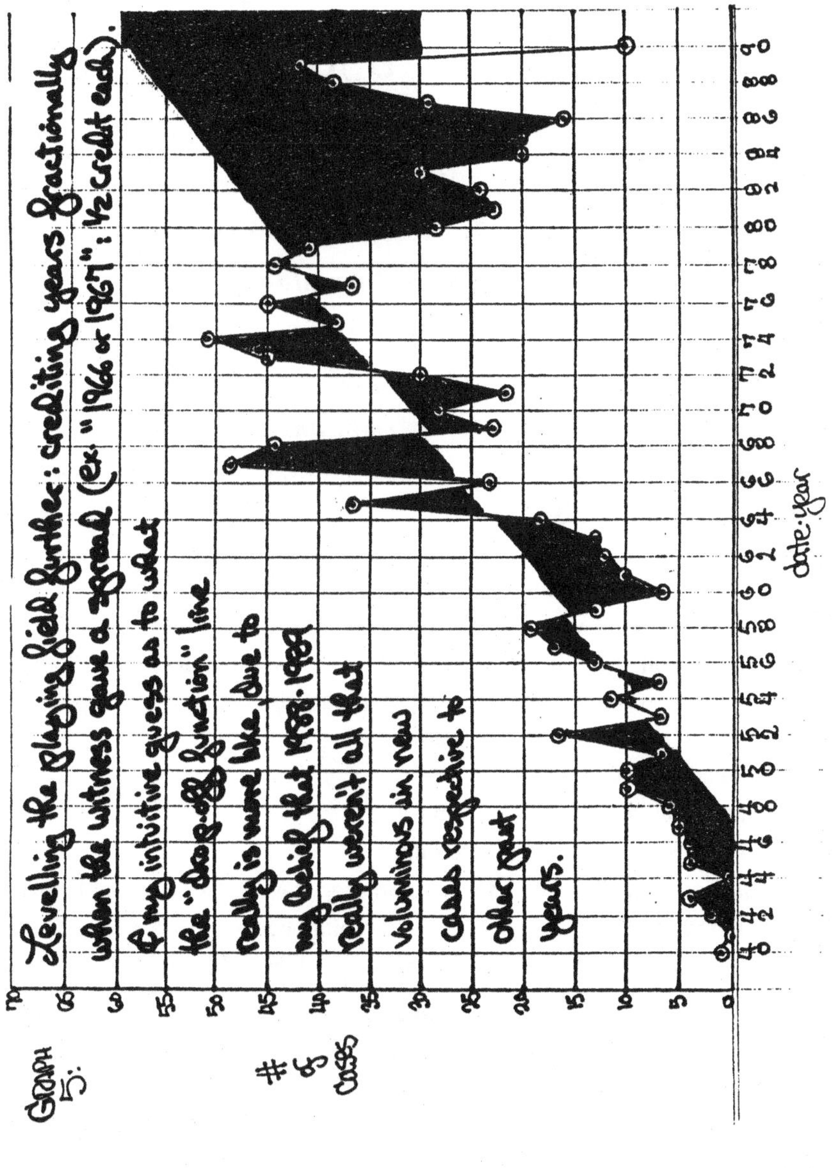
Graph 5:
Levelling the playing field further: crediting years fractionally when the witness gave a spread (ex. "1966 or 1967": ½ credit each).
& my intuitive guess as to what the "drop-off function" line really is more like, due to my belief that 1988-1989 really weren't all that voluminous in new cases respective to other past years.
# of cases
date·year

Section 4:
Lights with unusual motions

One of the earliest mysteries of the UFO phenomenon was the apparent denial of the laws of physics by the objects in their motions. Whether these abrupt motions arise from external reality or imperfect observation (i.e., was it really instantaneous or just really fast?), is partly beside the point. The weight of observation suggests extremely odd changes of motion whether they are "right-angle turns" or "instant reversals" or not. A few of many cases in the Timmerman files follow.

Scottsville, New York – *May 1983, early evening*

Four persons were driving to a birthday party when they spotted two lights on the horizon. The lights were side-by-side and stationary. They then became extremely bright, and one light leapt upward to create a vertical rather than horizontal relationship with its partner. They then took off rapidly into the distance until they seemed to merge into one.

At that point smaller red lights began to drop from the larger about halfway to ground level and rise back up to it, rapidly yo-yoing towards and away from the larger. Witnesses did not remember how lights ended.

65 miles north of **Prince Albert, Saskatchewan** – *early August, 1977 and 1978*

Two years in a row, a camp advisor at a Girl Guide camp witnessed the following phenomenon. At 3:00 A.M., a light like a streetlight switched on

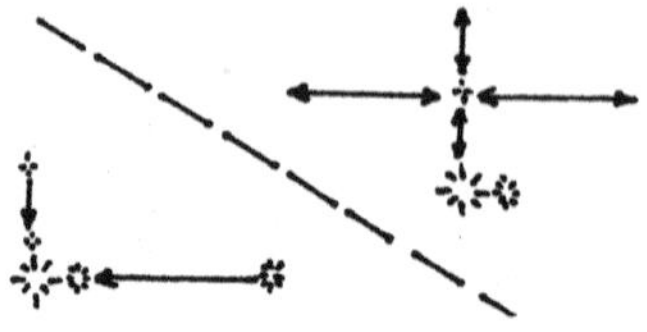

across a large lake in an area occupied by Boy Scouts but above the trees. A smaller red light approached it flying in from the east at rapid speed and stopped close by. Then a very small white light came in rapidly from the north and stopped overtop. The smallest light would rapidly bounce up and down, shoot off to the east, west, north and back, always coming to dead stops, and always bouncing up and down on its return. The smallest light then left, the big one switched off, and the witness can't remember how the red one disappeared.

Indian Lake, Ohio – *August c. 1967, 2 to 3:00 A.M.*

The witness noticed a very bright star in the sky where neither a star nor planet should be. It seemed to get a little bright and move very slowly. Then it came directly beneath Polaris (the North Star). It moved to the right and stopped, then returned directly beneath

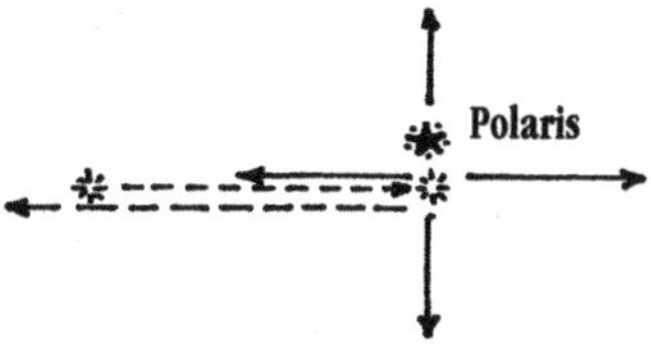

Polaris. Then it moved to the left and stopped, and returned. Then it went below Polaris for a while and back up. Then above Polaris, and back down. "What it did, it formed a cross." It did this cross slowly but then: "all of a sudden it went from the top to the bottom of the cross so fast [and several times] it was almost impossible for your eye to follow it. And then it came up under the North Star and to the left and to the right so rapidly that you could hardly follow it. Then it came back under the North Star and just sat there." This whole performance lasted about two hours.

Teston, California – *fall c.1975, in the evening*

The witness saw four red lights in the sky. The lights were individually shaped like little crosses in that they had spear points of light extending above and below and to the right and left. They were arrayed in the sky like

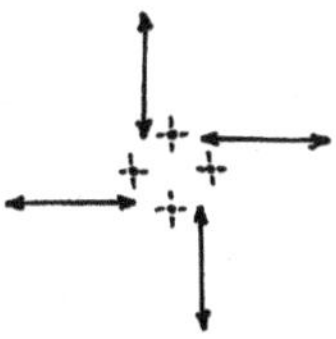

a diamond, or a cross without a central light. As she looked at them, the array went up and then down; then to the left and to the right, drawing another element of the cross motif in the sky. Although you could see through the middle of them, she still felt that they were somehow connected together. The array then backed straight away from her and disappeared.

Lima, Ohio – *1967, early summer, about 2:00 P.M*

Four family members were driving when they saw cars pulled over watching something in the sky. It was five bright lights in a V-shaped formation. The objects darted very rapidly and erratically. "They went from twelve o'clock maybe

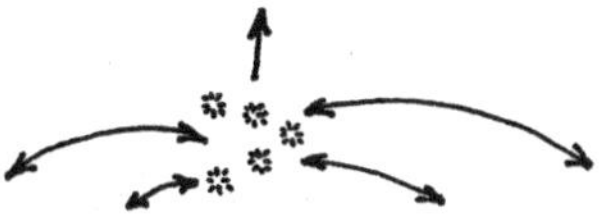

to slide down to a four o'clock position, stopped in midair, then went backwards over to maybe a nine o'clock position, stopped; and these were very jerky movements, very quick...then after several seconds they went from a nine o'clock straight over to a three o'clock position, stopped, hesitated for a minute or two, and then back at let's say an eleven o'clock and just extremely fast shot off until they disappeared from sight."

Dolton, Illinois, *near* **Chicago** – *1958 or 1959, 8 or 9:00 P.M.*

Three friends were playing out in a field (a ballpark) when eight to ten lights came in overhead flying in (some unnamed) formation. They seemed very high and their speed was fast. Then they abruptly stopped. The formation broke apart and the individual lights began making all sorts of uncoordinated maneuvers: "like they were actually playing out there." These rapid changes of motion continued for 30 or 40 seconds, when they all returned to formation and sped off at extreme speed.

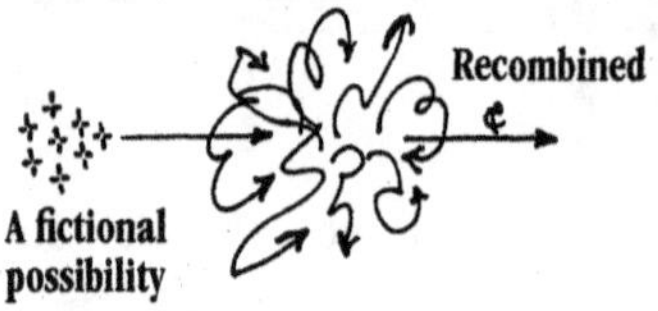

Newbury, New York – *1957, around 7:00 P.M.*

A large group of college students had just exited the dining hall, probably in the fall of the year. Over the hills from the west came five yellow-white lights flying in a straight row. Their motion was so straight and so quiet that it had an eerie feeling about it. When they got just past overhead, they stopped. The line then broke apart and flew off in five different directions. "It was almost like they came to a point, all split in different directions, went off, did whatever they were supposed to do, only took a short time, they came right back together in the same formation, went right back over the hill." All the maneuvering motions were very rapid: "they just went *zip, zip,* up and back, just right angles quick."

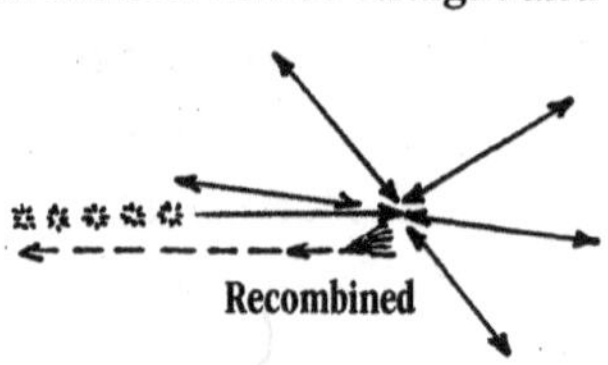

Middleboro, Massachusetts – *late summer or early fall 1979, c. 9:00 P.M.*

Two young males were fishing at night when they saw a group of red fireballs coming in the sky. The objects were small to the eye, but seemed to have a round shape, when viewed through binoculars. There were seven objects in a hexagonal formation with the seventh fireball in the center. The array stopped in the sky and hovered for 10-15 seconds.

Then they scattered. "They just started scattering all around the sky and doing loops. Not loops, but circles. Zigzag patterns, weird patterns." All this performance lasted about five minutes. Then the objects regrouped and shot off across the sky.

Williamsport, Pennsylvania – *October of 1972 or 1973, about 8:00 P.M.*

Two persons were talking in the driveway, when they noticed an array of three bright lights in the northern sky. One extremely bright light was in front and two slightly less so stacked vertically behind. The array was past the zenith, heading south, and being pursued by a jet. The lights made a sharp 90° turn to the east, and the following jet made a sweeping, curving turn.

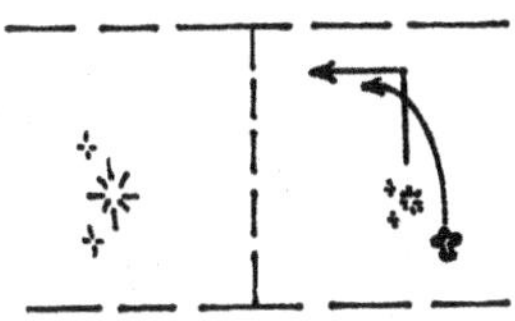

Both lights and jet disappeared to the east. In about 30 seconds, one of the lights (assumed) returned from the east. It made a descent from significant height down to about 500 feet (still appearing as a ball-of-light). As it did so, blue flashes began to appear and race along the power lines near the house. The flashes stopped; the light ascended, and went on to the west. About five minutes later the light recrossed the sky again, going west to east and was gone.

Snoqualmie, Washington – *January 1975, at night*

Three persons were watching television in the evening when the sound went off in the set. A new, different voice came on instead. It said: "Go outside and look north," and then the television returned to normal. They went out and located the Big Dipper and Polaris, and then another unusual "star". This "star" began flashing all different colors of light

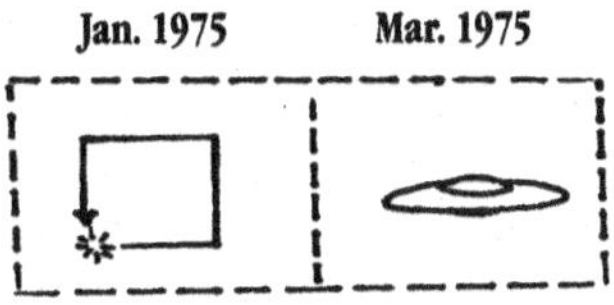

and moved in a pattern which outlined a square. Then it raced away rapidly. About a month and a half later (in San Francisco) he and a friend saw a large spinning disk enter the water, and 20 minutes later reemerge and fly away (March 23, 1975).

Section 5:
Balls-of-light, up close

In principle, the simplest UFO phenomenon should be the Ball-of-light (BOL). It's not. Many ufologists have wondered whether the BOL should even be considered a part of ufology at all. Skeptics have said that if the phenomenon exists at all it is just ball lightning or swamp gas glow. None of this is obvious, and most BOL cases bear little resemblance to ball lightning or glowing gas. This is not to say that some BOL cases may not point to some natural phenomenon** cousin **of ball lightning but as you will see from the following cases, even the BOL remains plenty mysterious.

Fort Saskatchewan – *fall 1950, about 3:00 P.M.*

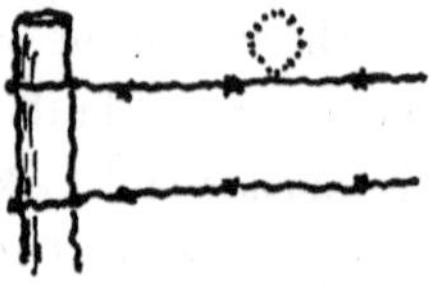

The witness was going through a field to fetch a pheasant that his father had shot from the car. He saw an orange ball, like a fireball, sitting on the wire of the nearby fence. It was round but a bit fuzzy at the edges. It sat in place for ten to fifteen seconds, then quickly followed along the fence wire, and just disappeared. It seemed to simply vanish. It was the size of a softball.

Oquawka, Illinois – *summer 1945, around midnight*

Several people were sleeping out in the neighborhood and watching a meteor shower. Across the street and about two hundred feet away was a large oak tree. Near the base of the tree were dull white spheres, radiating like a diffused fluorescent light. They were the size of basketballs and seemed to be circling the tree. There were three or four objects and they kept up this motion for 45 minutes to an hour. The observers ultimately got tired (no one went over to investigate) and went to sleep.

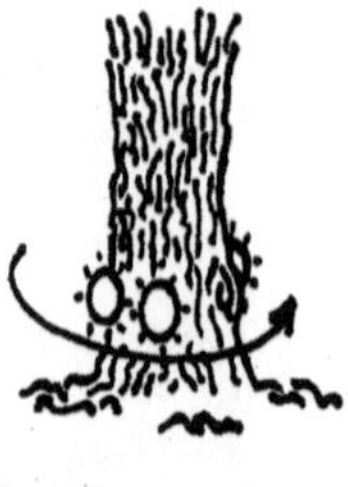

Rochester, New York – *sometime during 1962*

Four family members were sitting at their dinner table and looked out their window into the backyard. A very large, very bright object was entering it. The light was yellow and round. It was bigger than an automobile. It moved in quickly, then hovered for a few seconds, lighting up the whole yard. Then it moved off rapidly. No one heard any sound associated with the experience, and all of them thought of it as a "UFO".

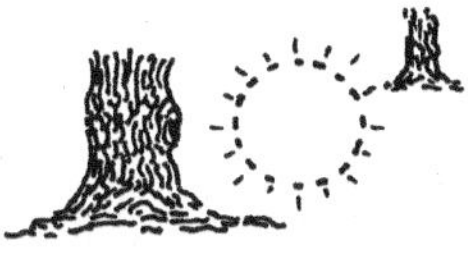

Biggar, Saskatchewan – *summer 1970 or 1971, c. 10:30 P.M.*

The witness was driving on the highway outside of town when he spotted a ball-of-light which seemed to be rolling in the sky. The ball was composed of a smear of all the colors (yellow, orange, and red) at the fiery end of the spectrum. It seemed to be spinning. It flashed across the road directly in front of his car, and lit up the whole highway, as if it were day. The object seemed huge, far larger than, say, a beach ball held at arm's length in apparent size. The whole experience lasted only several seconds, and the object moved rapidly away.

102 miles east of **Winnipeg, Manitoba** – *September 1968, in the evening*

A couple was walking in the vicinity of Caddy Lake, when a strange light appeared above some distant trees. It slowly meandered closer over a period of 25 minutes. As it approached, the couple hid behind a sign and watched the light move over a marsh. The two people flagged down a car and got a second couple to watch the end of the performance. The object moved just above the trees, their tops swaying as it passed. The temperature seemed to markedly drop, though they felt no wind. The ball seemed to spin and gyrate slowly and emitted a very light humming noise. It was self-illuminating with a soft, white fluorescence. It was somewhere between a car and a house in size. When it went over the marsh it just continued on until it was out of sight.

Suffern, Saskatchewan – *late fall of 1973, in the evening*

One night shortly after supper, the daughter of the house was looking out a window to the west, and spotted an odd yellow light. She watched for a while and then said to her father: "That light out there was yellow and now it's red." The father went to the window and saw a large round red ball, perhaps a mile away. It was bobbing up and down. The daughter told her dad that it had been doing that even before when it was yellow. It kept bobbing and every so often would shrink down to nothing, and after a ten-second delay would *Pop!* back up to full size. This cycle repeated every three or four minutes for an hour and a half. The object then seemed to just vanish, and seemed to reappear much farther away to the south.

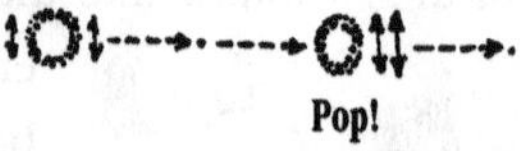

Findlay, Ohio – *fall 1957, around midnight*

An engaged couple had gone to the drive-in, and were on their way home, getting slightly lost in the process. All of a sudden the whole area around them lit up like daylight for about a quarter to a half mile. Then dark again. They kept on and a few seconds later it happened again. A huge ball-of-light was rising from the ground behind a barn. The BOL would rise, illuminate brilliantly for about five seconds, shut off, then on again. Each time it rose a little higher in the air. Finally, at some height, it shut off its brilliance, and a shower of tiny white particles rained off it. The object, half the size of the barn, scared them badly and they drove away.

In air over **Waycross, Georgia** – *late January or February 1970, 7:30 P.M.*

Two gentlemen were flying a small plane over Georgia, ultimate destination: the Bahamas. They were about to take a break and land in Waycross. Over the right wingtip a glowing red ball appeared. To check whether they were misperceiving something astronomical, or perhaps a ground reflection, they made several maneuvers over a ten-minute period and the ball stayed right there. The object was level with their craft and about one hundred yards away. They were flying at about 6500 feet and 125 knots, and the sphere stayed with them through even a 360° turn. Although the witness would not guess at size, he said that it seemed "pretty large," its apparent size equally that of the rising Moon. The air traffic center advised them that nothing but themselves appeared on radar in that location. Then, almost instantly, it was out of sight.

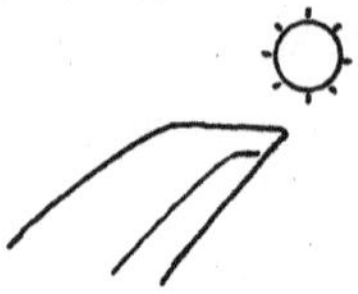

In air over **New Hampshire Air Force Base** – *about July 1958, at night*

A 509th Air Refueling mission was returning to the base from Goose Bay. They were flying a KC97 at about 17-18,000 feet. A light appeared, traveling as if it were a moving star. The object got closer and resolved to be a spherical shape and the brightness of Venus. It was beneath the cloud

cover. The officers were informed of this, and as it continued to close, it resembled the Moon in apparent size, and brightly illuminated the bottom of the clouds. The sphere was brilliant, blue-white light with two dark spots in it, possibly indicating some structure. The commanding officer was asked: "Why don't you turn towards it and flash your lights or something?" He replied: "No way. I'm not flashing lights at *that*. They might think it's a raid or something." The object then angled upwards and within about five seconds was out of sight.

Fort Saskatchewan – *fall 1988 or 1989, around 5 or 6:00 P.M.*

The witness, with a young child, was patrolling the roads surrounding her property in her car. She was looking for illegal hunters using her land. As she parked on a hilltop, she heard three bangs, like shotgun blasts. Out of her woods came three balls-of-light, about the size of baseballs but of an orange-yellow color. They seemed to be rolling,

turning in the air. They passed over the car at about treetop level, stopped in the air, and then flew away. Shortly there were four more bangs, and four more objects emerged from the woods and repeated the performance. With the exception of the bangs, she heard no other sounds. Both an older child at home, and a neighbor heard the blasts, but just she and her younger child saw the spheres. The Royal Canadian Mounted Police interviewed her and her neighbor, and told her that it was an airplane in the area.

Section 6: Even more unusual lights

Lights display an unlimited variety of phenomena, many of which are difficult to regard as some non-intelligent natural activity, and many of which seem just beyond explanation at all.

Topeka, Illinois – *sometime in the 1970s, late in the evening*

Half the family was in bed asleep, and the mother and her son were finishing tidying and locking up the house before retiring themselves. Outside the house, something a little larger than a car's taillight appeared, and a bit too high off the ground for a car. The mother told the son to get a flashlight and a gun, and they went to check it out. She shone the flashlight on it and the object went from red to green and whizzed away up their lane.

Grand Lake, New Brunswick – *November 1972, 10:30 P.M.*

A man and two of his children were hunting deer. They saw a very big "star" moving very slowly. It moved across the lake a ways off, and the father began shining the flashlight toward it and "signaling": 1 flash, 2, 3 flashes, 4, etc., up to 10 flashes, then stop and resume. The object turned and began coming back up the lake toward them. And it descended as it came. The children became scared and begged their father to stop flashing the light and take them back to the cabin. At that point the object just clicked out, and was apparently no longer there. Five to ten minutes later the air over the lake was swarming with Air Force jets, which criss-crossed the area for a half hour.

Junction City, California – *time unstated, in the late evening*

The witness was walking in a camping area and noticed a very faint red object moving very high in the sky. It was extremely difficult to follow, and he used his peripheral vision to keep track of its location. He decided to hold up his flashlight and click it on and off in the direction of the object. The light then "flew directly down the beam of the light, the flashlight, toward me." He quickly turned the beam off and the object stopped over the top of small trees on a ridge, perhaps 1500 feet away. It began twinkling white, blue, and red. It then changed to a bright (red) magnesium-like flare color, and moved to the left. It appeared as a round ball which then turned pure white and was lost in the trees.

Mona Island, Puerto Rico – *summer 1971, about 9:00 P.M.*

Two counselors had taken 19 students on a camping trip to the island. It is fairly remote, containing not much but a lighthouse, other than the natural environment. An orange light about the size (apparent) of the Moon came across the island. "As it passed over the lighthouse, the lighthouse shone its light, the thing all of a sudden stopped. As its light moved, it moved. And it did that three or four times until all of a sudden it just disappeared like you turn off a light… then, in 20 seconds, it just came back up. Right in the same place." The light moved on, went out again, and did not reappear.

Arcade, New York – *July 4th of 1976 or 1977, late at night*

Two people were about to turn in at their campsite when they thought they spotted a fire still going at their camping neighbors. It seemed reddish and a little angular at first, but as it rose, appeared as a round white ball, between a golf ball and a baseball in size. It floated slowly, but its motion was enigmatic. It would blink out and then blink on to its right, without seeming to move through the intervening space. Then it would do it to the left, and continued several times. Then it utilized this strange form of motion to come straight on, finally flying only two or three feet above their heads. (It isn't clear how long this blink/blink action took place in its final route over their heads and beyond, but it's a small matter.)

Between **Ithaca and Elmira in New York** – *1982 or 1983, at night*

Two persons were driving up a hill somewhere along Route 13 when they observed an orange-ball-of-light hovering in the sky ahead. The object even then was quite large: larger in apparent size than a thumbnail at arm's length. It blinked out and appeared quickly, well to the left. Then it blinked again and was immediately to the right side of their car, though a little ways off the road. This was alarming enough that they kept right on driving without noticing what happened subsequently to the object.

Buckhorn, Ontario – *date unstated, 3:00 A.M.*

The single witness was night fishing off the local bridge. He spotted a light, larger than a planet but smaller than the Moon. It was the color of a white light bulb. It moved from south to north but in jumps, switching off in one place and appearing in another. "It would just light up there and then it would light up over there...I never saw it move and I never saw it streak or nothing." As he stood and watched, four Canadian Air Force jets came and flew straight for the object. What then happened? "Just disappeared. It was there, and it just disappeared...Just like you shut a light bulb off...I don't think I got any fish that night."

Thornville, Ohio – *summer 1973, around 8:00 P.M.*

Well folks, this isn't a light or a BOL, but it seems that it belongs here, after what we've been reading. Two people were driving home when they saw a bright light coming at them and above their auto. The husband stopped the car and got out. The object was round and brightly illuminated with yellowish-white light. The light emanated from a very large number of individual lights covering the whole bottom. "It was almost solid." There was a strange quiet noise, a light hiss. "And the object was able to change from one location to another, maybe three-fourths of a mile, almost at will. And almost instantaneously." It hovered over a house, and came back over to about 500 feet of their car; and the husband got back in and drove off. Later others reported seeing the object, and an undescribed trace was found near the house mentioned.

South of **Trinidad, California** – *fall of 1966, at night*

A group of college students was having an outing on the beach. On a beautiful clear night, they noticed some brilliant white lights on the horizon. They were spaced horizontally in a straight string which crossed much of the sky, north to south. At the rate of a slow heartbeat, the light at the southern end of the string would blink off and a similar light would appear, with identical spacing, at the northern end. This happened a few times, as if it were a means of moving whatever it was across the sky. The students panicked. "We have to put (our) light out. They're going to come and get us!" And they joined hands in the pitch dark and left the beach.

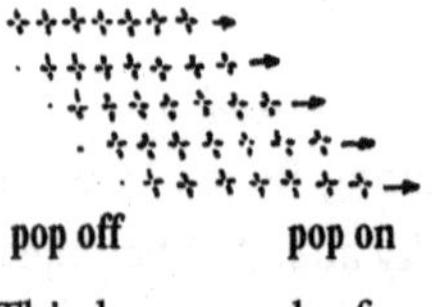

Jefferson, Maryland – *Easter Sunday, 1980, around midnight*

Two young people were standing in a field with their dog and three horses. A light, low to the ground, moved along the top of the hill. Nearing a tree, it hesitated and began to rise. It was a "pretty white" to begin with, but acquired a flashy orange tint. And it began to move toward them. The horses panicked and bolted away, running through a barbed wire fence in the process. The dog cowered and whined and went to hide in the barn. The object hesitated, rose a bit more, turned a brilliant orange, and zoomed away in a flash. There was no sound at all during the experience emanating from the BOL. It took the people three and a half hours to catch the horses, which were covered with heavy white foam lather.

Esterhazy, Saskatchewan – *October of 1976, 10:45 P.M.*

A couple and their daughter saw three orange balls in a triangular formation moving slowly across the sky at low altitude. The objects had

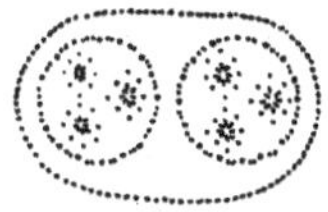

halos of orange-yellow light around each of them, and a larger halo around all three. A second set of three showed up, which were identical to the first. They moved in a choppy motion, as if they were rocking on a sea. Even in binoculars, there was no further shape, just an indication of red sparks emitting from the ends. "And it was so quiet, you couldn't hear a bird chirp, you couldn't hear a dog bark, it seemed as though I was the only person on earth, in a way."

Newark, Ohio – *summer of 1979, 9:30 to 10:00 P.M.*

A couple saw an unusual light from their rural home, and ran outside to watch. It was bright, but at the same time it was milky white. They watched it just hover for several minutes. No noise. Then, very quickly, it split and shot off in two different directions. "And this same thing happened several times within the next few weeks... almost identical spot."

Gulf of Mexico, out of Jacksonville, Florida – *fall 1981, around 9:00 P.M.*

A Naval Junior ROTC unit was on a cruise when a light source was spotted off the left side of the ship. Everyone came on deck to watch. It was a fiery orange ball which seemed to spin on its axis. The object would hover and then shoot up and down at amazing speed. It did the same off

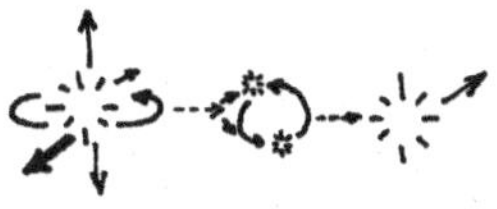

into the distance horizontally and back. This routine went on for thirty minutes. At one point "it separated into two balls, went around itself, and then it went back together." This happened more than once (but how many wasn't said). Finally it sped away into the distance.

Lake Scugog, Caesarea, Ontario – *spring 1983, about 4-5:00 P.M.*

Parents and daughter were fishing on the shore of a lake, when they noticed a large light (two feet in diameter) under the water. Standing up, they could see perhaps a dozen or so of these lights, generally in a cluster about 45 feet in diameter. The nearest light was as close as ten feet away. After about twenty minutes two young men came up and watched the phenomenon in silence. When they turned and left, the phenomenon

moved in their same general direction going down the lake. The water depth near the fishing pier was only eight feet and the lake 22 feet at its deepest, but the object, whatever it might have been, was not determinable.

Near the **Azores Islands** – *February or March 1971, at night*

The U.S.S. Saratoga was on mission toward Scotland, when a huge scraping was felt at the bottom of the ship, and it came to a shuddering, near complete stop. The bridge crew noticed a large blob of light moving rapidly away underwater. The crew was told that they had hit a whale, and not to talk about it. The next night, a large blob of light was seen following the ship. The crewman/witness says that the object was two times wider than the 35-40' wide ship itself. This latter pursuit lasted for about ten minutes.

Fort Worth, Texas – *August or September 1978 or 1979, 9 to 10:00 P.M.*

Parents and son were returning home in their car from a bowling league. A light appeared ahead, hovering over the electrical power lines. As they approached, the father stopped the car. No sound. The object, a round ball-of-light, hovered there three to four minutes while electricity seemed to flow up off the lines into the sphere. The ball, ten to fifteen feet in diameter, was relatively dull when they first saw

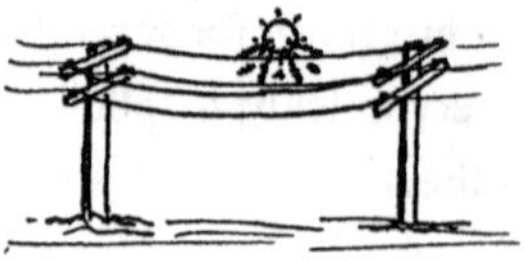

it, but it became almost daylight bright by the time it was finished. It then dropped a little in height, raised up, stopped, and then *pffst* out of sight.

Russells Point, Ohio – *summer of 1957, around 11:15 P.M.*

A husband and wife were returning from a roller rink, when they saw a shooting star. The husband asked his wife to make a wish, but she informed him that this wasn't any shooting star. The star turned green with a glow all around it. The glow dissipated and in place of the green fireball

Color change

were six elongated cigar-shaped objects. They continued to move in a formation, flying across the face of the Moon. As they continued on a glow again grew and enveloped them and they passed on appearing as a single reddish fireball.

Section 7:
Cases where the structure wasn't describable

Although John's files include plenty of cases covering almost any imaginable element of the UFO phenomenon, and cases in which the witnesses could describe the structure of the objects involved often in great detail, he received many cases where the witnesses couldn't honestly say that they'd seen enough to say what the object looked like. I could have just skipped these cases, as there are so many others to recount, but I felt that a small flavor of these was of some value, so here are ten such reports.

Morrison, Illinois – *October 1982, at dusk*

A policeman was returning home from a departmental function when he spotted "a tremendously bright light, almost white, solid white in color; a hundred times brighter than any airplane landing light." It appeared to be low and nearly stationary. As he drove nearer, it began to move, first slowly, then accelerating so that it beat him to the intersection that he was approaching. As he drove up, it slowed down. He stopped his car and got out. Over the top of the intersection were street lights which covered the area, but above those lights only a dark object: "I would estimate the size of two boxcars." On the dark object were many multicolored lights (reds, blues, whites, yellows) with the colors all smeared together. "There was absolute silence, no noise whatsoever." It moved slowly across the top of the intersection, and then arced away at tremendous speed. The bulk gave the impression of being verging on transparent "like you could see through it; yet you couldn't." [Maybe, say I, like it was not quite totally there.]

Garretson, South Dakota – *around October 10, 1972, at 4:00 A.M.*

Dogs were barking and the wife woke her husband to ask him to look into it. It wasn't the dogs. The distant sound changed and got louder: "woof/woof" turned into "beep/beep/beep/beep/beep." He and his German shepherd went outside. The noise appeared to be coming from the sky but he couldn't see anything. "Beep/beep/eee/eee/eee." It moved, now north, now east, now south. The German shepherd turned tail and ran back to the house. Another big "beep" occurred over the cattle feedlot, and a light came on which lit up the whole area. The wife ordered her husband to get back in the house, which he did. Then the sound "Oo-Oh-Oo-Oh" and it, whatever it was, trailed off into the distance. In the following days, two neighbors said that they'd seen a powerful light over his house that morning.

Sacramento, California – *spring of 1974, 2:30 A.M.*

Two women were on a balcony observing local traffic when an object approached in the air intermittently shining a light. They thought it must be a helicopter but there was no sound. In fact: "The whole city seemed to have quieted. It was weird." The object approached in a zigzag pattern as if on a search mission: 90° out, short sideways, 90° back, etc. It moved very slowly, and shown an occasional pure white light which seemed not to illuminate anything below. The light occupied a dome in the bottom of whatever the object was. "It was startling, because normally you'd think you would light up the buildings." The object drifted slowly and "then all of a sudden—*shhooo*—it was gone... It was deadly still in the city. The bars normally get out at that time, and there's traffic, but it just seemed that everything was deadly still."

Over the **midwestern United States** *in the air – sometime in the late 1950s*

A pilot and copilot of a commercial airline were flying a DC-3, when a lighted object of some sort came up right near their right wingtip. The object, which appeared to have some structure to it, was covered with a pulsating, light green glow. The object then began to loop over and under the plane as they flew, literally flying circles around them. It then shot off and was gone.

Oshawa, Ontario – *fall of 1974 or 1975, at night*

A phenomenon which happened more than once was reported by many people in town and publicized in the newspaper. It would appear at night and usually around the Pickering Nuclear Station. You would see three lights (red, green, white) hanging stationary in the air. There was no noise, but you could feel a pulsing. "We sat underneath this object for a good hour one night," but you could never make out a structure. On one occasion a plane came nearby, and the object went straight up through the clouds and out of sight "in a flash." The motions when it moved were extremely fast. The Air Force, to whom it was reported, seemed to ignore it.

Kamsack, Saskatchewan – *July 11, 1989, at 11:00 P.M.*

A few hours previously there had been a tremendous rainstorm and hail, and the power had gone off. The family dog was barking and the wife went out to look. The husband then followed, and they saw something flashing, zigzagging in the air over the neighbor's field. "The most beautiful purply blue you ever saw." The object flashed this way and that, sometimes only two feet above the ground. Its motion was like a butterfly, but the light itself seemed as big as a small car. Its shape seemed something like that of a...[the tape recorder was indistinct]. "And there was not a sound, nothing." The husband asked the wife what she thought it was, and she said "I don't know what it is; like a giant firefly." The husband, flashlight in hand, never even thought to shine a light on it.

East of **Hastings, Nebraska** – *date unknown, in the evening*

A couple driving in their car saw a light high in the sky to their rear, but coming nearer and downward. Then the object altered its course and went ahead of them and blocked the road. It began to move toward them, hovering just above the road. The husband threw the car into reverse and tried to back away as rapidly as he could. Meanwhile the object was flashing lights at them: 1 on, pause, 2nd on, pause, 3rd on, pause etc., until the total of 9 to 12 were all on, then all off, all on, all off; then start the sequence again. Not ready for extraterrestrial communication, the driver careened backwards as fast as he was able, and the object gave up and went away. They stopped and tried to call ahead to tell people where they were, but no phone lines worked in that direction, though service was okay elsewhere.

Near **San Jose, Costa Rica** – *sometime in 1979, at night*

Five persons were in their house when they noticed flashes of different colored lights outside. They looked and saw an object about 400 yards away and above house height. It seemed round, and also seemed to be creating a huge amount of wind. There was, otherwise, no noise. It hovered for about twenty minutes, then moved slowly, showing multicolored lights all around "like you have color flashlights crossing each other...this was wide, very wide, and you can see nothing, nothing but big lights." The wind, which had begun with the appearance of the object, suddenly stopped blowing when "that thing just went out."

Litchfield, New Hampshire – *early fall 1965, early A.M.*

Six children were living with their parents/aunt and uncle (i.e., three children of the aunt and uncle, and three of their cousins) in a dorm-style bedroom for all six kids, when they all awoke to the presence of a "thick red light" coming from the window. Metal was rattling at a basement door, but the adults did not awaken. The kids went to the kitchen and two crawled up on the sink to look. The witness (speaking to John) said that this was the last thing she remembered till morning. Her sister told her that she jumped off the sink to the floor and hid by the cabinets. The sister said that she saw a craft. No one could remember anything else until they woke in the morning "all of us being soaked in our beds." Two of the children went into the backyard and found a circular mark out there imprinted in a sandy area.

Onion Springs, California – *July 1988, at night*

Four people had gone camping in the area of Mt. Lassen, and were lying out looking at the stars and talking about UFOs. We said, "wouldn't it be so neat if one would come down?" and "we got real excited." All of a sudden, a light like a strobe light began flashing high up. It was like a powerful spotlight and would intensely illuminate circular areas where it hit. Clouds began to form in the area and covered most of the sky except the area above them from which the beam came. "It was strange. Real weird." They looked back at the sky, and the position of the Moon had changed—apparently much unaccounted for time had elapsed. "That meant something happened, but it didn't dawn on us." When they returned to their motor homes, they realized that what should have been a couple of minutes was more like an hour and twenty. The two women were ultimately hypnotized separately and reported onboard craft experiences with large male-seeming persons in glowing white helmets and shapes. Now all four persons believe that they're getting information or contacts via dreams. This report was unusual in a lot of ways, not the least in that three of the four witnesses were there at the mall to give their mutual assent to the details of the experience.

Section 8:
Good ol' disks

Flying disks are the historic staple of ufology, dating right back to the early 1947 wave when Colonels George Garrett of the Pentagon and Howard McCoy of Wright-Patterson Air Force Base (writing for General Twining) concluded that the United States was experiencing flyovers of such technology. They are also the definition of a UFO in the minds of the American public. Many of the witnesses who reported their cases to John undoubtedly had the image of the disk so fixed in their minds that they didn't even bother to mention the shape unless John specifically asked for it. For them, and most of us, "UFO" generally means "disk."

Grants Pass, Oregon – *midsummer of 1979 or 1980, during daylight hours*

A large number of people were enjoying a swimming hole in the middle of a warm day. They saw a large, mechanical object approaching in the sky. The device was a silver disk, smooth on the upper and lower parts with a middle section composed of square windows. It moved like a slow dirigible until it got overhead. Then it began whirling about "like it was showing off what it could do." It produced no sounds. After the aerobatics show, it resumed its slow motion in the direction of northern California.

Man's Lake, northern New Brunswick – *fall 1981, various times*

A family who regularly went camping in this area saw the following object several times during the fall of this year. Other friends, including two Air Force men, also witnessed it. The object would come down over the lake "a little bit like a wavering action," and then stand still in the air. After awhile it would lift up and rapidly move away. It was a disk with a dome, and (usually) red and white lights flashing around it. It seemed to rotate on its axis, and made no sound.

Near **Hudson Bay** *(the town)* **in Saskatchewan** – *early fall 1974, at night*

A brother and sister noticed a bright light in the sky out of the window. They phoned a neighbor who went out and viewed it through binoculars, and they watched it from their place through a rifle scope. They phoned the RCMP in town, and an officer also went out and looked at it. The object was a disk like two plates joined together. Somewhere on the object was an extremely bright (welder's arc-quality) light. This was so bright that it was difficult to make much out of the object's shape. There seemed to be portholes, and maybe something moving inside, but hard to say. The object would move slowly, hover, then "just go—*swwhhh*. You could barely see it, and all at once —*chhhh*—come right back and hover again." Finally it just blazed off at tremendous speed. They'd watched this show for two hours. Two days later the RCMP interviewed them extensively.

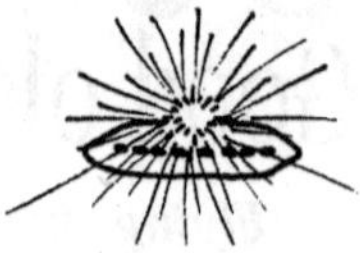

Carlisle, Ohio – *spring 1988, in the evening*

A man was walking his dog when a large object was spotted overhead which moved and then stopped in the air. It was an unlighted object of dull gray and shaped like a dull metal disk. Then two smaller disks came up from behind and stationed themselves on either side of the large one. Then they moved in front like an honor guard. Finally a third small disk came in and occupied a position behind the large one. All four objects had a light glow around their edges. The objects made no sound and seemed very low, and the man got scared and went in to try to wake his wife up, whereupon she regarded him as if he'd gone nuts and didn't go outside.

Oshawa, Ontario – *fall 1984, 1 to 1:30 A.M.*

A man saw a huge light pass overhead. It resolved into a circular device, flat on the bottom but with all sorts of technical pieces attached to it: "parts stuck out here and parts stuck out there...it looked like something on TV that I've seen quite often in a show called *Battlestar Galactica*." The object was the size of a city block, "at least 500 feet long." Shortly afterwards, his sighting was corroborated by two coworkers who viewed the same object from different positions.

Baltimore, Maryland – *October 1949, during the day*

A man was delivering mail at 10:00 A.M. when he heard a small plane overhead. The aircraft was a Beechcraft training plane, and it was the apparent target of another *plane* which was diving on it. *That* plane turned out to be a flying disk. It was bright, silvery white, and as it got nearly overhead simply and abruptly stopped. It then proceeded to corkscrew back up into the air. The disk seemed to have observation ports both on the top and bottom surface, and as it spun rapidly the witness had the impression that he could see right through it. The object reached height, did a sharp angle turn, and flew off toward Washington, D.C.

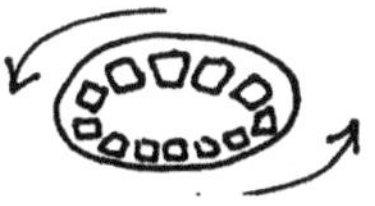

Lima, Ohio – *September 1955, during the day*

A group of men was working on a house when they spotted a silver disk the apparent size of a dime held at arm's length. It came across the sky east to west, taking about three minutes to make the crossing. Then it returned and was joined by three similar disks in a V–formation coming out of the north. At the nearest point, the four were about the size of a quarter at arm's length. The first disk took up a position in the "V" to create a diamond formation, and they stopped briefly in midair and took off rapidly to the east and were gone.

Kingston, Ontario – *November 1967, around 8:45 P.M.*

Two men were working guard tower shift at the Kingston Penitentiary. The guard in the Northwest Tower called the other and alerted him to a large object approaching from over the lake. It was an oval object, a structured disk, moving in a slow, floating manner at about 1500 to 2000 feet. Occasionally, it shone a strong spotlight beam down on the lake. There was no noise as the object continued its slow approach over the next minute and a half. The guard went out to the catwalk and turned the prison's spotlight on it. The object stopped and began to move slowly away. At this time he noticed a rotating circle of lights around the craft. Then, at terrific speed, it "just disappeared altogether."

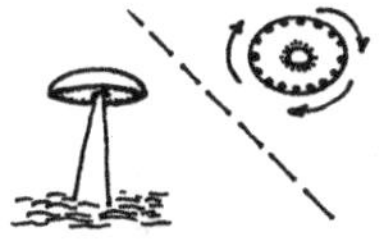

Dallas, Texas – *June or July of 1985, about 3:30 A.M.*

The night was steaming and people weren't getting much sleep. Nine people gave up on it, and were sitting with open windows hoping for a little relief. All of a sudden a wind came up. The tree outside was moving, and there was a large object in the sky. It was a disk composed mostly of windows. The object, estimated 5+ miles away, came a little nearer, dropped a little,

went up, hovered, and then took off rapidly. When it left, the wind which had been emanating from that direction died away. The witnesses thought that the object was quite large and very bright but no one else reported it.

South of **Webb, Saskatchewan** – *midsummer 1984, late at night*

A farm family had been having sightings of fiery BOLs on or near their property since 1981. Typically, they'd be awakened but not, they thought, by any noise. Out the window they'd see round BOLs looking like fire in the fields. They'd go out looking but never could successfully approach one. They had ten or twelve sightings of this sort. Then, in 1984, they spotted a silver disk coming from the west over the hills. It hovered and everyone gaped at it for a minute or more. And then "it just absolutely vanished, at an incredible speed." The youngest daughter was terrified and barricaded herself in the house, crying. No sound accompanied any of these events. It was larger than your whole hand at arm's length.

Near **Renton, Washington** – *date unknown, around midnight*

A husband and wife were watching TV, when a strange light reflected on the wall. Out the window there were three small disks flying in the trees near the mountain. When a truck would come up toward the mountain the disks would seem to hide and reemerge later. High in the sky was a larger craft. Through binoculars they watched the small disks rise to the larger. A "hatch" was open in the bottom "and they just seemed to go into this hatch one after the other, *zap, zap, zap.*" The big saucer glowed red, then bright white, and just zipped away.

Section 9:
Cigars, and variations on the disk theme

Whether the shape is described as a cigar, fuselage, blimp, football, oval, egg, top, or sphere, ufologists have tended, rightly or wrongly to lump them together on the basis of one form or another of radial symmetry. Still, in many ways, these shapes seem quite different, and, knowing nothing about the physics and technologies of these objects, who is to say why so many display this symmetry? Whatever is going on, John interviewed people who reported almost any radially symmetrical shape you'd desire. Here are a few.

Near **Dawson City, Yukon** – *winter of 1980, at night*

A trucker was just rousing from a roadside nap in his cab, when he was surprised to find that he'd slept all through the night and it was daylight outside. Except it wasn't. The light was coming from a slow-moving object traveling over the valley. "The whole Blackstone basin for about forty miles was just lit up like daylight." It took two minutes for the object to traverse the valley and go on. He estimated the device's length at three-fourths of a mile. It was a long cigar-shaped craft with row after row of lights on the bottom. The witness had a feeling of fear and dislike to the thing and was happy when it left.

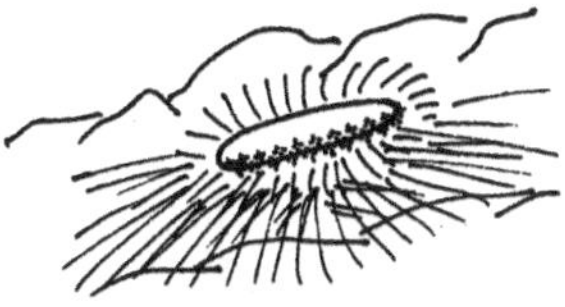

Cadiz, Ohio – *sometime in the early 1970s, during the day*

Five family members were driving on Route 22 when they saw an object which seemed connected to a cloud. The object was cigar-shaped and a dull grayish-silver. Its apparent dimension was that of a semitrailer if you viewed it from a "block" away... so the family felt that it was huge. The cigar would

descend from the cloud, sit there, and then rise back into the cloud. The family drove underneath the object's position and when they could look again, both it and the cloud were gone.

South of **Buffalo, New York** *in the air – February, early 1970s, post sunset*

Three American Airlines employees were flying out of LaGuardia to Chicago. They were in clear weather well above an undercast of clouds. Suddenly, a large, close object crossed in front of them, taking up three-fourths of their windshield. Its speed was so great that it was gone in an instant. The pilot asked air traffic control about traffic and received a hesitant "No," but "do you want to report *it*?" The captain said: "No. We didn't see anything." The witness said that he has talked to ATCs and they have been told not to admit to pilots when they have such a sighting on their scopes. The object was hot copper color, and created no wake disturbance for the plane.

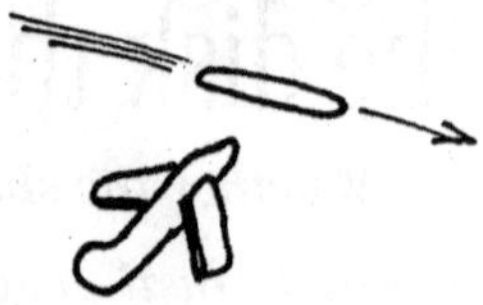

Between **Walla Walla and Seattle,** *in air – September or October 1980 or 1981, midnight*

A commercial flight was going to Seattle when the crew spotted an object coming toward them. It came alongside and "parked" there. The pilot made an evasive action, but it stayed with them. He called the flight center and was told "Well, don't be surprised, there are several of them reported this evening." United, Continental, and Braniff had all reported in. The United pilot thought that the four objects that he saw must have been an Air Force scramble from Portland, but was told no. The witness of this report felt that *his* object was between a saucer-on-edge and a cigar, with an upper and a lower row of lights. Between the light rows was an area that seemed to glow on its own. The lights were around twenty in number and red and green with the intermediate white glow. The object paced them for about seven or eight minutes, and then whizzed away to the rear in a matter of a second or two. During their encounter, the pilots heard the following exchange between the Braniff pilot and the traffic controller: (controller) "There's been several reports of UFOs in the area." (Braniff) "Oh, it's going to be one of those nights again." (controller) "Yep. I think so."

Lima, Ohio – *sometime in the 1970s, date unknown, before sunrise*

A man was driving to work early one morning while still dark. Ahead of him in the sky was a brilliant, hunter's orange-colored object. It was cigar-shaped and oriented horizontally. It then began to tip upward into a vertical position. Another, much smaller orange object came up to it and seemed to go inside. Then the cigar pivoted again and became horizontal. It began to move out, slowly at first and then just accelerated away.

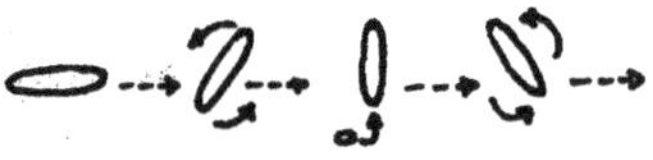

Near **Mount Vernon, Washington** – *1977, date unknown, at night*

A husband and wife were driving home when they noticed a bright "star" in the sky, growing brighter and coming closer. It passed, went behind, and passed again well off to the south. The couple was curious and turned off the road to find a dark spot to look for the UFO. Nothing showed so they went back toward the highway. The husband wanted to remain looking, but his wife said, "No. If they want you to see them, you'll see them." Then a very large dark object passed overhead, emitting no sound. It was as big as the Goodyear blimp. Another similar object approached its twin, each with a flashing red light on top and a white light on the bottom. The flashings were out of synchronization but as they got close, they synchronized. Once passed, they lost synchronization again. Only a small motor sound was heard.

Clinton, Ontario – *early June 1958, 9:15 P.M.*

Five members of the Royal Canadian Air Force were driving outside of town, when they saw a glowing orange light over a ridge near a farmer's field. It was oval in shape and very large: its apparent size being that of a football held at arm's length. Its distance from the road was between 300 and 400 meters, and its altitude about 500 meters. No sound was emitted, and the object seemed to be simply an oval of orange pulsing light. The air force guys decided to drive off the road and into the field after it, but it rose straight up and slowly drifted away at a leisurely pace. They never reported it.

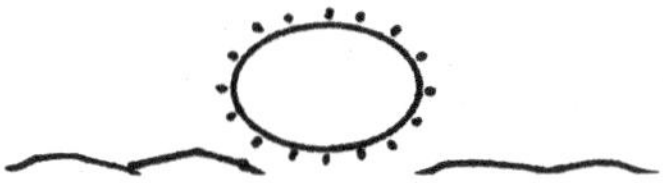

North of the **Grand Canyon,** *in air – January 7, 1978, 8:00 P.M.*

A commercial airline was flying from Phoenix to Salt Lake City at 35,000 feet. A glow appeared that encompassed most of the western sky. The glow approached the aircraft, and illuminated both the exterior and the cockpit of the plane. In the center of the glow was a spherical object. Its apparent size was that of the full moon at the horizon. Its color was light metallic with "a little bit of mottling effect." The object suddenly stopped

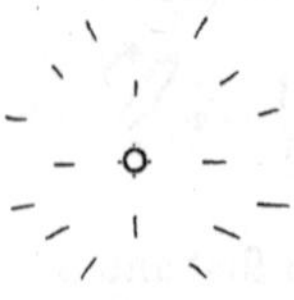

about a quarter mile away from the aircraft, off of the left wing, whereupon it paced them at 600 mph. Air traffic control said that the only unusual traffic was a Vandenburg rocket launch. The object left them in an upwards direction rapidly. The pilot said: "If I've ever seen anything from outside this world, that was it...and I'm glad it was friendly."

Pasadena Freeway, California – *July 1980, 11:00 P.M.*

A man (one of the few persons who wouldn't give John his name) was driving on the freeway when he saw two large objects coming from the other direction. They were shaped like old-style children's pump-tops, and they had lights around them. The two giant tops were one behind the other, and were "tipping", but not in unison, as they came. They passed overhead showing large numbers of small marquis-type lights on the bottoms. The general color of the bodies of the objects was silver. One top tilted on its side and flew off at terrific speed. It tipped for a while, then raced back to its companion and continued on down. There was no noise.

Barstow, California – *multiple events in 1976, around noon*

Teams of people working for NASA at the Goldstone Tracking Station would see the sudden appearance of a silver sphere hanging in the sky. This object would just be there, and then just vanish. Its appearance was always around noontime, and it would stay visible for three to five minutes. This happened about ten to twelve times over a 30-day period. The nearby Air Force base said that they had nothing in the area at any of the times, and that they could not pick up anything on their radar either. Looking at it with a television camera with a closeup lens showed no features to the smooth sphere, either to the eye or on video. The object always appeared in the same place at about the same time, but not every day. "You know, we see this stuff all the time."

Section 10:
Disk cases with a difference

The following cases include aspects which most of us, I presume, would view as exceptionally strange, even though the cases do not qualify as "close encounters" in the Hynek "500 feet or less" arbitrary yardstick. One wonders whether hidden in these odd events is a key to the greater mystery. At quick glance, this first case seems just another odd motion in the sky, but does it contain a hint of the mathematical and technical bending of space which allows UFO travel?

Southeast of **Corinth, Mississippi** – *late December 1981, about 3:00 P.M.*

An ex-USAF officer and a friend were out hunting quail. One directed the other to two bright shiny metallic-looking objects traveling one behind the other, and holding an exact straight line toward the horizon. As they nearly reached the horizon "they reversed direction, with no slowing, no turning, it was an exact straight line abrupt reversal of their speed and direction." They then proceeded back across the sky until they achieved a position generally overhead. "At that point the one in front made a direct, complete right angle turn, exactly a turn with no stopping, no slowing, no turn other than just a right-angle turn with continued high speed." The second disk continued in the original straight line until it got to the point where the first made its turn, then it turned with mathematical precision at the same point and in the same way. Shortly, the first object got to a point in the sky and simply disappeared. The second object continued to that same point in the sky when it simply disappeared.

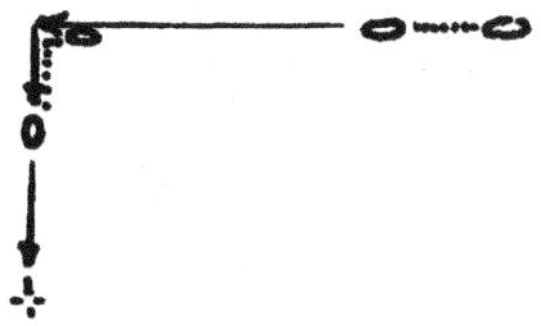

Brandon, South Dakota – *fall 1968, 9:30/10:00 P.M.*

A woman was driving home from work when she had a strange feeling and looked up to see a dark mass above her to the left. She panicked and sped home with the object pacing her all the way. The next evening,

though she left work later, she was again paced by an object, only this time it was brightly illuminated. This time it stayed and hovered above the house, disturbing the television her mother was watching inside. She got her father to get in their car and drove off while the silent round object paced after them, perhaps 300 or so feet in the air. The object ultimately sped off to the horizon.

Biloxi, Mississippi – *January 1974, during the day*

Two college co-eds were driving from Gulfport to Biloxi to see a movie at the mall. They were driving on a highway which was constructed quite close to the Gulf. Suddenly, out of the Gulf, emerged a big *something* right near their car, startling them so that they ran off the road briefly. The round object was midway between a ball and a saucer in shape, and had lights on it. Despite its nearness and emergence from the water, it was soundless. The girls were so scared that they just drove back onto the road and kept on going.

Grants Pass, Oregon – *summer 1987, at night*

Very late at night a young man in his twenties was out walking when he saw a large, very strange "balloon" in the sky. The top was not illuminated, but the bottom was full of square windows from which came white light. In the center of the bottom was a hole from which emerged four smaller objects which gave him the impression of an octopus reaching out to try to grasp something… but these were small detached objects which cruised away. The small things were different colors (yellow, red, and green, perhaps). There was no noise. The objects left a short ways and simultaneously returned. Then the big craft ascended slowly out of sight.

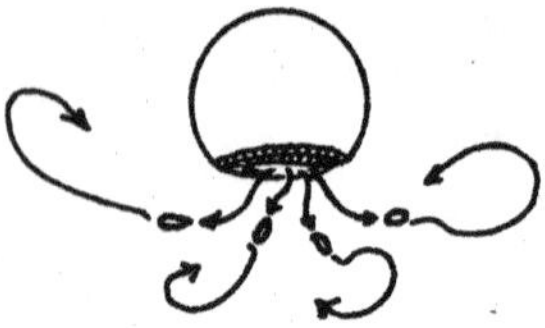

Pontotoc, Mississippi – *June 10, 1975, at night*

Three young men were out running their hunting dogs in a pasture with low ridges on both sides. They sat in their truck on one ridge. A light was seen moving, flickering among the trees on the opposite side. It was in the sky, but at tree height. About 600 to 800 yards away, it broke into the clearing and was revealed to be a disk with a dome. It slowly meandered down in a waving drift, headed toward the first of a few isolated houses on the ridge side. At the presence of the object, all the dogs but one came

running scared back to the truck, and jumped into their boxes. The object proceeded to drift over the houses and hover briefly above each security light, which would dim a bit.

The young men wanted to get out of there, and they hollered for the other dog to return. "And at the instant we did that, that flying saucer or whatever it was, it turned and started coming right back straight toward us. And we thought: Oh boy, we messed up now." As the disk approached, it encountered another security light from one of the houses, and stopped and dimmed the light as it had been doing. When that was over, the object meandered on its original course (perhaps *forgetting* about what it had just been doing?). Getting a ways away, it stopped and began to turn. It took on a dull red glow, like a dirty taillight, and then, over a period of five seconds, ramped up to extremely bright red. And the next instant it was gone "it just wasn't there anymore."

East of **Cave Junction, Oregon** – *October 7, 1974, around dusk*

Two persons were driving toward the Oregon-California border when they rounded a corner and saw a large saucer in the sky. They stopped

their car and watched. The saucer was stationary but a violet vapor trail still extended behind it. From the edge of the craft came a blue light which extended powerfully all the way to the ground. The light was emerging from a ring of octagonal windows. In about two minutes, the craft put out a cloud of black smoke ("like a squid") and moved away rapidly. They saw it diminishing in the distance. Continuing to drive along the road toward where they thought the object originally was, they came across a heavy redwood sign which said "Leaving Oregon" at the border. On or about that sign, the women saw pairs of oval, slanted green eyes, though it was too dark to see what they were attached to. Several pairs...possibly several entities. One woman said: "Stop! Stop!" but the other said: "You must be crazy! We're not going to stop. They'll get us." Later when they told their husbands, one was frightened by the story and told them not to talk about it. *Coincidentally* in a month or less, the redwood sign was removed.

Orange, California – *June 1981, 11:00 P.M.*

A woman was walking her dogs when she turned a corner and saw a light shining on her with a flickering action. There was no sound, and the light flickered again, and her dogs, uncharacteristically froze. She looked

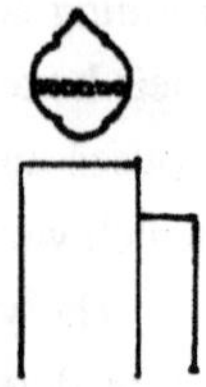

upwards and saw an odd object on the top of a building. It was round and had sort of a cone on the top "and I thought, that's a weird looking helicopter." The top-shaped object had windows around its middle, and the light from its windows was multicolored like a kaleidoscope. She felt like she was in some sort of hypnotic spell. Then it rose slowly in the air, a vapor came up around it and "it looked like it just kind of disappeared."

Oshawa, Ontario – *spring 1990, time of day unknown*

A mother and child were driving in her car in an unusual area of the country (for her). An object appeared in front of them, and they watched it through the front windshield. It was a grayish disk with red and green lights around the top, and a line of bolts running around. The object flew upwards, over the vehicle, then came back, and just disappeared. The mother is completely flummoxed by the experience, because "I didn't remember it until he mentioned it. Then I can see it in my mind's eye. And that's weird... I mean I can't see me erasing it from my mind...I don't even remember truly where we were. I have no reason to be out in the country with him."

...from child's drawing

Kent, Washington – *late 1970s, date unknown, around 9:00 P.M.*

A senior in high school heard a buzzing or humming outside and grabbed his camera to go out and look. Near the school there was a large disk object with domes both above and below. A series of lights around the bottom was beaming down on some new construction. The student raised his camera to take a picture and one of the beams hit him in the face. That was the last thing he remembered until he came to and saw that his watch read 3:00 A.M. He has no idea what happened.

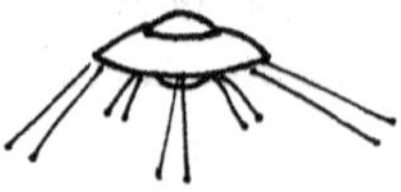

Newark, Ohio – *summer 1977, between 3 and 4:00 P.M.*

Husband, wife, daughter and daughter's boyfriend were driving and saw a flying saucer landing in a field: "so we pulled over to see it." Then the saucer opened up, and you could see shiny golden-colored metal on the inside. A second, small roundish disk then rolled out of the opening and rose up and left. The larger saucer did, too, so the witnesses drove on home. When they got there they realized that they were at least two hours late in arriving. None of the four of them had any recollection of the time. "Yes. And we were all very surprised." John asked if they'd told anyone else about the experience, and what was the reaction. "Well, they think we're crazy. What else?"

Medford, Oregon – *August 1976, during the day*

The witness was working on his cabin (a mobile home) up in the forested hills. It was a clear, bright day with no clouds. He was distracted by an intensely bright light ("like burning magnesium") coming across the skies. He squinted at the lights (he now realized that there were two of them, side-by-side), and saw that they were coming so as to pass over his home. He heard no noise—puzzling, but not as puzzling as what he saw next. These intensely lighted objects were disks, curved on top and more or less flat on the bottom, and in between them was a third dark gray object. It was a World War Two-vintage bomber. The plane had two propellers, which were not turning, and a bubble-like gunner's hatch on the front. The tips of each wing seemed to rest on the luminous disks on either side, as if they were ferrying it. The trio of objects moved silently overhead, over the hill behind him and were gone.

Section 11:
Triangles and boomerangs

Two of our more-or-less modern UFO alternatives: John received a few of these case types as well.

Peru, Indiana – *August 1957, at night*

A young woman was driving home after work and noticed a group of people standing alongside the road looking into the sky. They directed her to look overtop the nearby trees where sat a large black object. It hovered about 100 feet in altitude and made no noise. The shape was a "soft delta" with window-lights underneath within which some movement seemed to take place. In the middle of the bottom was a round area which looked like it might open up as an entryway. The object was estimated at a thousand feet long. As it slowly moved, a small sound like a vacuum sweeper arose, and it drifted away to the horizon.

Oshawa, Ontario – *1984, date unknown, at night*

A man, who had seen two entirely different types of UFOs in the year previous, was looking from his apartment building toward the Pickering nuclear power plant and saw two triangular-shaped objects. They would turn toward each other, point-to-point. Each of their sides was illuminated with a different color (red, green, white). When they completed their turn, these lights went out and they blended into the darkness.

San Jose, Costa Rica – *July or August 1981, 11:00 P.M.*

In a small town outside San Jose to the southeast, the witness was camping with the Red Cross. He saw a triangular object, well lit, about 300-350 yards off the ground and maybe 400 yards away. There was no noise. The triangle hovered, then turned and moved, made another sharp turn, and another, drawing a triangle in the sky back to its original spot. Then, rapidly, it went high and came back low. Then a

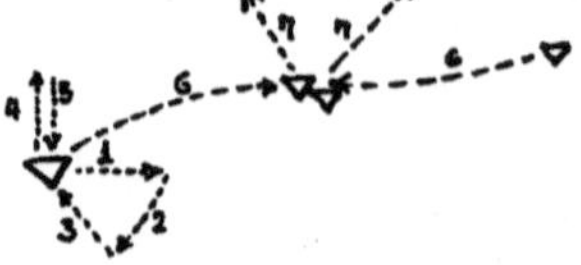

second triangle came into the area, and the two moved to meet each other. They stopped together for about thirty minutes. Then they split and rapidly disappeared into the sky.

Wooster, Ohio – *October 18, 1973, around 11:30 P.M.*

A person was sleeping at a friend's house and was awakened by him and told to come outside and look. There were a group of people watching a bright object, pulsing in the sky. The object seemed like a triangle with three different-colored lights on it. Each light pulsed differently. When the object moved, the red light would pulse brighter. It went right, left, up/down for 25 minutes. People had time to gather in their lawn chairs to watch the show. The object dropped low finally, then shot straight up and away. The witness said that he felt that the object was an "alien" presence, even "evil".

Bossier City and Shreveport, Louisiana – *September 22 and October 6, 1987, at night*

A young couple was returning home from a movie at about 9:00 P.M. They were sitting outside, talking, and noticed a startlingly large object passing in the sky. It moved silently despite its bulk (they guessed at its length as being five football fields long). The thing, a large conical triangle, proceeded across to the local air force base. It had sparse lighting on the bottom, and seemed metallic and solid. "It looked to me like a Starship." Two weeks later ("no doubt in my mind that this was the same object") he saw the same object moving in the same direction.

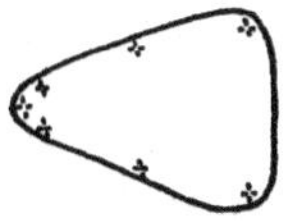

South Bossier, Louisiana – *January 21, 1989, about 10:00 P.M.*

A woman was called by her mother and told to go out and look for a UFO which was moving in the direction of her home. The two lived about six miles away. She did so, and spotted it crossing the sky to the west, and it ultimately disappeared. People in the area have seen it several times moving in the direction of Barksdale Air Force base. Looking at it through binoculars, it is triangular in shape but has blue and white lights which seem to flash on and off around the exterior. The close approach it made to the mother's house was still accompanied by no sound. The television news has passed these experiences off as weather balloons.

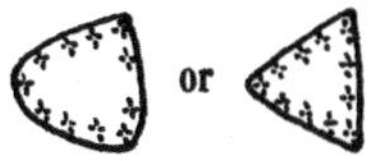

Waterford, Connecticut – *November 7, 1974, 3:00 P.M.*

Two schoolgirls were biking home from school when they saw a ball of fire in the sky. The girlfriend remarked that it couldn't be a meteor because

it was falling too slowly. They rode home, got one of their moms, and went out in the car looking for what it was. They saw it again from the beach, and one girl took several pictures. Several other people had also stopped to watch. The object was shaped like a triangular space capsule with rounded corners. Flames were coming out the back as it did elaborate rolls and maneuvers in the sky. Then it took off into space. The film came back with no negatives and only one picture, a picture which was loaned to a man to duplicate and that, too, has disappeared.

Lake Decatur, Illinois – *summer 1986, between 8:30 and 9:30 P.M.*

Three persons were fishing off a dock when they noticed a light moving above the trees across the river. The object turned and lit up the bank alongside them, and then turned back down. It began to slowly make its way across the river toward them. They became frightened as it got nearer, and turned their lantern off. The object seemed to react to that, and turned away to follow the river's course. The object seemed triangular, with dull glowing lights at each corner, but the interior section of the triangle seemed empty, as if the lights were on some girder-like structure. In the middle was a blue glow, however. And, as usual, no noise.

North Canton, Ohio – *March 30, 1983, 7:45 P.M.*

A father heard his son excitedly beating on the house door and yelling for him to come outside and see the strange plane in the air. It was a slow-

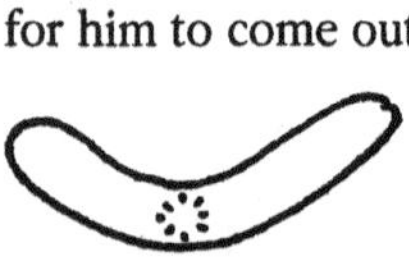

moving boomerang with a large, but dull, light on its nose. The son said that it had turned on a very bright searchlight which had lit up the neighbor's woods. The wingspan was about 100 feet, the width thirty to forty feet. It seemed about ten feet thick. The object moved over the house and slowly away, whereupon jets came racing through the area. The object never hurried as if it thought, "Hey, I'm the big cheese, ain't nobody going to touch me."

Dover, Ohio – *February 6, 1947, 7 to 8:00 P.M.*

A woman was on the phone to her sister, and saw a lighted slow-moving object coming in the sky, and beaming light off the front of it. She opened the nearby door and could hear no noise. She said: "You won't believe it! This thing is going too slow. It's coming in your direction." Her sister then went and saw the same object. It was a boomerang-shaped thing with lights along both wings. She was reminded (later) of the Stealth bomber today. There were colored lights sparsely positioned along the wing so that you could make out some shape. You know, folks, it's funny, but back in Blue Book days of 1952 Captain Ruppelt was tearing his hair out trying to find cases of simultaneously viewing from different locations, and John found several of them.

Newark, Ohio – *spring 1989, about 7:00 P.M.*

Two weeks after seeing a domed disk with lights structured all around the bottom (with her two daughters), a woman spotted an unusual object after getting off from work. This woman, who was (apparently) Latino, described the object as a "big boat" in the sky, but directed John's attention to a picture of a boomerang from another UFO case. The object had many lights on it and made no sound. The night was foggy, but she's confident in what she saw. It drifted away to the south on a straight course.

A "boat-in-the-sky"

Near **San Juan, Puerto Rico** – *February 24, 1977, in the evening*

Several friends were in a town plaza when one of them noticed an object up in the air with square windows and lights within. The object was moving around, or its lights were. They were all sorts of colors. She immediately thought that this was an OVNI, the Spanish term for UFO. People were afraid that it was a plane going to crash, but she said: "No. No. It's an OVNI. It's beautiful." She thought "If you are a UFO, brothers, I want you to come near me so I can see you better." Instantly the object began to move in their direction. "So big, so enormous, bigger than a Boeing. And he came like 200 feet above us, and stood there in midair." It was a boomerang with multicolored lights "Beautiful… like a Christmas tree." The lights were huge (bigger than a Harley headlight) and you could see a rim around them. And smaller lights encrusted its belly.

"The UFO itself was like a great cloud… it was like smoke… you could see the shape of the UFO by the bulbs." In the middle of the boomerang's belly was a round, dark area. She got rather hysterically excited and began to shout: "Hey, take me up! Take me up!", like, as she says, she was crazy.

Immediately there were two openings, one in each wing, and two spotlights beamed down: one covering her and her husband, the other, three other people. The light bathed them but that was all. The end of the story? Ask John and the tape recorder demon, as the tape then ran out.

Newark, Ohio – *August 1956, at night*

Two young men were camping out in the backyard one evening and they had a camera handy. They saw five very bright lights enter the area

flying in a V-formation. The object(s) flew erratic and sharp patterns for about five minutes, which included 30° high speed turns. Sometime during the performance, one of the witnesses managed to get a picture of the formation. The picture was developed and the case reported to both the local newspaper and to the Air Force. It made the newspaper, and the Air Force came and confiscated the young man's negatives. The newspaper was also visited and their copies of the picture taken. Not only were none ever returned, but on later inquiry, the Air Force denied having ever taken a report on the case.

Section 12:
Odd shapes

The public considers "UFO" to mean disk, cigar, sphere, with the odd triangle or boomerang thrown in. One would expect that persons coming up to John were there to report those kind of shapes and it would be a rare individual who would admit to a non-conforming UFO. Still, John got a few of them.

Chillicothe, Ohio – summer 1985

A husband and wife had decided to go outside and relax on their patio, when the husband just froze with a stunned look gaping at the skies. The wife looked up in time to catch a huge craft going directly over their trailer.

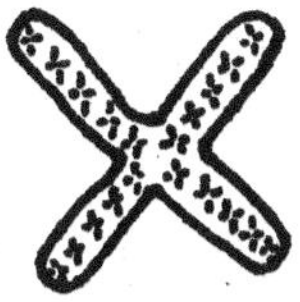

It was X-shaped and covered with lights, and silent. She ran to get a neighbor lady—too late to see the big ship, but in time to see a sequence of four individual lights cross the sky following the same path. The wife said: "Since I saw my first spaceship or UFO or whatever you wish to call them by, my life has totally changed and it's for the better. I am a much better, happier, calm-centered person. I know that there's intelligent life out there and I feel very secure in knowing that someone's out there kind of watching over us. And are available to help us."

East of **Swift Current, Saskatchewan** – *winter 1966, 2:00 P.M.*

A boy was ice skating in an outdoor rink on a windy, cloud-covered day. He looked up and saw the clouds part for a few seconds. There in the cloud opening was a large black object, slowly moving to the east. It was shaped like a swastika and was rotating. Along the long struts of the cross were windows. Then the clouds rolled back together and it was gone.

Cross Lake, Shreveport, Louisiana – *sometime during 1946 or 1947*

Three amateur sailors were testing a sailboat on the lake when they spied three round, bright objects flying overhead. These were followed by three more, and these by three more still. The three groups moved upwards toward a large object shaped like a kite with what looked like a solid tail. The groups seemed to fly into the kite object and disappear. The kite oscillated for a bit, and then, *zip*, it was gone.

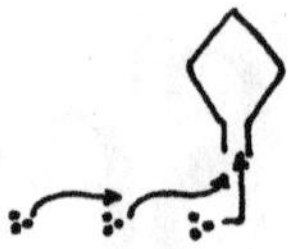

Oshawa, Ontario – August 1990, 5:00 P.M.

A large group of people in several cars saw a weird object in the sky and went down toward the lake to watch it. It was a clear, cloudless day except for this thing which appeared like a low, solid, slow-moving cloud. The "cloud" was almost round, or oval, but exiting it in all directions were bolts of electricity, which would illuminate the whole mass. It drifted south over the lake and the whole performance lasted three hours.

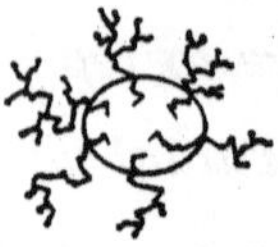

Odessa, New York – August 1972, 6:00 P.M.

A family was driving in their car when the father said, "Hey, anybody want to take a look at a UFO?" and they stopped and watched for twenty to thirty minutes. The object was a cylinder, apparently very high and stationary. A cloud surrounded and occluded it, but out of it came a small disk of light. The disk circled around and went back into the cloud. Another one then did the same thing on the other side. The cloud dissipated and there were two disks playing around the cylindrical object. The cloud formed again, and the disks would occasionally reemerge. "My family finally got cranky and after about a half hour I left."

Northern Florida – *sometime in 1985, during the day*

A husband was driving a sleeping wife northward near the Florida border on a clear, cloudless day. But suddenly a single cloud appeared out the front windshield ahead of them. As he watched, the cloud would disintegrate and become eight to ten smaller roundish objects with the remaining body of the original cloud nearby. That cloud would totally disappear and then reform. This weird activity persisted (three times) and he woke his wife, and she witnessed it a further two.

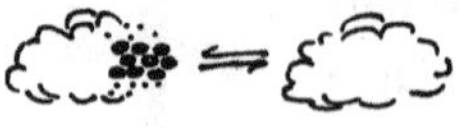

Near **Sioux Falls, South Dakota** – *fall seasons, 1963-65, late at night*

A farming couple had a series of UFO events on their property, which concentrated in fall seasons in the late evenings. Most of these events involved lights, singly or in pairs, and changing in color from bright hot white to duller orange. One evening, however, produced an entirely different object. This thing was a square-shaped object rather like a squat urban building with square lights on it arranged in rows. The thing seemed large, the apparent size of a boxcar about a block away. The windows shown a bluish light and were numerous (15 to 18). It just seemed to hang in the area but though they tried to get in their car and chase it, they never seemed to be able to get any closer. As usual, no sound.

a wild guess

Tupelo, Mississippi – *summer 1979, around noon*

Two persons, activity at the time unstated, saw an odd object in the sky at small airplane speed (c. 100 mph) and fairly low altitude (c. 500 to 1000 feet). It seemed to be one or two objects depending upon your definition. They were like two silver metallic "spheres" (the witness actually means "disks") which were on their sides and connected by a structure like two wheels with an axle. They passed silently overhead and went on about their business.

Dixon, Illinois – *March 1967, 10:00 P.M.*

A husband and wife were driving when they spotted a starlike light to the right front of the car, which was flashing several different colors. The light continued to approach as they drove, until the husband stopped the car and backed into someone's driveway. The object was at this time just across the road and hovering above the telephone pole wires. The colored lights were flashing around a boxcar shaped vehicle; also the same general size as a boxcar. It had two large windows in the side, and made no noise. There seemed to be some movement behind the windows "and that's when I got back in the car." The object quivered like a leaf, then began drifting across the road and away. At a distance there was a "big bright light like a flashbulb going off, and then it just disappeared."

West of **Champaign, Illinois** – *October 1988, 5:40 A.M.*

The witness was driving to work when he saw a strange object about 300-350 feet off the ground and perhaps 150 yards away. It was hovering over the top of a house, and emitting no sound. "The description of the craft: if you can picture in your mind a tiara, a crown jewel tiara..." The rest of the object was like a regular disk, and he assumed that the tiara was the front end. In

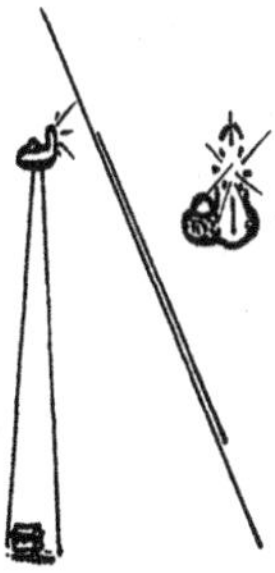

the tiara was an extremely bright light, and from its bottom came a thick blue beam which encompassed the house. The disk part looked like it was encrusted with multicolors of stained glass, with light coming from inside. The blue beam seemed almost solid, and of laser-light coherence as it sharply outlined the house. The driver didn't want to be late for work so he drove on.

Swift Current, Saskatchewan – *January 1971, predawn*

The witness was driving to work when he noticed a long tubular object moving along with his car. It came across the field and changed into an orange balloon-like thing with something hanging below it. Then it changed into an aurora borealis-like wall of multicolored light. It went on the other side of some trees, and emerged as a rolling orange ball. No sounds were emitted. The witness claimed that three others saw this, but wouldn't give his name.

Whitby, Ontario – *October 1976, 8 or 9:00 P.M.*

A son was driving with his mother on a divided highway with a central guardrail. Ahead they saw a T-shaped object coming down the middle of the division. The "T" was tilted over so that the crossbar was coming toward you like a ram. On its front face were a series of shutters each of which partially covered a light. The long shaft of the "T" trailed out horizontally behind, and contained several round windows, one of which shown a beam down on the road. No noise. Low to the road. And it passed on.

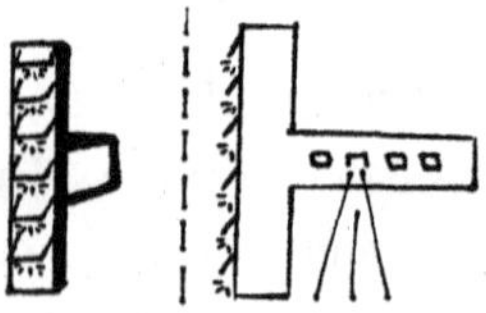

Ashdown, Arkansas – *late November 1988, and after, at night*

A UFO flap was in evidence, as far as this lady was concerned, and she and friends had seen several light events, beginning in November 1987. But shortly, she and a friend had a closer encounter. They saw a large "star" coming in their direction, and when it came nearby, it had the shape of a long house trailer, with long rectangular windows. It turned an amber color, and two small objects approached it from the west. It then turned blue, and they went inside. It pivoted and left the area at leisurely speed. She then felt that this thing began to follow her around, and on one evening she picked up her unbelieving husband and pointed it out to him. When they got home, he was screaming for her to come back outside because the thing had just come back over the house again. When she got out to see

it, there was a tremendous flash of light. They recovered, asked each other if they'd seen what they saw, and went back inside. The television show, which she had just begun to videotape, was already off the air, and neither had any recollection of the time.

Altoona, Pennsylvania – *August or September 1988, time unknown*

A husband and wife were driving from a mall and were stopped at a light. In the sky in the distance they saw two objects. One was high, but the other fairly low. He was curious and altered his course to try to get a better look. They drifted slowly, so he was able to get right beneath one, and get out of the car to look. Two other persons did likewise. The objects were shaped like Christmas trees with their tops whacked off. At the end of each of about six "branches" was suspended a large shiny metal ball. There was no noise, and the objects drifted on. He engaged one of the other men in discussion:

(Man)	What is that?
(Witness)	Buddy, I don't know.
(Man)	Well, what do you *think* it is?
(Witness)	Well, it looks to me like some kind of a UFO or a big Christmas tree or something.
(Man)	Man, that's crazy stuff. UFOs are something that people *think* they see. I'm standing here looking at this.
(Witness)	Well, so am I.
	Ultimately, the objects picked up speed and went over the mountain.

Section 13:
Close Encounters

Ho hum. Just another dozen or more cases of multiple witnesses seeing obviously "impossible" technological devices at close range. Yes, skeptics, they didn't *leave any traces of themselves behind...could it be that they have a bit better engineering than we have, so that the odd hubcap or fender isn't falling off? And, could it be, that they're a might careful and disciplined...you know, a million miles from home and all. Whatever...pardon my prejudices. Rather than tell all the stories this time, maybe a short info-stack with a drawing guess could do.*

Note: "d" refers to diameter.

Springfield, Pennsylvania – *April 24, 1962, around dinner time*

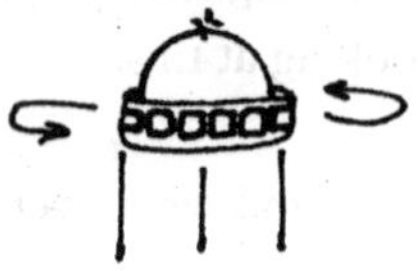

Witnesses: at least three
Duration: 3 minutes or more
Size: 30 feet d; 25 feet high
Distance: about 30 to 40 feet away
Miscellaneous: see *International UFO Reporter* article, Jan./Feb. 1985

East of **Oshawa, Ontario** – *fall 1978 or 1979, dusk*

Witnesses: four
Duration: several minutes
Size: 30 to 40 feet d
Distance: about three telephone poles high
Miscellaneous: separately drawn sketches

St. Paul, Nebraska – *January 19, 1980, in the evening*

Witnesses: four
Duration: a couple of minutes
Size: about car-sized or more
Distance: near collision with car
Miscellaneous: report to sheriff

Fredericton, New Brunswick – *July 19, 1965, 10:30 P.M.*

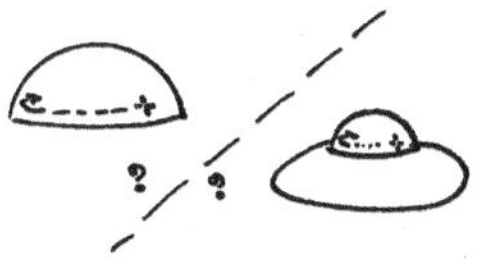

Witnesses: four
Duration: about one hour
Size: 40 foot d
Distance: about 200 feet up
Miscellaneous: many reports to airport

Dayton, Ohio – *May 1988, just after dark*

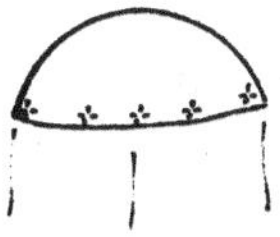

Witnesses: three
Duration: minutes
Size: size of a baseball diamond
Distance: about telephone pole high
Miscellaneous: police car also saw it

Cleveland National Forest, California – *April or May 1983, at night*

Witnesses: many
Duration: minutes
Size: about plane-size
Distance: close over car
Miscellaneous: simultaneously sighted miles away

Oshawa, Ontario – *fall 1980, early evening*

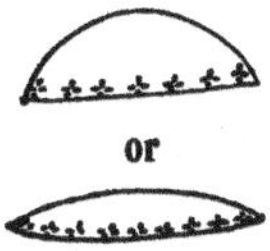

Witnesses: two
Duration: seconds to minute
Size: about 300 feet d
Distance: 100 feet over car
Miscellaneous: instant acceleration

Lipton, Saskatchewan – *January 29, 1950, 9:00 P.M.*

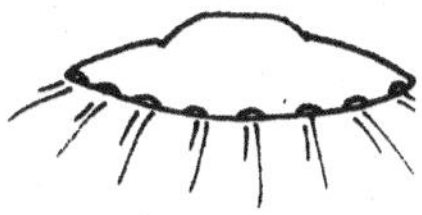

Witnesses: two
Duration: 20 seconds
Size: 50 to 55 feet d
Distance: 100 feet up
Miscellaneous: perimeter exhausts

Springfield, Illinois – *fall 1978, 2:00 A.M.*

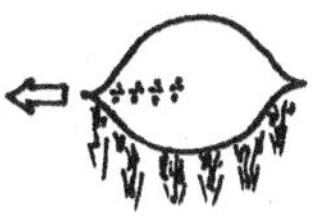

like gas jet flames

Witnesses: one
Duration: several seconds
Size: large
Distance: sixty feet up
Miscellaneous: (windows placed somewhere)

East Corning, New York – *1967 or 1968, early morning*

Witnesses: two, separately
Duration: seconds to minute
Size: 150-200 foot d w. 3 foot d lights
Distance: couple hundred feet and low?
Miscellaneous: hummed

Elmville, Ontario – *winter, 1968-9, 7:00 A.M.*

Witnesses: at least three
Duration: 30 minutes
Size: (wouldn't guess)
Distance: just above the house
Miscellaneous: patrolman later saw it; object hummed

Near **Norfolk Naval Base, Virginia** – *late August or September 1974, 9:30 P.M.*

Witnesses: many
Duration: three to five minutes
Size: 150 feet d; 10 to 15 feet high
Distance: 50 feet above drive-in
Miscellaneous: slight buzz; jets scrambled

Huffman, Texas – *August or September 1974, after midnight*

Witnesses: five
Duration: several minutes
Size: perhaps small plane-size
Distance: about 10 yards away
Miscellaneous: light hum; feeling of peace

Newark, Ohio – *summer 1956 or 1957, 10:30 P.M.*

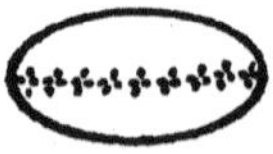

Witnesses: three
Duration: a minute or so
Size: bigger than two cars
Distance: near and low in field
Miscellaneous: felt she had to go to it

Towanda, Pennsylvania – *sometime in 1974-1975, at dusk*

Witnesses: five
Duration: three minutes
Size: big with three large lights
Distance: 40 feet overhead
Miscellaneous: mother yelled to get in the house

I'm glad I'm talking to someone that believes us because there's nobody else who believes us. I kept this secret for years, my mother and I. We'd always talk about it, and stuff, but it was like "Yeah, right, if we go and turn it in, everybody is going to laugh at us!" (So) I never turned it in...I just... everybody that comes around says: Oh, Bull; and I say: Oh, Yeah? Well, wait until you see it!

Webster, South Dakota – *September 1956, 9:30 P.M.*

Witnesses: two, plus police
Duration: three to five plus minutes
Size: 150 feet d
Distance: about 100 feet overhead
Miscellaneous: The witness said that after their close encounter, and with the object still overhead, they drove by police and three other cars watching the object. The witness thinks that the policeman (highway patrol) must have reported the object through some channels, because he believes that he has read about his case from the other's point of view in some later publication.

There were quite a few other CE I cases, but they'd go on interminably. Typical CE Is are amazing but they just come and go without stories.

Section 14:
Close Encounters with different shapes

All those beasts *in Section 13 could be legitimately called disks, or flying saucers. These aren't quite the same, and many of them have enough distinctiveness that they deserve their little stories.*

York College, Nebraska – *sometime in 1961, during the day*

A bunch of college boys were off-campus, fooling around playing interfraternity games in a rural undeveloped area. Out of the southeast came a huge cigar-shaped object, perhaps 150 feet long and forty to fifty feet in diameter. All around the structure were orange lights. The object cruised in silently at 300 to 400 feet and came directly overhead. Only a displacement in the air was heard. The college boys ran to their cars and drove away fast.

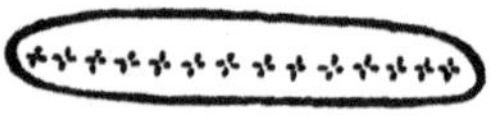

New Berlin, Illinois – *summer 1964, during the day*

Four people were watching television when the set went fuzzy and they heard a high-pitched whine. They went outside and saw an object hovering over some high tension power lines. The pitch was initially loud, but stopped when the people emerged to see it. The object was very slow (c. 5 mph), shaped like an egg with three colors of lights rotating around it (red, green, and white). There were "windows" at the top, and it was about the size of an automobile. One of the young men ran under it waving and yelling; and the object shot up and away. (Witness was the local police chief at the time he told this to John.)

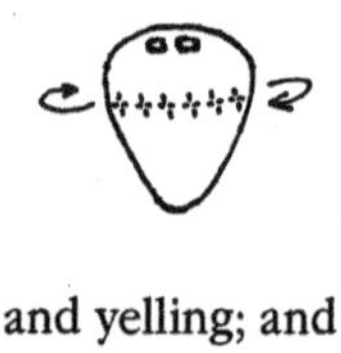

Belleville, Ohio – *fall 1983, at night*

A father and his sons were training their dogs in the woods and noticed an odd light in the trees. They investigated and came within about 75 yards of an object with large orange lights. They jumped a fence, and heard a light humming noise, and suddenly the "ship" was right overhead. It was conical, "kind of a Christmas tree shape," with orange lights on the side and a tripod and one light on the bottom. It then zoomed away. No landing trace was found the next day, only a "rotten" eggs odor.

... a guess

Cass Lake, Minnesota – *summer 1964-1965, at night*

Six youngsters were alone at their aunt and uncle's cabin when they saw a light outside. There was a cigar-shaped object hovering over the water and a boat at the dock. It was tilted at an angle and made the water move "like an air boat would do." The object looked silver with red lights all along its midline. It seemed to be about twenty feet long. No noise, almost no feeling at all as they watched: "that's what was probably the scariest thing about it." They ran back inside, heard a *whoosh*, and the object went into the air and away.

Wallingford, Connecticut – *spring 1985, about 9-9:30 P.M.*

Three persons were driving when one of the passengers yelled: "Oh, my God!" and began shouting about an object overhead. The object was huge, "sort of like a mall," and shaped in an octagon. Multicolored lights (red, yellow, blue) were flashing all about, and the bottom was very intricate "like a giant microchip." The lights seemed as big as mall entryways. No noise, but a slow drifting motion that allowed several (20?) minutes of viewing. Other cars on the highway slowed to watch. "I should have written all this down; but, of course, I didn't. I didn't even tell anybody who would care, you know, until today. That's why I'm so nervous."

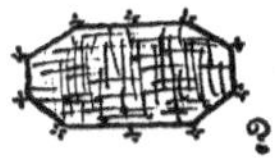

Sioux Falls, South Dakota – *sometime in 1975 or 1976, daytime*

There had been two cattle mutilated on this farm, and the witness had taken to always carrying a gun, loaded, in case he ran into whoever was doing it. He saw a light off in the distance and playfully pointed the gun at it and pulled the trigger. Almost at once, the object came to within thirty feet of him. It was a glowing egg, and hovered there noiselessly. Ten feet tall and six to eight feet wide and self-luminous like a light bulb. He hollered for someone to get the camera, but before they could the object began to move and then streaked away.

Horseheads, New York – *around November 1968, early evening*

A husband, wife and their son saw two "flying saucers" hovering near their residence. They were shaped like children's tops, but flattened on top and bottom and one a smaller version of the other. The large one would move and the smaller one would follow. This went on for about an hour. The odd thing was that before it would move the large disk would intensely glow. "I'd never seen anything glow like that...the glow seemed to drip off when it went up... seemed to be sort of a residue."

West Seneca, New York – *August 1973, 10-11:00 P.M.*

Three friends were sitting in lawn chairs in the driveway when they heard a low hum and looked overtop the garage. There was an object which appeared like half an egg, silver metallic with an orange and blue glow about it. It was slowly descending to about twenty feet from the roof when one of them yelled: "Stop! You'll crush the garage!" Whereupon it *did* stop, and flew away rapidly. Two days later, one of the witnesses heard the same sound, went outside to his dog and saw the same object, now at street level. It was about twenty-five to thirty feet in diameter, and only three to four feet off the ground. He walked toward it, *compelled* to do so; and he felt sensationless. The dog barked and he snapped out of it and backed away. The object then drifted away, angled upward and was gone.

Smyrna, Tennessee – *February 1979, predawn*

A late-night employee was cleaning up a diner, situated by a small lake, and was taking a smoking break. Above him in the sky hung an object, possibly a ball, very large, silent, although it's shape was somewhat difficult to accurately ascertain. It began to drift away down the lake. He flashed his lighter and it stopped. Flash again: closer. He kept doing this until it was about fifty yards off and he began to change his mind. As he was also night watchman, he had a gun inside, and thought about getting the gun and shooting this thing. Simultaneously with his thought, the object made a jumping, leapfrogging move which placed it thirty feet further away. Then it turned in the air...and disappeared. As the witness thought more about this he felt that the morning couldn't have gotten as late as this had, and he

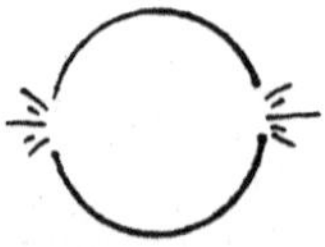

wondered why he couldn't fix on a shape.

New London, Connecticut – *spring of about 1983, 10:30 P.M.*

A supervisor at a local hospital was driving to work when she saw a round object stop above the treetops ahead. She was curious, pulled off and stopped. The object had red, blue, yellow and white lights flickering around it, and shone down a white beam. Suddenly the thing was right in the road ahead of her. And very strangely—no other cars on the road. "All of a sudden a peace came over me." She remembers only walking late into work that evening, feeling wonderful; except that when she snapped out of her feeling on the road, she realized that she was sitting with the car off and window down, something she'd never do, for safety's sake.

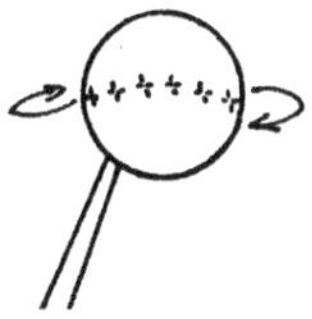

Section 15:
A few stories with disks up close

Near **Wapakoneta, Ohio** – *September 1972, just around dusk*

A husband and wife were in their home when the National Weather Service announced that a tornado had been sighted. A huge storm was going on, and the husband walked out to see if the tornado was close. As he did, an object with red and white lights came into view: low to the ground (thirty feet), very slow, and soundless. It moved behind the barn, across the road, into a gravel pit, all with instant angular changes of motion (no *turns*). Then the object took a path directly toward him and his wife, who had joined him on the porch. She got terribly frightened, ran into the house and hid in a room, refusing to leave, and denying that there was something out there (she later calmed down and admitted what she saw). The object was a metallic disk, thirty feet in diameter, eight to ten feet thick, with a band about the middle within which were the red and white lights. Above the lights was a two-foot wide band of translucent material out of which light shone. The whole performance took several minutes with the final Mexican standoff (hovering fifty yards away just over the power lines) being a full two to three minutes. The object then moved off, rose a bit in the air, lit up so brightly that it was extremely difficult to look at "and then it just, it almost instantaneously disappeared."

Somewhere unstated in **Colorado** – *April 1979, 2 to 3:00 A.M.*

A mother and her young son were staying with her parents at the old family home in Colorado. The mother and son were both awakened to find pulsing orange light shining into the bedroom from the outside. The first thought was that there were police cars outside for some reason. She got up to go to the window to see. The orange light now was gone, but across the street and up a little in the air was a bluish pulsing light. It was on a domed disk object from the bottom of which pulsed this light. It was very close.

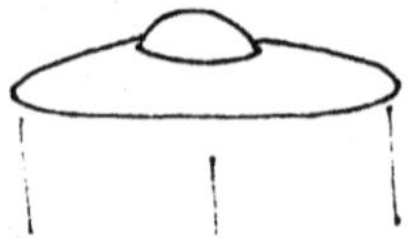

I looked at it and I said: Oh, my God!; and the way that I felt was I had just hit an invisible brick wall. I looked at it and I didn't know what to do. I should have went and got my dad, but I was just transfixed and I... it was like there was no place to go. I had that feeling... I wasn't afraid that people wouldn't believe me, just I was observing something that shouldn't be there. I remember that my mind was like shut off. I kept looking at it for maybe a minute; I turned around; I got back in bed and I went to sleep. I know that sounds strange...

Utica, Ohio – *sometime during the 1970s, around 10:00 P.M.*

A mother and her three children were driving home when they came across a huge disk hovering in the air. The diameter was at least as much as a semitrailer is long, as it was wider than the house near which it was hovering. She pulled the car over and watched for about five minutes. The disk had very large windows near the top. [For a rare change, this case had a witness drawing attached to it so I don't have to be too creative.] From these windows came a soft pale blue light. The ship was about fifteen to twenty feet tall, a large rather thick-looking affair. From the bottom of the object came a pale yellow light... a light which had the sense about it of being soft or textured, as if it were thick, "the beam might be thick to walk through." There was no noise from the craft, but plenty of noise from the kids, who were now screaming that they were afraid, so she started the car and drove away. At the point where she had stopped the object could have been no more than 150 feet away.

Wells Township, Pennsylvania – *December 27, 1967, 9:00 P.M.*

Two seniors in high school were driving back to their homes on a dirt road when they noticed a triangle of lights near the horizon. One of them thought it must be a radio tower, but the array moved and began to come nearer. The driver parked the truck. The lights resolved to be on a large disk, at least 100 feet in diameter, moving 300 to 400 feet off the ground. It banked, showing its underside to contain squared light panels, three of which were lit. But as it banked the whole bottom of the craft suddenly flashed into life:

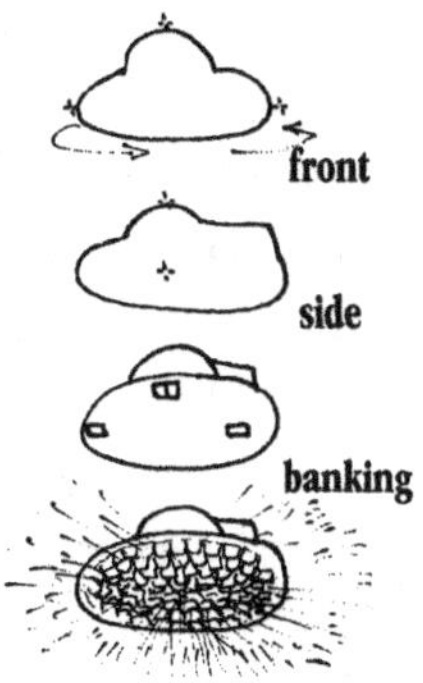

"hundreds" of panels. As it releveled, the light in the dome of the disk came on, and it began to follow the dirt road making no noise whatever. As it came too close, the witness insisted that his friend get back in the truck, and physically pushed him to do so. They then drove rapidly away. The object banked off and went in the direction of Elmira, New York, where, coincidentally, there was a power outage twenty minutes later. [This was another rare instance of a witness attaching drawings.]

Near **Madison, South Dakota** – *1967 or 1968, date unknown, at night*

Two brothers were horseback riding south of Buffalo Trading Post heading back toward their farm. As they rode up a hill, they saw something overhead, and one of the two brothers completely blanked out, and can't remember anything else which occurred for the next several minutes. The second brother remembers hearing a sound, *whizz*, and seeing a disk overhead. Everyone was scared, including the horses, who were trying to break loose and run (the brothers had dismounted). The object was spinning: "It was just like it had seen us because it slowed down." It had small windows encircling it, and in the bottom the outline of a door or hatch perhaps, which might open and extend down. The object, about treetop level and just above them hovered for "quite a while," and then moved away over their neighbor's house, and beyond to where it looked like it might be landing right in their own backyard. The one brother snapped the other out of his memory loss by informing him what just happened, and they decided not to go look for the saucer, but get straight home. Everyone else was asleep, so they told them the next morning. "They all laughed at us, of course, but I guess we let it go at that."

West Middlesex, Pennsylvania – *late September 1957, at dusk*

A husband and wife were driving to his mother's home when the wife saw an object which was trailing them in the air. He sped the car up, slowed it down, but the object paced them and stayed right there. When they passed through areas which were built up, it would rise and move away, but in rural spots it would come back in close. It seemed to leave them as they turned toward his mother's house, but when they arrived in the driveway, there it was hovering just 100 yards away. It made a low thrumming sound, "like a very large diesel motor, which quite frankly scared the hell out of me." The disk was shaped a bit like a pie, with red, green, and gold/white lights going around the perimeter. Beneath these, on the undercarriage,

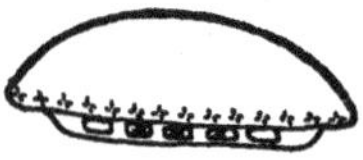

were squarish windows within which the wife says she saw silhouettes reminiscent of the top portions of people. As they watched, the mother came out of her house to greet them. The mother, a very religious person who never swears, turned to look at what they were watching and yelled: "Jesus Christ!" and ran back into the house. The wife went in after her, and the husband grabbed a rifle just inside the door. He walked out: a 24- to 28-foot diameter target at fifty yards would be an easy mark. He clicked a shell into place, and the thing just vanished. "So help me God, the thing disappeared." He made a call to the local air base and within minutes the air was split by the sounds of one or two jets scrambled.

Benton, Louisiana – *January 19, 1988, 5 to 5:15 P.M.*

A father and his daughter were driving in a thoroughly urban area to pick up the mother from work on a bright sunshiny day. They parked in the lot next to the wife's place of work and sat for a moment to wait for her. The daughter said: "Look! What is that?" Over Interstate 20 was a flash, a streak of light. The "streak" then suddenly came right in front of them and hovered over the ground. It was a disk, like a flattened top, about 150 feet away, and about fifty feet off the surface. It stopped in the air and spun. The metal was grayish steel in color and the midsection of the object was punctuated with what the husband called turbines: apparently wind-scoop or exhaust-type openings which he felt were associated with the propulsion of the object. From the top of the machine, there emerged a sheath from which extended rotary blades, as if they had helicopter like function. The device was twelve to fifteen feet in diameter, and about five feet tall: "about the size of a car." The nugget in this case is this:

> This machine sat there and looked at us, and we looked at it, and I guess it must have been a good minute and a half. And it seemed at this time there were no cars moving, didn't hear a thing in the world. Nothing. Just like the world stood still – it just seemed like I was in a trance... like there was nothing else in the world but us and the machine. As soon as the machine left, traffic on I-20 came alive and the parking lot became active.

Section 16:

UFOs which leave their mark, and marks with no UFO

"Landing Traces" have been seen by some ufologists as a possible key to establishing the phenomenon scientifically, as they are one of the few (some say the only) things that are permanent and physical enough to be taken to the laboratory. Embarrassingly, although there are many hundreds of "landing traces" in the UFO literature, almost none have been so studied. Exactly who should be embarrassed by this I'm not sure, but the fact remains. John received several trace case reports as you shall read; he also received a group of "traces-without-a-UFO." These latter are of dubious value, but they are included here for your interest. The first case mentioned below did not leave a trace, but is included due to the effect that the object had on the grass, which one could imagine creating the well-known swirled and matted grass trace had the object been lower and the conditions of the vegetation appropriate.

Near the **California/Oregon** *border – summer 1980 or 1981, 7:00 P.M.*

A husband and wife had raised some livestock and were making a meat-delivery run to the butchers for restaurant sales. They were returning home and stopped on a hill to take a dinner break in the truck. There, coming out of the middle of a field was a simple disk: silver, curved top, flat bottom, about 200 feet in diameter. It silently hovered above the field for about five minutes: "I didn't do much breathing in that length of time either." Beneath the disk the hay was wiggling and swaying around. The disk then rose in the air and shot away becoming a small dot in the sky.

Shelby, Ohio – *August 1953, at night*

Most of the family was already in bed when the woman of the house looked out the bathroom window and saw a red-lighted object wobbling downward. She looked more closely and saw a round object on the ground with three round openings (ports) in it from which came a fiery-like glow. Trying to rationalize this she wondered if something was burning in their burn-barrel out back. She looked again (she was trying to take a bath at the time, and curiosity kept getting to her, so she was up and down, observing) and saw something different which would float up in the air near the garage almost as if it was inspecting the copper cable which hung there. This second thing was shaped like eyes (ovals) but perpendicular (one on top the other?) And would glow (pulse) and the round object would glow (pulse) in return. "I was sitting on the bathtub for two hours, at that time, very… you know." She finally got her husband up to look at it, too. The days following saw the nearest evergreen tree turn brown and die.

Waldron, Saskatchewan – *sometime in the late 1970s, about 1:00 A.M.*

A couple woke up to a roaring sound (like a jet) and bright fiery red light shining into the house. The woman ran into another room to see if the house was burning, and by the time she ran back the light had disappeared. Another young woman, a half mile away, was also awakened by the sound. The cattle panicked and bolted, running through a four-wire fence and ended up five miles away. The next day, at the neighbor's property, a trace was found where tall grass had been disturbed (the shape of this trace was not described).

Weatherford, Texas – *sometime in 1959, 9 or 9:30 P.M.*

A young man was going to pick up a friend on a motor scooter. He saw a lighted object off to his left, and went to approach it. He became afraid and stopped and pointed his headlight at it. He seemed to expect to see the object, but saw nothing except a glow; when he pointed his headlight away, then he could see the object. The thing, whatever it was, was hovering. But he went on. The next day there was a depression in the tall overgrown grass, and the plants were slightly discolored toward brown. The light seemed about a foot in diameter, the trace, six foot. The object seemed about two to three feet off the ground. The light was like a translucent sphere, internally lit in a magenta color.

Pekin, Illinois – *late May 1967, during the day*

A grade school student was goofing around in class staring out the window. He saw a silver disk descending outside but some distance away.

The disk was skinnier at one end than the other and went slowly down behind some nearby low hills. A couple of days later, after he had told his father about it, he insisted to his dad that they go and take a look at where it went down. The place was an illegal dirt track, but there in the middle was a large circle where the grass was browned and dead (size of trace unstated: "huge").

State of Washington – *October 1963, 9:30 A.M.*

Two people were out bird-hunting (probably somewhere near Seattle) and came upon an object just sitting in a field about 100 yards away. It was an oval, metallic saucer, very shiny and with blinking red lights. The two hunters got into a disagreement about who would go get the police and who would stay, and so both went. By the time they got back, the thing was gone. In its place was a very dark brown, oval-shaped trace which seemed to have been singed into the grass. The longer dimension was about twenty feet across. The police? "they didn't make no comments," but "I was telling my wife not too long ago that I would like to go back. I wish I could go back and see that spot."

Smiths Falls, Ontario – *sometime in 1979/1980, probably autumn*

[This is a not-quite-firsthand case, but close enough to report.] An adult sister was back to her old hometown to visit her brother and mother, and everyone was buzzing about an event which had just occurred. They had seen a very large flying saucer come down and apparently land near an abandoned quarry. When it had gone, they had discovered a patch of vegetation sixty feet in diameter which was both depressed and burned. The sister was all excited by this and wanted to go up and see the site. When they got there, they were blocked by barbed wire, "no trespassing" signs, and the presence of two military patrolmen.

Lebanon, Ohio – *date unstated, event at dusk*

[To the readers: many of these "date unstated" cases happened because the witness said something like "I could tell you the exact date, but I'd have to look it up," whereupon John, the endlessly trusting nice guy, would get them to agree to send in a report form, which then (apparently) never happened.]

A father, mother, and son heard a high-pitched whistle outside the house and went out to investigate. They saw a large object with many lights around it "parked in the field." The mother became afraid, ran inside and flipped a set of security spotlights. The object immediately raised up fifty feet in the air and came at the house. It made an abrupt 45° angle upwards and accelerated away at very rapid speed. Over in the field was a scorched area of grass, circular and forty feet in diameter.

Langford, Saskatchewan – *late 1970s around Thanksgiving, around dawn*

Several women were out in different locations and noticed flashing lights and looked up and saw an unidentifiable object taking off in the direction of a small mountain called Stearns Mountain. The object seemed to land. The object took off and the site was mobbed by curiosity-seekers. The trace that they found was triangular, equilateral, twelve feet on a side.

Braintree, England – *1959 or early 1960, unstated time of event*

Three gradeschoolers saw a bright light come out of the sky and seem to land among the trees. The next day they went over to investigate and found three holes in the ground in an equilateral triangle and the inside portions of two nearby trees charred up to about four feet in height.

Bath, Ohio – *April 1969, in the morning*

A bunch of kids were getting off the school bus when they saw a white light in the sky. They went into school and when they came back out for a break, it was still there. It was moving about quite a bit. The students went back inside and were told that an object had landed on the football field and they were not to go outside. The superintendent and the principal both were named in the newspaper as having seen the object landed. On the field was a trace of three spots.

Harrison City, Pennsylvania – *fall 1970, at dawn*

Two men were on their way to work when they saw what looked to be a water tank on a hill, but there had never been a structure up there before. On the way back from work that day they noticed that the structure was now gone. Curious, they drove up to take a look. There, in a small area of grass, were three burnt areas in a regular triangle. The grass was burnt down to bare ground and the ground slightly dished. The circles were ten feet in diameter, and the triangle fit into a thirty foot area.

Wycombe, Pennsylvania – *late October 1973, time unstated*

A father and his daughter were returning home to their farm and, as they parked the car, saw a sixty-foot diameter disk with portholes along the perimeter hovering over some trees, 500 to 600 feet away. Lights were flashing sequentially from window to window. The object then silently descended (apparently behind the trees).

A few days later, the father and daughter decided to walk over to the area and see what they could see. The trace described is not easy to recreate from the words on the tape. The sure things are: three D-shaped depressions set in a triangle, and a rolled-out path which extended a couple of hundred feet from one side of the triangle and circling back to another. Confusion arises from the statement that the "Ds" were six-foot long and "crossed one another" in a triangular shape. One possible rendition of this is sketched here. Caveat emptor. The father took film of this trace, and was later questioned by a member of Johnsville Naval Air Station as to whether he had seen anything that evening. When told yes and that a trace had been filmed, "he got quite excited, said he belonged to some kind of observers UFO reporting group." He had the captain of the station contact the farmer and request his films. "Of course I refused."

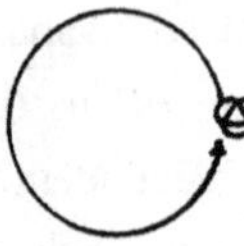

Cedar Rapids, Iowa – *early fall 1970, 5:30 P.M.*

A woman heard what she thought was a loud humming of the power lines, but it turned out to be coming from an object which was sitting in an alfalfa field up near the fence. The object was a disk resting on an extended tripod. It had bolts or rivets around its perimeter, and above them three oval windows. Within these windows were three silhouettes, about which she could make out only that they wore drab green clothing and were moving about. The object rose and the sound moved off with it. It slowly and smoothly went over the trees and away. She went out to investigate immediately and found a trace consisting of three marks set in an equilateral triangle, the sides of which measured twelve feet. The marks were circular, about fourteen inches in circumference.

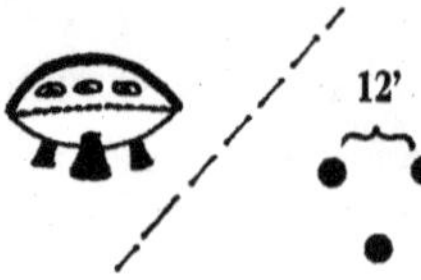

West Yellowstone, Montana – *summer 1953 or 1954, during the day*

A grandfather and his granddaughter and grandson were standing by a lake when they saw a disturbance in the water coming nearer and hesitating beside their boat dock. The surface water was agitated as if something was spinning underneath. The grandfather went to get a camera, but the thing took off across the lake and disappeared. When they walked into the water, they found a sandy bowl-like depression about five feet in diameter. John asked if the witness thought the object was fish spawning and was met by, shall we say, skepticism.

And a gang of alleged traces in search of an object:

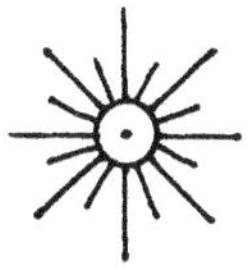

Location: Wauseon, Ohio
Date: March 1984
Type: Circle of dug-up ground with a two-inch diameter hole in the middle, and lines extending like a sunburst.

Location: New London, Connecticut
Date: June or July 1985
Type: Thirty-foot diameter area of flattened grass in the field, the central part of which was "somewhat charred." Grass swirled.

Location: Lestock, Saskatchewan
Date: unnamed 1976
Type: Circular trace found while swathing wheat field. Sixteen feet in diameter. Wheat would not grow. Just black dirt.

Location: Queensland, Australia outback
Date: unnamed 1979
Type: Two traces, one a thirty-foot diameter donut (three foot wide ring with undamaged middle); other an eight foot diameter donut. Grass in rings burnt black.

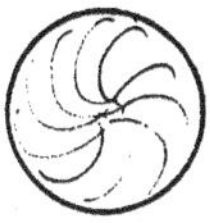

Location: Minden, Nebraska
Date: mid-June 1976
Type: A large circle of heavily bent down and clockwise swirled corn plants in a field seen to be normal one week earlier. Plants were also burnt. Size = "14 rows."

Location: northeast of Yorkton, Saskatchewan
Date: date not given
Type: A burnt circle of fifteen-foot diameter in a "grain" field. In the middle were four holes marking a one-foot by one and a half foot rectangle. Hole = one-inch diameter.

Location: Kingston, Ontario
Date: 1965
Type: Twin rings of depressed and badly destroyed wheat (one inside the other). The rings were nine-foot and twelve-foot diameter with a one-foot undisturbed patch between.

Location: Winnebago, Nebraska
Date: early summer but year unspecified
Type: A circular spot somewhere between 75 and 100 feet in diameter in a corn field: "sterilized" so that no plants would grow.

Location: Lancaster, Pennsylvania
Date: July 1970
Type: Family discovered twenty-foot diameter ring in front yard of grass matted down. Surrounding this was six to eight-inch annular ring with "black beads" (like graphite) all over it. This ring died. In center was a two-inch "dent" in the ground.

Location: Westlock, Alberta
Date: no date
Type: A ten-foot diameter circle in a barley field. The grain was burnt away. Three pod marks inside the circle (about one and a half-foot penetration) and a depressed "belly spot" in the center.

Location: Stockholm, Saskatchewan
Date: August 1973
Type: Found eight to ten-foot circle in wheat field while swathing. Clockwise swirl and four areas where soil blown away. "Time of Langenberg, Saskatchewan, incident." Center area flattened.

Location: Waldron, Saskatchewan
Date: 1974
Type: Found four different diameter circles while swathing barley (fourteen feet, ten feet, seven feet, four feet). Barley flattened hard to ground and counterclockwise swirled. Circles aligned north/south.

Location: Cookson Hills, Oklahoma
Date: June 4, 1991
Type: Several traces in grass, all squashed down and counterclockwise swirled. Single twenty-foot circle; array of four with a connecting path (15', 20', 12', 6'), and a half-circle which also was counterclockwise swirled.

Location: Kingston, Ontario
Date: no date
Type: Five circles in a field of grass with nothing growing inside. Circles were basin-like holes in ground, five feet in diameter and one and half to two feet, deepest point.

Location: Salisbury, North Carolina
Date: early 1970s
Type: Circular trace (ring fifteen to sixteen feet in diameter, about nine inches wide of disturbed grass in front yard. Three circular pod marks within. Three or so feet away was a small "insignia" traced a la the Lonnie Zamora case. Much "wadding material" like cigarette filter was scattered about.

Location: Fairmont, Minnesota
Date: late spring, 1953 or 1954
Type: In the middle of pasture was an eight to ten-foot diameter scorched area with three extra black places, and curled metal filings scattered about.

Location: Swift Current, Saskatchewan
Date: winter, sometime in the 1960s
Type: In ultra cold weather (c. minus 30 to minus 40° F.) A couple, driving home at 2:00 A.M., came across a dense but extremely localized area of fog. Stopping the car, they observed that all the snow in the area was melted and the ground was steaming. All snow outside the area was intact. The trace was not perfectly circular, but gave witnesses the feeling that something hot had been hovering overtop the area.

Section 17:
Close Encounters involving physiological effects

People are concerned over whether UFO encounters are dangerous, and that is still controversial, but here are a few cases wherein people claimed to be negatively affected by the experiences.

Greenville, Tennessee – *fall 1968, 7:00 P.M.*

A husband and wife were driving their car on a rural dirt road. As they approached the highway there was an object hovering overtop the power lines. (The shape of this object was not specifically stated but the report seems to be speaking of something circular or oval.) Very bright light pulsated from the object in blue, green, pink-red, and all smeared together. "It had a pulsating rhythm to it, which did not correspond to my heart rhythm, and it was upsetting my heart rhythm. It seemed like my heart wanted to go faster and faster… and I wanted (to be) gone. I finally told my husband, please, I want to leave."

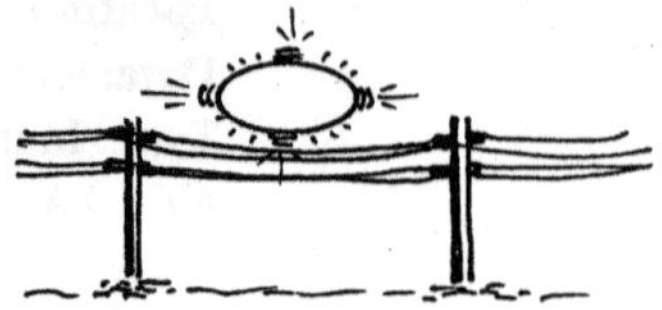

Hopewell, New Jersey – *September 1979, 8:30 P.M.*

Two men were working in a cabin when the power went out and a reddish light filled up the whole room. One man was terrified and wouldn't even look out the window. The other did, and saw a "ship" (apparently a disk) of metal with brightly colored, "flowing" lights going around. He felt paralyzed then, and thought that he was being "probed". An image appeared in his mind of two alien beings (small, chalky white, hair, large eyes, "they were humanoids but not exactly"). Then everything just disappeared (the ship was gone), and the power came back on. Witness said that in two months his whole life crumbled, a fact that he seems to relate to this experience but without knowing any causal link.

Emmaus, Pennsylvania – summer 1979, 8:30 P.M.

A woman saw a strange "star" moving in an odd manner, and pointed it out to her neighbor. He said that he didn't know what it was, but got in his car to go to work. As the object in the sky moved up and down, another object came in closer to the house just over the trees making a whirring sound. At that moment she was paralyzed. Both objects resolved to be disks with flat bottoms and curved tops. The smaller, closer one, had rectangular lights (bright white) on the bottom. The nearer object hovered over the trees, and then began to move away. It got out of her sight momentarily and then she could move. She checked her watch and the "few seconds" of paralysis had lasted ten minutes. She looked up at the larger distant object, and the smaller one was going up to it. It hovered beneath for a few minutes and then both whisked out of sight. That evening she had a sore throat, a small lump, which the doctors couldn't figure out and ultimately went away. Otherwise, she felt great: "I was different for about two weeks. I was very calm. I'm usually a...not a hyper person but sort of tense, and I was just very calm about everything. Nothing bothered me."

Troy, Pennsylvania – *August 1975, about 9:00 P.M.*

Two teenage sisters were walking back toward their home in the country, when a disk-shaped object dropped down from the sky near them. It hovered a few moments and then slowly moved closer. The sisters could feel hot air on their faces, and decided to run. Now, the hot air was on their backs as the thing kept behind them, emitting a hiss, like soft air brakes. They got to a creek bed and tried to climb up the bank. The object was right overtop. The older sister got up to where there was a railroad track, but her sister didn't make it. She went back and found her standing, like she was frozen with her hands out and looking skyward, still in the creek bed. The older sister shook and slapped her till she fell to the ground. She pulled her to her feet, and they continued to run home. How the object left, they didn't notice. It was huge (bigger than a barn) and obviously menacing in their minds. On arriving home, the "twenty minutes" that this terrorizing chase seemed to take registered about an hour and a half on the clock. Needless to say, the sisters did not follow through on their earlier plan to sleep out in their tent that night. The

younger sister, rather, went right up to her bedroom and crawled under the blankets. She still will not talk about the incident. As an aside: while the girls were running with the thing overhead, the older sister noticed that the hay around her was spinning counterclockwise and laying almost flat to the ground. By the next day it had popped back into place, but you could still see the path that the girls made when they ran.

New Philadelphia, Ohio – *June 30, 1982, 2:45 A.M.*

A man put his dog out for the evening in the garage and she was whining and crying. When she settled down, he went to bed. He awoke "in sort of a hysteric state," feeling that there was somebody in the room. He fully roused himself: no one there, walked to the bathroom, checked the time, and laid back down. He looked into the mirror and saw the reflection of a small green pyramidal object. The object may have been just outside the window. The pyramid seemed to have light orange bands around it and the green areas flickered. In a few seconds, the thing disappeared and he heard a noise like something going over the roof. The next day the witness was violently sick and had to leave work.

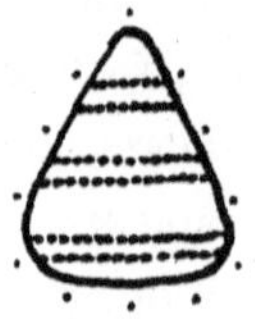

Arbutus, Maryland – *summer 1954, late at night*

A young girl was awakened by a bright light shining into her bedroom window. She got out of bed and went over to the window. Just outside were lights arrayed in a triangle, flat to the ground level, and pointed at her. They were white and illuminated everything in detail in the surroundings, but no structure of an object was obvious—just the lights. All of a sudden the lights were just gone. The next two or three days she had a fever which forced her to stay home. John asked: how do we know this wasn't a dream? She said: "Can't be sure… I had a fever… maybe I dreamt that. But it seemed to me that it was real, that I got up and went to the window, and saw this."

North Canton, Ohio – *fall 1954, 8:00 P.M.*

The witness was walking in his neighborhood when he saw a small red object high in the sky. It changed colors through orange to white as if someone "was welding all the way through the sky." Then it dropped lower and went back to a dull orange "like it was cooling off." It came at him, wobbling like a leaf fall, and settled over high tension power lines. The thing was a disk about 100 feet in diameter. The witness then felt like he was paralyzed and had the sensation of floating upwards. He seemed to get as close as three or four feet from the bottom of the object, seeing and feeling a "whole bunch of electrical sparkles, just twinkling in front of my

eyes." Then he blacked out. When he came to he was 100 feet up the road and in shock. The object was still high above, and another smaller one was low above a building. This second one exhibiting six exhaust "furnaces" around it as it rose. The small one left in a *swoosh*; the larger simply vanished. The witness began getting nightmares and had recurring sickness in cyclical intervals of about three months. These bouts of chills and fevers would last about a week. The nightmares are repetitive dreams involving lying on a table in a paralyzed state, whereupon he usually becomes agitated enough that his wife wakes him out of it.

Near **San Juan, Puerto Rico** – *1986, date unstated, 7:00 P.M.*

The witness was driving toward San Juan when the car was engulfed in a bright white light. The intensity was such that everything seemed to visually bleach out like the color of snow. The light was emanating from above, and the driver stopped the car. He got out but was afraid to look up at the source of the light. He inspected under his hood and found that cables had been burnt out. [The witness testimony is confusing here. My guess is that what he meant is that he drove on to work, refusing to look up at the light. *After* work, his car wouldn't start. He *then* found burnt cables. Tinkered everything together, then drove back home.] When he got to the same spot where he'd had the encounter with the light, it was 5:00 A.M.

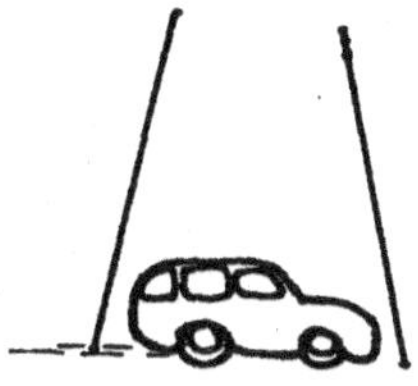

Unaccountably, he stayed there sitting in his car till 8:30 A.M. Afterwards, he had what he feels are symptoms related to this: hair falling out, sensitivity to light, vomiting, and the need for an operation.

Concord, North Carolina – *March 23, 1987, 9:20 P.M.*

The witness heard a crash outside and went to see if someone had had a wreck. There in the backyard sat a domed disk, larger than 25 feet in diameter, which was its height. There was a six-foot diameter top dome, and an 18- to 20-inch wide ramp extended from the bottom. The craft was silvery blue and the dome shone so blindingly orange that it hurt the eyes to look. She went back inside and stole peeks at it, till the shooting pains in her eyes forced her to stop. Then it was gone. The light had been seen by her neighbor as a thick orange, bright fog. The dog never reacted to the object at all, but she said that the light "was so dense that my outside light looked like a small light bulb, couldn't even see the post at all." The lady's eyes had pain for three days due to all this. Two days later, her grandson came over, heard the story, and detected remnant magnetism in a metal pipe near the landing spot (his keys attracted toward the metal).

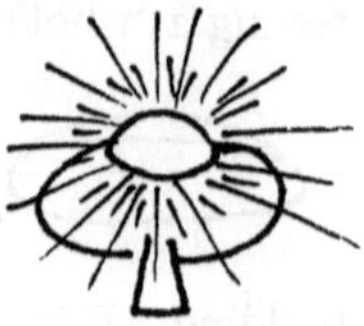

Shelby, Ohio – *around February 1979, at night*

A woman was visiting her aunt in the country, and they noticed a bright light outside the window. It was like a spotlight hanging in the air in the field near the dog kennel. The one light became two, as the witness went outside and the aunt stayed to watch. The aunt says that two lights went under the third brighter one and disappeared. Once the niece was outside the object's appearance was now a set of red and green lights and they were moving. She started toward the field, thought better of it, and stopped. The red and green lights were on some huge object, much bigger than the house. It made a soft whir and as it went overhead she could no longer see the lights on the upper surface of the oval object. She *could* see *five- to six-inch* diameter bolts studding the bottom. The dog which was with her began crying and whining and, for whatever reason, she thought of her former dog, which was very brave and protective. At that exact moment she received a pain in her head which drove her to her knees. And, in an instant, all her memories of herself and her former dog flashed across her mind. Then she got back to her feet and watched it move over the house, but the aunt said that it never came out the other side, merely suddenly appearing across the road, and going away. Going inside, they found that the five-minute experience had lasted fifty minutes. And she had a persistent two-week headache.

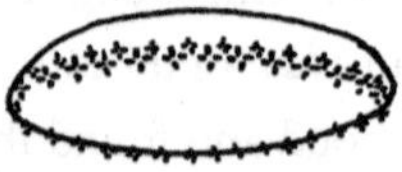

Section 18: Close Encounters involving vehicle interference

One rare and potentially valuable close encounter is the "engine stop" case, where it could be possible to measure not only permanent physical effects (the "magnetic signature" of the iron/steel orientations in car body structures could be seen to be altered), but also some estimates of the forces required to do this could be made. Despite Mark Rodeghier's catalog of about 400 such events, the UFO research community has rarely done anything with these cases. John detected about nine of them during his travels, none, unfortunately, recent enough to pursue.

Hamilton, Ohio – *mid-November 1965, 9:00 P.M.*

Four persons were driving along a river road when they encountered an object which caused an "almost" engine stop. The object moved extremely

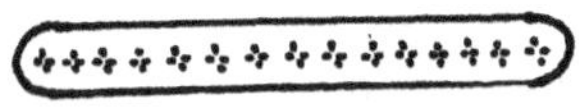

slowly and passed overhead, whereupon they stopped the car to watch it go overtop. It was a long blue-metal cylinder with multicolored lights arrayed along its length. As it silently went over, the radio went out and the lights dimmed, but the engine kept running.

Trail, Oregon – *sometime in the 1980s, at night*

A lady in her eighties was driving on a country road to her home, when a brilliant reddish light illuminated her car from above. The engine stopped and her car rolled to a parked position near a corral. She was momentarily blinded, and then the light went out. She restarted the car and went home. A neighbor then told her that she had had the same experience in that spot sometime previous.

Bowling Green, Ohio – *sometime in the 1970s, during the day*

A mother and her daughter were driving by an area called Van Tassel road which has a wooded area alongside. These woods had been the site of another UFO experience by friends of theirs (although they didn't know it at the time). The car was brand new. As they neared a corner, they saw two saucers, one stacked on top of the other, hovering over a cornfield. The radio died, then the car died, and the daughter got hysterical. The craft(s) went off into the woods, and the car was able to be restarted, and they went on.

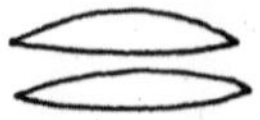

Possible rendition

West of **Columbus, Ohio** – *April or May 1971, about 4:00 P.M.*

Two adults were driving and had come to a stop sign, when they noticed a "funny plane" in the air. The object had a dome on the top with a steady blue light, and a large number of flashing white lights in irregular patterns on the body. The object flew just ten to fifteen feet above the nearby trees, but made no sound. The color of its body blended with the sky so that its shape was hard to determine. When they decided to try to follow it, they found that the car engine was dead and it would not start for about five minutes.

a guess

Flint, Michigan – *fall 1965, 10:00 P.M.*

A family was driving home in the evening when a bright light went across the sky in front of them, very rapidly. The transit took just a few seconds, but the car engine died and the lights went out. The car was only two years old. The engine would not start for about a minute, then went normally.

Springfield, Illinois – *summer 1956, 11:30 P.M.*

A bunch of people in different cars was driving up to a set of streetlights, when the stoplights went "red" in all four directions. Above the intersection was a cigar or blimp-shaped object with "windows" aligned along the perimeter from which came an orange glow. One car coming to the intersection died. The object seemed to be pulsing, and then suddenly went upwards out-of-sight. The appearance of the object had seemed abrupt, almost instantaneous, but the leaving, though rapid, was viewable. Many of the witnesses were local pilots.

Carthage, Texas – *mid-September 1973, 11:30 P.M.*

Can a *boomerang* stop a vehicle? The witness was returning home late from a date, when a large shadow passed over his car. He slowed to look. He saw a huge boomerang (length not given, but fifteen-foot middle width) going over the trees and the road. He decided to drive home even faster and the thing paced him. Finally it veered and went directly overhead, cutting out his 8-track, lights, and engine. So he sat there dead for awhile and the thing hovered. It moved off and he drove home. His parents didn't believe his excuse.

Alger, Ohio – *October 1938, about 7:00 P.M.*

A father and son were out in the cornfields with their tractor preparing the corn rows for picking. An object came coasting up toward them until it got overhead, about 500 feet up. The tractor then conked out. The object hovered for a bit with lights of different colors pulsating all around it. The thing then turned at a sharp angle and moved away to the horizon. The tractor was able to be cranked right back up.

De Soto County, Mississippi – *sometime late fifties or early sixties, predawn*

Two duck hunters were in their motorboat headed toward a location on a lake near the Mississippi River. Two lights suddenly appeared over their boat and the outboard motor died. The thing was of an unknown shape (no structural definition could be seen on whatever connected the lights). The lights were small and the distance between about equal to that of a small plane. But the object was extremely slow and silent. It maintained its low altitude, turned, and drifted away. They checked the engine and it still had plenty of fuel.

Section 19:
Close Encounters and a mixed bag of effects

Just for fun and completeness, here are some other things that witnesses say that UFOs can affect.

Saskatoon, Saskatchewan – *sometime in the early 1950s, midafternoon*

Two youngsters were playing along the railroad tracks on a bright, clear day. They noticed the presence of two very bright balls of white light, four to six inches in diameter, "softball-sized". The balls were "dancing" along the tracks. The kids were frightened and left for home. The balls-of-light followed them. When the kids split up for their various homes, the BOLs split up also, each following one to the house. The witness ran inside and into the bedroom. Peeking though the drapes, the BOL was just outside the window. Then, suddenly, it *dissipated*. Inspecting the outside, the witness found a bible studies book which had been left near the window, and it had burns on its cover.

Sudbury, Ontario – *August 1978, 3:30 P.M.*

A father was driving his two children on a country road, when his daughter saw an object overtop the trees near the road, perhaps only 100 feet away. It seemed to be like the rounded top of a silo, but it was up in the air. As it silently hung there, it looked like an oval with no bottom half, discolored by a "burn mark". They drove on, but the father later went and inspected the area, finding that the tree over which it had hovered was scorched, but only on the top.

In the middle of nowhere, **New Mexico** – *sometime in 1949*

A husband and wife were driving through New Mexico on their way back to Houston, Texas. An object came overtop their car, went over, hit the ground, and exploded. They stopped and inspected the hole: "The hole I would say was 35, maybe 45, feet wide, and it looked like it was about fifteen or sixteen feet deep." The husband picked up a largish piece of metal, and it was still warm. It was hard but had a spongy perforated appearance. Brownish-red colored. He took it to authorities in Houston, where they confiscated it and swore him to secrecy. [I've included this case because it gives me the opportunity to say that, if you put aside the several allusions to Roswell/crashed disk stories, this is the only case John received which had a solid remnant left behind, and even it was New Mexico in the forties.]

Riley, Alberta – *February 1974, around midnight*

A woman was driving home through the countryside. When she turned a corner near her home, she saw a bright light in the sky, which seemed to be lighting up the area. She drove nearer, and saw an elongated object, maybe 100 to 150 feet long, and that same distance in the air. To get to her house she had to drive right under it. The cigar had many windows in it. Its lights, though bright, seemed of a purple-tint. It sat there silently. "So I thought, well, if they're going to do something to me, they're going to zap me up whether I turn or whether I go underneath it." So she bravely went on. Just after she got to what should have been the other side of it, it was gone. She got home, went inside, and her husband told her that the television set had just blacked out.

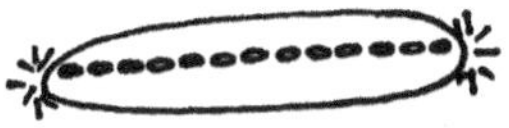

Tigard, Oregon – *summer 1972 or 1973, around 11:00 P.M.*

A daughter was waiting for her mother to come home from the three-to-eleven work shift, when the television went blurry—no images, just lines and fuzzy patterns, and an insistent honking was blaring outside. There was her mom, honking the car and pointing up to the sky. The daughter and several neighbors rushed outside to see what this was all about. A huge circular dark object was overshadowing the entire court between several houses. Around its perimeter were many lights, perhaps windows, perhaps not. It moved very slowly for a few minutes, and then simply was gone.

Harvey Station, New Brunswick – *early November (no year), at night*

A husband and wife had just put their children to bed, when their dog began to whine and act up, and the television set flickered and went out. Outside the window was a slowly moving object about 100 feet higher than the house. It was a disk, flat on the bottom, and forty to fifty feet in diameter. There were glowing red and orange lights around the perimeter and it moved silently. When going to get binoculars, the kids woke up and they

came and saw it, too. Its motion was toward the air base. It then stopped, shot very quickly to the side, hovered, shot quickly back and on the other side of the base, meandered a bit and then *whisss*, gone.

Alliance, Ohio – *summer 1976, around midnight*

A woman was on her way home from work and driving on a country road to miss the traffic. She got the feeling of being watched, and her car radio went staticky and then went out. Above her car to her left, about telephone pole high, was a "large" domed disk. It was silently pacing her car. She tried to shake it by changing speeds, speeding unsafely, even stopping, but it wouldn't quit. She looked at her watch and it had stopped functioning. Suddenly it hovered down directly in front of her, spun counterclockwise, spun to the right of her car, then did a "huge backwards S" in the air and was gone. She felt that the car was sluggish during the encounter, but it and the radio functioned normally when the object left. The watch's battery had to be replaced.

Atwood, Kansas – *August 23, 1988, around midnight*

Two people were working on a project in a house in the country when they got an "eerie feeling" that they should go outside. (They were both flying saucer aficionados, by the way.) They did so and felt the air charged with electricity. They saw a yellow-ball-of-light which may have just risen from the nearby field. The light moved toward them. It had a very definite (hard) outline despite the glow. When it was just overhead, it momentarily expanded to greater than ten times its original size. All this took place silently. It then continued on and was gone. The next day in town they were told that the town had a brown-out that night.

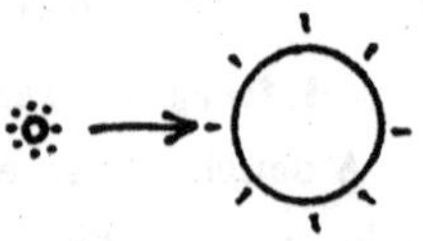

Swift Current, Saskatchewan – *September 1967, 11:00 P.M.*

A family of five were in their home in the country when they saw a light-in-the-sky which seemed unusual. More or less simultaneously, the power went out in their home. They tried to phone, but the phone service was also not functioning. Looking at the object through binoculars (it was about 400 yards away), it appeared like a disk with a conical dome containing glass windows, and an array of lights circling clockwise around the bottom and changing colors. They watched this stay in position for four hours, gave up and went to bed.

Fresno, California – *summer 1983, late at night*

Three teenagers were returning from a party, driving the back roads. They turned down a road which ran through fruit farms near the foothills and there was a large domed object hovering over the middle of the road. It glowed with an orange light, and was making the power lines on both sides of the road swing violently. The teenagers stopped their car and rolled down the windows. The night was clear with no wind. Still the power lines were strongly agitated, yet the object was silent. They panicked, turned around, and rode out quickly in the opposite direction.

Love Field (Dallas), Texas – *sometime in the 1970s, late night*

A man was sitting in his apartment when his lights dimmed and the television set began distorting its picture. He went outside to see if he could see any reason for this outage of power. Overhead there was complete cloud cover, except that in one area there was a hole in the clouds. In that hole (or beneath it) sat a house-sized, circular, glowing object. The exterior was translucent and he could see a light source revolving about inside. It was sitting above power lines "and obviously it was drawing energy from the lines." In about two minutes "it just was not there anymore" and the hole in the clouds closed up. Later, those lines arced and sparked so that they had to be replaced.

North of **Swift Current, Saskatchewan** – *summer, mid-1970s, at night*

A livestock farmer was out late at night and he noticed an odd light (a "UFO") hovering over in the northwest from his property. Later that evening, his stock set up a great commotion in the barn, especially the bull. But he didn't go back out. In the morning he discovered that two of his pigs were missing and he never found any trace of them, subsequently. And the power company had its trucks out there all over the area. Apparently one of the main power lines had been literally cut off, and had to be replaced.

Bellingham, Massachusetts – *fall, mid-1970s, 9:30 P.M.*

A woman was driving home from work when all of the nearby streetlights went out. She looked into the sky and saw a large black mass with colored lights flashing on it, but could make out no shape. It hovered above her car briefly and then took off making just a humming noise. An article appeared in the newspaper the next day about others calling the police to report a UFO.

Fort Saskatchewan, Alberta – *end of August 1989, 11 or 11:30 P.M.*

A woman was driving home when she thought she saw a motorcycle headlight coming toward her. She slowed down, but it seemed to stay just a certain distance away. She stopped, was frightened, and made a U-turn. Going quickly, the object stayed behind her. As she turned a corner, the light simply cut through the corner and followed. It seemed to get a little larger,

and the white light acquired a little yellow-orange spectrum around the edges. Most puzzling to her, all along the road as she raced home the yard lights were all out. "Everybody has a large yard light. And none of them were working. I didn't notice one light on the whole strip of road." The light stopped as she neared her home and rose a bit. She then saw the object as a roundish shape with a large light on its top and a smaller one on the bottom. She ran into the house, peeked at it briefly through the window, went to call her friends, and it was gone.

Near **Cheyenne Mt., Colorado** – *winter 1987*

This is one of the few reports where the individual would not give John his name. The witness, a captain in the Air Force, was flying into NORAD with another officer, a major. About ten minutes from landing, an object

came up parallel to their flight path and paced them. It was estimated to be parked about 5000 feet away. It hung there for about two and a half minutes, whereupon their guidance system was malfunctioning, although the F-15 still flew normally. "We were in some kind of field energy; you could tell it." [The pilot was saying that the flying controls were okay, but that the gyrosystem was spinning, I believe.] It made a sharp right turn and rapidly moved away. Upon landing, the incident was reported, and "We were debriefed. Extensively." John asked: What did the debriefing officers say to you? "Shut your mouth. Absolutely. Not a word."

Section 20: Old-fashioned Close Encounter IIIs

The case report of a UFO with entities moving in the windows or around it on the ground seems a thing of the past, or at least a great rarity today. But there used to be hoards of these: a fact which inspired the excellent researcher from the early high-quality CSI-New York group, Ted Bloecher, to begin the collection of humanoid entity cases, HUMCAT, which unfortunately has never seen the light of day in print. If it ever does, then these CE IIIs from John's cases could join it.

Wellsboro, Pennsylvania – *summer 1958, midafternoon*

Two teenage sisters were in their home when they sensed an odd vibration. They walked out on their porch and saw an object hovering over the barn, and larger than it. It was like a giant cigar or blimp, and it had porthole-like windows all along the side. Some smaller structure was suspended underneath. The device was metallic silver and moved slowly and silently. Within the portholes, "people" were waving. The object disappeared over the trees.

South of **Bermuda Island** – *early spring 1967, at night*

On cruise with the HCMS Annapolis, a lookout spotted a light and reported a "UFO." A second lookout reported the same. Officers confirmed this and even the captain was roused to see. The object was an elongated cigar (c. 250 feet) with several windows in it, within which "people" could be seen walking around inside. Seamen were told to keep their mouths shut about the incident.

Cedar Rapids, Iowa – *early fall 1970, 5:30 P.M.*

We've already told this lady's story (see Traces, Section 16). But here was a nice little backyard disk with entities in the windows.

Oshawa, Ontario – *November 1989, 7:00 P.M.*

Two brothers were walking in the middle of the street near their home and saw a disk silently moving through the sky. Its form was dark, but it had four large brightly lit (yellow) windows. In each window, an entity was staring out. They had oval-shaped outsized heads on small bodies. The disk moved on.

Renton, Washington – *sometime in 1974 or 1975, 9:30 P.M.*

A husband was outside his home when he noticed unusual lights over the nearby Boeing plant. The object shot upwards, dropped again, and hovered. Then it made a rapid arc and came much nearer his place. It hovered about 300 yards over the house. It was an "aluminum" metal disk (about 50 feet in diameter), and it had windows in the bottom area. He saw images of beings moving in them. He yelled to his wife to come out and look, and she told him to "put his cork back in the bottle," which exasperated him. The UFO hung there silently for two and a half to three minutes, with a radiant glow covering the bottom and a single small light on the top. When it left, rapidly, he went inside to tell his wife that she should have come out. She told him she watched the whole thing from the bedroom window.

Shelby, Ohio – *sometime in 1950, morning*

It was early in the work shift at the Air Force Depot in Shelby, when someone tapped the witness and said to come outside and see what's overtop one of the buildings. They were two disks, shaped like tops, more or less side-by-side. The bottoms of the disks were solid but the tops were clear, like Plexiglass. Inside the top dome you could see the "operators," looking just like humans, walking about, looking down, and making notes. Then the disks "stacked" one on top of the other, moved slowly, then very rapidly accelerated. The Air Force produced a bulletin that evening saying that the objects seen in the morning were not what the men thought they were, but instead two new National Guard jet planes.

Middleton, Ohio – *fall 1979, 7:00 P.M.*

A brother, sister, and a friend were driving around when they saw an object very close overtop their car (perhaps only fifty feet away). It was silently pacing them. [It's not clear in the transcript—the witness was excited telling John—but it "seems" to be that the object was a disk, and that the driver

stopped the car to watch it.] The object had a lot of lights on it and at least one window. Within that window was the silhouette of a figure seeming to have a bird-like head. The sister wanted to rush out of the car to it. She tried, but her brother held her in. "A good feeling overcame me and made me want to get out of the car." When the object left, they drove on to her girlfriend's house and found that they were two to three hours later than they should have been. "My brother... he doesn't like to talk about it."

Decatur, Illinois – *summer, about 1970, possibly dusk*

Two girlfriends were riding their bikes, when one noticed that her house seemed to be glowing reddish. It wasn't on fire, because they then saw a large "craft" sitting nearby in the air. There were windows and you could see entities moving around inside it. The girls got scared and tried to bike quickly home. The object followed, hovering nearby. They dismounted their bikes, but the one girl's pants were caught as her girlfriend ran to the house. The object "was sitting there looking at me." She doesn't remember anything else until she woke up inside the house. Her girlfriend and her mother filled in the story as follows: her girlfriend ran in to tell the "stuck" girl's mom. The mom ran out to see a light go off in the air, and no sign of her daughter. Ten to fifteen minutes later, the missing girl knocked on the door (something she never bothers to do in her own house). She was "standing there white as a ghost. I didn't blink. I didn't say anything. I just stood there. I don't remember anything." The only vague memory that she has is looking up (at the craft) and seeing some "figures." This is the kind of old-fashioned CE III that serves as the "bridge" to the abductions phenomenon. It is also the point where many persons interested in UFOs would like to draw an emotional line: it's all kind of "fun" until you get to cases where the phenomenon is messing around carelessly with our daughters, isn't it?

Fresno, California – *around December 26, 1978 or 1979, after midnight*

A man was driving late at night and was sleepy, but didn't want to stop the car and nap. He took an old dirt road, which more or less paralleled

the freeway, to avoid traffic and drove on. Then he did park and slept behind a walnut grove. He woke up suddenly to light bright as daylight and thought that he'd overslept. He got out of the car and the light went off. He looked up and 100 feet away was a disk coming slowly and silently nearer. It was very low, only eight feet off the ground. It was radiating neon blue light at first, but changed to a powdery orange with white associated with it. He heard a *zzzhhh* sound (like air and soft mechanical) and a rectangular window slide open. There were three or four "persons" inside looking out. They had heads too large for their bodies, seemingly small framed. The facial features were difficult to see, but they appeared to be without ears or hair, and had large eyes. Their clothing seemed to sparkle. The ship pulsed its light at about the same rate as the witness' heart. It changed color again to a milky white and blue, and with another *zzzhhh* a door seemed to fold down out of the side. [Witness is confused about this: whether it folded down or just slid into the wall.] He panicked and jumped back into his car. It wouldn't start. He sat there shaking, trying to get the engine to turn over. Finally, after a "hundred" tries, the engine fired and he drove off. As an aftermath, he had persistent eye burning and itching (a sort of rash) and his nose felt raw for three or four months. The doctor said it was an allergy. He's not convinced because the symptoms started in the car on the way home.

Lake of the Ozarks, Missouri – *December 10, 1987, at night*

A man went outside his house for a smoke, and felt that something "overwhelming told me: Turn around." He did and saw what looked like two headlights in fog, but there was no fog. The lights-in-fog were coming overtop the trees. They came closer, and another set of lights appeared behind, then a third set, all following the same path. The first object stopped and the others came alongside. The first raised up a bit, and the last dropped down. The objects were more or less disks, forty feet in diameter and maybe eight feet thick. On their rear ends they had twin "pods" ("like a Lear jet"). On each pod was a green "crystalline" area emitting light. The objects created "fog" around them as they moved, which dissipated behind. On the fronts of the vehicles were windows ("portholes") [or perhaps he means along the sides: this is hard to determine. My drawing shows them on the side, meaning that the objects lined up side-by-side, but lengthwise in their array extending away from him.]. He could see humanoids easily in the windows: large eyes, no ears or hair. He was scared and wanted to yell for the rest of his family, but was paralyzed. He then received a dense information exchange by telepathy: things like nutrition and reproduction. Then the

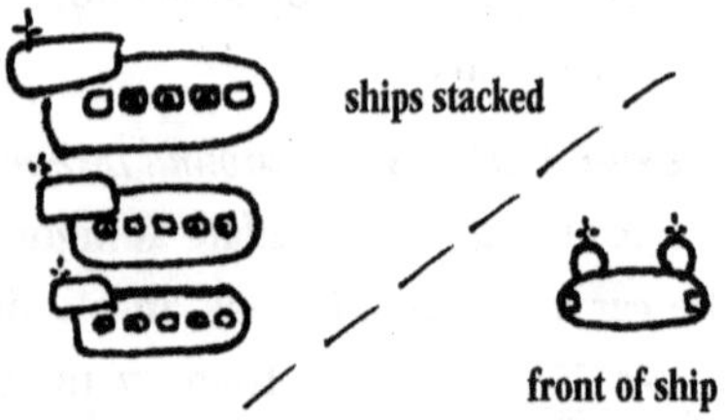

craft began to move off, and he could scream for his family. Eleven people scrambled out and watched the craft (now 200 feet away) as they leisurely left the scene. "About all I can remember, right now. I feel a little weird standing here, man." John replied, "That's all right." He could have added: I've heard a lot stranger.

Section 21: New-fashioned Close Encounter IVs (abductions)

At times, it seems that everybody has been abducted left, right, and center, if you read current UFO literature. John found very few such cases. Of course, one can imagine all sorts of sociological reasons for him not receiving such reports at the malls, and my friends, Budd Hopkins and Dave Jacobs, would probably say that a great deal of what I've already abstracted in this book were really hidden abductions (I know that Dave at least feels this way). But what do we really know, and can say, about John's cases? Each will see it as they choose, but, to fuel the fire, here are the CE IVs that John heard.

Franklin, Pennsylvania – *June 1973, at night*

The witness was at a campsite with many other people, but was lying on a blanket off to herself looking at the stars. She closed her eyes but couldn't open them. "It was like I almost lost consciousness or touch with physical reality." The next awareness that she had was of being inside a craft with short bald beings doing a physical exam on her. The procedures seemed to take about ten minutes, and then she was aware of being back on the campground, but on the other side of the road from her blanket, and with many people standing around her. They were concerned for her condition, and her children were there saying: "We couldn't find you. Where were you?" She felt disoriented, dizzy, and just sat on the ground for awhile. Her body felt tingly, her skin very sensitive. She had laid down at about 10:30 or 11:00 P.M. and it was now 4:00 A.M. She got herself together, went to her camper, and tried to sleep. Other people alleged seeing a UFO somewhere in the area that evening.

Dayton, Ohio – *sometime in 1978, at night*

A woman was in bed when she woke to the sound of her windows vibrating. She was frightened and wouldn't get up to look. The next night the same thing happened. This time she looked.

Outside was an object composed of three round sections linked together, and concentric rings of colors (white, blue, red, white, blue, red) going from the center outwards. "It was like a dream, but it wasn't a dream because I remember it." Then she remembers being inside the ship, undergoing the typical ET-examination by big-headed little characters with white mushroomy skin. "I did not find it to be a pleasant experience, but the feeling that I had was that they weren't there to harm you. I would compare it to being tagged as an animal." The dream or memory then ended. Later she heard that a local television person had videotaped a craft, which she felt was the same thing. That video turned up missing.

city unstated, **Ontario** – *July 1968, time unstated*

A woman had just finished preparing food for her dogs in her kitchen when "I was just taken, immediately, right from inside the house." She found herself outside, standing paralyzed, watching a thirty-foot diameter disk descending. Three aliens came out and dragged her aboard the ship. The rooms were all like pie-slice wedges and she went by several until

coming to the "medical center." There she was placed on a levitating bed and told that they were going to do "brain surgery." They calmed her with a wave of the hand and opened the front of her skull. They resealed it without a trace. "What I believe is that they were using a tracking device." Then she was returned. She believes that this was the first of several abductions.

Houston, Texas – *late September 1979, at night*

A woman was home alone watching television. The set malfunctioned, getting very fuzzy. Her patio lit up brightly. She looked out and saw a being coming straight for her. She thought: "You're not human." It thought back: "I'm humanoid." The being was less than five feet tall and had a metal gray suit, large, soft eyes without pupils, no eyelids, nose, ears nor hair. The mouth never opened. The skin seemed not skin, but rather a fabric. It was white. Three fingers and no palm to the hand. Wearing gloves. "Come with me." "I'm afraid of you." "Oh, you'll be prepared and you won't be afraid." She then blanked out. When she awoke at about 3:30

A.M., she was sitting on her bed. Then she remembered the fill-in material: she was taken out onto her patio and under a spacecraft: An oval disk with a dome, small windows and a light beam which came down from the bottom. Once standing in this, it acted like an elevator and drew you up into the ship. Once inside, she recalls no examination, only that she was allowed to wander about the craft and talk to the other beings. She got the impression that the entities had gender and that there were both male and female onboard. Once she heard a *squishing* sound and turned to see some sort of vortex in the ship, and a being stepping out. "It was just like a whirlwind, you know, and he just stepped out. Like—you could see him coming, actually, just a split second before he stepped out…kind of startled me." After this event the witness thinks that she's had other communication over the years, but not (apparently) onboard experiences.

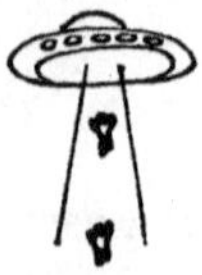

Indiana, Pennsylvania – *June 14, 1978, 11:30 P.M.*

A husband, who is a great UFO buff, and his wife, who shares his interest in this and other esoteric topics, were watching a drive-in movie when a light passed over and he got out and photographed it. [The film never was returned to him.] On their way home another red flashing light went over. Then a blue light. Back home, the wife was worried about the lights they'd seen. Upon sleeping, she had a dream of being taken aboard a craft by small creatures (both her and her husband). The transition from within her home to outside was "like I was floating between…I was outside and inside at the same time." Communication was by telepathy, and they were there because the husband had so many UFO books. She had a few dream-sequence-like shifts and woke up three hours later. She has come to believe that the dream was real, and that bruises on her arms, appearing a couple of days later, were due to this. And she believes that she had a two-week early period. "My whole life has been upset since then… I just get all shaky… right now I'm just a total wreck because I don't want… I never had nobody to talk to about it." The drawing above, by the way, is a drawing made by the wife according to her 11-year-old *daughter's* description of an entity in a dream that the daughter had: of several of these chasing her mother. Now, the

witness drawing

husband has read Whitley Strieber books and noted that his wife has said that entities have told her that she is "a chosen one," as they said to Whitley. The husband thinks that he gets information in dreams via a pyramidal cap, which concepts come true. Now their 2-year-old son seems fascinated with the cover picture on *Transformation*. All this seems a bit troublesome to me for reasons having little to do with UFOs.

San Bernardino, California – *May 1988, etc., various times*

A very young son has been telling his mother about having entity experiences since he was two and a half years old. She says that her son had not yet been into any environment which would have predisposed him to this element of pop culture—no preschool, no television. His first report to her was that little people came into the living room and took him out the window. Little people, gray skin, big black eyes. Later she read *Intruders* and began to freak out: "I looked for scoops all over my body at that time." She put the book away, because it made her nervous. Later she picked it up again, and her son saw it. "Those are my persons!" He placed the open book on the floor and kissed it. "He's very emotionally attached to them." He designated the "woman" and the "man," and described their craft and some of the physical examination they put him through.

Unusually, both the mother and her son were there at the mall while she was telling this to John, and John asked the boy a few questions. Some answers: "I flown out the window." What did you see? "A spaceship." Big or little? "Big. It got some lights around it." Colors? "Brown, green, and orange and blue and purple and red." Did you see anybody? "Persons." Just one? "A lot." Were they alike? "Yeah...short ones and tall ones." Did they talk to you? "I...know...I think so." What did the lady say?" (his mom's question) "Don't be afraid." Did they hurt you? "Yes...on my eye and my forehead and my mouth." Then the child began whispering to his mother, and she explained that he thinks that he shouldn't be telling this because "they'll get mad at me; they're my friends." The mother's way of coping with this is to get him to ask the beings to stop hurting him by asking them if what they were doing was okay with Jesus; and hoping that some reflection will make them stop.

Section 22:

Entities in the vicinity of a UFO, maybe

Sometimes the cases John heard make an obvious connection between what we would call a UFO and sometimes they don't. Here are a variety of incidents where you can decide for yourself whether we're dealing with ufology or something else.

An unnamed military base in **Texas** *– 1966, around 2 or 3:00 A.M.*

An employee at a base used for overhauling aircraft was on a late shift to strip a C-133 to be moved out. He was on his way down to the pit with the crew, when a workmate (already there) radioed: "Call security! As I started to go in the entrance door of the aircraft somebody pushed me down and ran out into the bushes." When they all arrived on the scene, the radioing worker said that a "small guy" pushed him over. He believed the person was an alien and that the push was accompanied by an electric shock. The crew saw a flattened silver ball-like object raise up out of the trees in the direction that the small man was said to have run. "Just sort of like a silver cloud-type thing." It went straight up, then moved slowly away to the east. As to the friend who had been pushed down, his girlfriend told the witness that the incident had screwed her boyfriend up regarding their relations and she wasn't happy about the alien interference with their love life. [Sorry, folks, I'm just explaining what the witness said: a "physiological effect", after all.]

Lawrenceville, Tennessee – *August 3, 1988 and afterwards (three incidents)*

A man was working in his garden, and his dog began to bark. He looked up and saw a ship: a large fifteen-foot diameter ball. The dog ran at the ball and it lifted up and left. It allegedly left marks on the ground and a high radiation count, other investigators said. About three weeks later (at 1:00 A.M.) He was awakened by the dog barking. He rose and saw a similar-sized ball, this time looking translucent and orange. All the lights had been out in the house, but now they mysteriously turned on. He was disturbed enough that he called his sister to come over, and went back home with them for the evening. Then, three more weeks later (about 11:30 P.M.) he heard a loud knock on his door. His security light went out. He investigated and saw two very tall figures outside his door. He asked them who they were and got no answer. He got his gun. Inquired again; nothing. He tried to shoot, but the gun wouldn't work. He got a rifle; it wouldn't shoot either. Finally, he asked what he could do for them, submissively. No answer, except one was now petting his passive dogs. Then two phrases: "We're not here to harm you," and "we shall return." The beings, though seven-foot tall, looked human except for a very wide mouth and long earlobes. One had a glowing flashlight-like watch, which flashed like a camera flash. When they left, the man said they seemed to rise up rather than walk away. All this allegedly happened just a couple of weeks before John heard the story. Who knows whether the seven-foot gun-jamming "aliens" dropped back in?

Ashland, Ohio – *June 21, 1968, 11:00 P.M.*

An 11-year-old boy was going to bed when a bright light "like lightning" shown outside his window. The light came into the room, filling it up. He felt paralyzed, and saw one entity, one figure inside the light. The being was four and a half foot tall with a larger head than he should have had but otherwise relatively normal. The entity tried to communicate with him by telepathy, but all he got out of it was "all my nerves just shaking and I kept hearing a sound like a humming or buzzing that just filled the room." It gave him a headache, which occasionally returns. He thought that the being was indicating that he would return, which did happen twenty years later (in the form of headache-producing "telepathic messages" but with no entity visible).

Guayrabo, Puerto Rico – *sometime in 1978 or 1979, late at night*

A young boy was sleeping when he was awakened for some reason. The mother reported hearing noises in the house but unaccountably just went back to sleep. The boy, in a different room, saw a light beam penetrate through the concrete ceiling, its green beam coming all the way to the floor. Down the beam floated two beings, one was very short, one taller. They had on clothing and helmets with lights on them. Very large eyes. He pretended sleep and they left him alone. They walked around the house, the boy following and spying. They looked into the refrigerator. Sometime during this escapade, he noticed that his father was missing from his bed where he had been sleeping with his mother. The beings finally left up the green beam. In the morning when everyone was rising, the son and the young daughter called loudly to the mother to come and look out the window to see the flying saucer in front of the house, but by the time she came over it was gone.

Newport Beach, California – *August 1975, 2:00 A.M.*

A man was driving back to his apartment after a night on the town. As he got out of his car, he felt compelled to immediately look to his right. At that instant a disk came overtop the building across the street. The object in a flash was above and in front of him about a story and a half off the ground. It was forty feet in diameter and a dull gray metal color. It was more, or less, than mere hovering. It was as if it had crystallized in that spot in space. Total silence. He took two steps toward the craft, very excited. Then he was engulfed in some sort of beam. He received a telepathic communication: "Do not move. Do not cry out. Do not... ", very authoritative orders. Then his memory gets hazy. He thinks that he sees two beings approaching—more as silhouettes than real seeing. They were about his height. Suddenly they were right there, and he remembers nothing more. "I found myself lying on my bed. And I was very much awake. And very scared, beyond belief. I was digging my fingers into the mattress and covers, and holding onto that bed like I'd never held on to anything in my life. I was sweating profusely and my heart was beating so hard the entire bed was bouncing up and down." Through this he'd kept his eyes closed. After 45 minutes, he turned his head and looked. "I instantaneously was back in that light beam again. I was hearing that voice again. I went through that whole scared thing again. I slammed my eyes shut and I was back in bed." He went through this odd experience three times before finally falling asleep. He woke up the following afternoon. He told one person about it and the whole thing then faded from his mind, only to return years later when he saw the movie *Interrupted Journey* about Barney and Betty Hill.

Duboistown, Pennsylvania – *November 21, 1973, 9:00 P.M.*

A high school girl was finishing a shift on her part-time job at a fast-food restaurant, and got in the family car and drove home. Well, that was the idea anyway. Once the car started, she heard a series of three musical tones. "That was the last thing I remembered until I woke up on a dark road. To my right was a Closed Road sign. Understandably I was confused and frightened and could not remember getting there... I just locked all the doors." She then noticed a red light moving in the sky from right to left. Then it reversed motion. Then reversed again. She got hysterical and screamed. She started the car, spun about and fled. She didn't know where she was or where she was going, she just drove. Ultimately she recognized the terrain and got back home. It was fifteen minutes after midnight, over three hours later. She went to her bedroom and eventually got to sleep. In the morning she still couldn't remember what had happened but went on to school. In first period the teacher opened the class by saying: before we start I want to tell you something—and proceeded to recount a red light UFO that he and his daughter saw last night. "At that point I almost passed out and threw up!" After that she tried to forget about it "thinking it's stupid being sixteen years old." But she couldn't sleep without a light on, didn't want to be out in the dark, and had nightmares of being held down by small creatures. This softened with time but fifteen years later the anxieties have struck again. She began keeping dream diaries about small creatures with large eyes, and following such a dream her daughter came in and told her of her own dream of her mother taken outside to a ship by small people. Needless to say, the whole scenario has been nerve-wracking for this lady.

Adequate Springs, Colorado – *sometime in 1957 or 1958, 1:00 A.M.*

A mine operator locked the operation up for the night and began driving home. The next thing he remembers was being on the street of the town four to five miles away with no recollection of driving the intervening distance covering very dangerous road. Under hypnosis, the following story unfolded: he saw a light around the bend of the mountain road. When he rounded the curve, two bars of intense light straddled the road with a single bright round light above. His car died and the headlights went out. He sat there in the dead vehicle watching the lights, and three entities emerged and came toward him. Needless to say he was petrified. The individuals came to the car and stood on the left and right sides and in front. He had a feeling of impending death. When the hypnotist (Dr. James Harder for you UFO cognizants) tried to push further, the witness developed a pain above his left ear and was not able to remember anything else. Subsequently, the witness believes that he and his family have had several other UFO experiences, plus other odd happenings involving psychic phenomena. (None of these latter seemed obviously UFO-related and are not recounted here.)

Section 23: Entities in search of a UFO

John received several tales of critters where no hide-nor-hair of a UFO could be (clearly) seen. For your fun and enlightenment:

Oshawa, Ontario – *in the 1960s in the middle of the night*

A 13-year-old boy awoke to find the door to his bedroom closed, which he never let happen. "I'm terrified of closed doors." There was this thing in the room. "All I could remember was the eyes. Big Eyes. I opened my mouth. I couldn't scream. I think I passed out...I told them [his family] and they said it was the Devil after me. So that really freaked me out."

Grants Pass, Oregon – *sometime in 1989, in the middle of the night*

An elderly lady was in bed, when she suddenly found herself going into a doorway to a stainless steel clean room. About ten feet away was a little man with an egg-shaped head and great big eyes. He communicated telepathically. He seemed to be saying something about her helping with the babies. John asked whether she was simply asleep. She said: I doubt it.

Roxton, Saskatchewan – *sometime in 1969, in the middle of the night*

A young man was sleeping in bed with his wife when he felt that something was protruding into his eye. He heard ("in my mind") voices speaking of him waking up. He felt a burning sensation on his lip. He began to open his eyes and was ordered not to. He peeked and saw two figures in silhouette at the bed. The dogs began barking wildly outside. Then he opened his eyes and no one was there. "That is the big focal point in my life. From then on I have an uncontrollable urge... to discover more and more about them." He thinks that depression has followed this, and loss of mental sharpness.

Richmond, Virginia – *sometime in 1965, in the middle of the night*

A young girl, age about seven, was going to sleep, but insists that she wasn't asleep yet. She looked over into the corner of her bedroom and there was a little man floating in the air. He was dressed in silver and had skin of silvery blue. He had white eyes and very red lips. He had a helmet with a clear mask. He looked at her like he was trying to talk to her but couldn't. She got scared and ran out of the room.

New London, Connecticut – *November or December 1988, in the middle of the night*

A 5-year-old boy woke up screaming and came into his parents' room. Oddly, they didn't get up with him, but just told him to go back to bed. The next morning he told them that he had a dream where little people were sticking needles into his fingers. He drew them with a big head but no nose or mouth. At John's exhibit he said they were like the Kelly/Hopkinsville creatures but without the big ears.

Oshawa, Ontario – *sometime in the 1960s, in the middle of the night*

Two children were asleep and woke up simultaneously. They got out of their beds and walked down the hallway to the stairs. They looked down and there were "two alien life forms" down there. They waved at them and the aliens waved back. Then the aliens just dematerialized, and the children went back to bed. The aliens were described as three feet tall with green skin. John asked: Do you dream much? "Constantly…and remember them quite vividly."

Redding, California – *sometime in the late 1970s, in the middle of the night*

A young man had been involved in an intense family prayer session for his uncle (which allegedly worked), and went to bed. About 11:00 P.M. he suddenly woke back up. "On the foot of the bed stood what you would call a little person, like you say from Ireland. Only this one—he had a really bad case of the super double-uglies." Big beaked nose with warts, ugly pointy ears, blond straggly hair, snaggle teeth, and snarling to boot. "I just told him in the Name of Jesus to go down to the middle of Walkermine Road and stay there and shut up and don't do anything or bother anybody until Jesus Christ comes along and tells you what to do next. And he instantaneously disappeared and I haven't seen him since. Of course, I don't miss him."

South of **Jackson, Mississippi** – *November or December 1960, 9:00 P.M.*

Five members of a family were driving back from a shopping trip and turned down a country road. They saw an "entity" on the side of the road. It ran in front of the car and into a ditch, and tried to climb up. It couldn't make it and just stopped and watched while their car passed. It was three and a half feet tall and very skinny. Pointy ears, claw-like fingers, but human eyes. A tight-fitting suit with a backpack, and a tube running from the backpack to a mouthpiece. No helmet, and somewhat balding on the head. They drove on by.

Omaha, Nebraska – *summer 1965, about 1 or 2:00 A.M.*

A family was driving in their camper (a pickup truck) near Omaha and the stockyards. Three beings raced across the road in front of them. The third stopped right in the road and they were going to hit it. It made a huge bounding thirty- to forty-foot leap from the Interstate and over a fence. The entities were very small with large heads and eyes, no hair and very pale looking. The stepfather was an ex-FBI man and wanted to stop to investigate, but the mother said: "No. No. Let's get the hell out of here." Later that morning they heard a radio report that some cattle had been found dead in the Omaha stockyards. The father then remarked: "Well, they probably dissected them to see what they're composed of."

Utica, Ohio – *sometime in the 1970s, around 9:00 A.M.*

based on witness drawing

A woman was driving home after dropping the kids off at school, when she came across an entity sitting in a ditch beside the road. The being was completely silver, including hair and face. "Somehow I had a zoom-in on his eyes and they were red. Now I could not possibly see that man that close in the car, driving." John asked if she'd slowed down. The reply: "I have no idea. I may have stopped and got out and talked to him, who knows? I don't know what I did. It's just a weird time."

Fredericton, New Brunswick – *fall 1969 or 1970, at night*

One day a woman was washing clothes in her basement when she saw a hairy leg outside the window. She didn't investigate and it went away. Another night she saw hairy arms out of her bedroom window, and pulled the blinds closed. Then a third instance, and she screwed up her courage and looked. There was "this big hairy thing; it had a bald head; it was talking." But she couldn't understand what it was saying. It had apparently taken the garbage out of her garbage can, and was now putting it all back. "It scared the living daylights out of me." The next morning she found a big round, brown spot in her yard, maybe two meters in diameter.

Man's Lake, northern New Brunswick – *July 1980, 11:00 P.M.*

A mother, two small children, and her dog were alone in the camp they'd set in the woods. All at once the dog got very frightened "and his hair all stood up." Then she and the dog were paralyzed. Six little men with antennae on their heads were dancing in a circle and chanting. "All of a sudden I was awake and the thing was gone."

Springfield, Illinois - *summer 1973, in the evening*

A woman went out into her yard to get her dog's water pan. Nearby a little man was floating in the air. He came over to about one foot away. He was small (about four foot), more or less human in facial features, puffy cheeks and a smirk on his face, a sickly pallor to the skin. His body was covered with a black cloth coverall which ended in a pointed hood. His hands and feet (covered) "came to a point." His arms and legs were thin. Well, despite her excessively close visitor, she was going to get that water pan with the creature drifting and smirking right alongside. When she reached for it, the being just became invisible.

Section 24:
Something in search of a UFO

Lots of things are simply now part of the UFO story whether there's a UFO around or not. We've seen it in abundance with traces, and now here are a handful of other things which the public tells John, because they believe that they must have been due to a UFO.

Missasauga, Ontario – *spring 1986, 10:45 A.M.*

A mother and son drove over to pick up his paycheck, a ten-minute drive. He was back out in five and they drove home. When they reached there, the 25-minute excursion had taken over three hours. No recollections of anything unusual.

Outside **Toronto, Ontario** – *midsummer 1970, 1:00 A.M.*

A father and his two sons were returning from a fishing outing. Despite being a brand new car, the lights and engine died. When it rolled to a stop, the father got out and tried to look under the hood. The flashlight wouldn't work either. He went back, got into the car, and everything (including the flashlight) now worked.

Waldron, Saskatchewan – *sometime in the late 1970s, 1:00 A.M.*

We heard this tale earlier under physical traces. This is the lady with the fiery light around her house who thought the house was on fire. Her cattle bolted through the fence and ended up five miles away. I included it here to make the ground trace and animal effects connection to these "near-UFO" experiences.

Baltic, South Dakota – *summer in the early 1970s, about 1 or 2:00 A.M.*

A woman woke up to a whirring sound outside her window. There had been some cattle thievery in the area, so she got her dog and a flashlight and went out. The dog came but very reluctantly and whining. She circled the mobile home and began hearing sounds coming down to her from the sky.

> Something tried to talk to me and it wasn't human. It was something with a vocabulary and growls between the words, and

> that scared the stuffings out of me. I didn't run but I was walking fast around the house. As I went in the door, I heard two or three other things of the same type of voice, just giving that one guy heck, probably for scaring me out of there.

As time passed she heard stories of several neighbors seeing something that same evening, including a farmer who had his tractor hovered over, and who just turned around in the field and went back home.

Groton, Connecticut – *fall 1974 or 1975, 2:00 P.M.*

Actually, in the witness' mind, this story starts two or three years earlier when she and a girlfriend were driving in the Devils Hop Yard area at 9:00 P.M. They saw a glowing light and got a cold, tingling feeling. Then their car died. They sat there a couple of minutes, and the environment warmed up again. The lights came on of their own accord, and they could drive the car home. Then in 1974 or 1975, she was hiking in that area with her dog. She began getting a funny, tingling feeling again and the dog began to act up. An hour and a half later she came to herself standing a long distance away and way off the trail. The dog was just sitting beside her. She was three miles from where she had parked her car, in an area where she never went into.

Mansfield, Ohio – *August 1988, 3:30 A.M.*

A lady couldn't get to sleep one night and took her dog out for a walk around the house. The dog was scared and went only with great urging. Finally, it just wouldn't go any further, and the lady turned to go back in. The leaves on the front yard's maple tree then stood straight up in the air, but there was no sound and no activity in any of the other trees. She felt a cold area come around, and felt that she was being pulled as if by a magnet. She had to struggle to get back in the house, and went down into the basement. The next day she told friends and they noticed that the maple tree had one limb high in the tree which was all wilted because it had been broken off and was just lying loose up there.

Orillia, Ontario – *sometime in 1973, 9:00 P.M.*

A family was tenting out in a camp west of town, and they heard what they thought was a dog with a chain coming up the hill. You could hear a chain clinking closer and closer. They shone a flashlight, but nothing. It was as if something invisible just walked by and on down another path. They tossed some stones down in the sound's direction. Suddenly there erupted an image of pulsing bright lights: green, red, silver; pulsing like a heartbeat. They packed up their camp rapidly, jumped in their car, ran off to report to the police.

Portsmouth, Ohio – *summer of the late 1940s or early 1950s, early afternoon*

A young girl was walking through the woods where she and her friends would often play. She was by herself and enjoying the sunshine and the quiet. She looked up at the trees and saw: "a tremendous amount of this—what I later read about and assume—I don't know what other language to use for it—angel hair. And there was quite a bit of it."

"And there were voices, but they weren't like you or I talking. And it wasn't at a speed you or I would talk. It was though a record would be put on fast speed." She can't remember exactly what went on then, but "there was a tremendous amount of fear when I left that spot." She had been crouching down to look at something on the forest floor when she spotted the angel hair, but doesn't remember standing up, turning, or walking away. She next remembers seeing the roof of her house, but can't remember having seen it from that area before. The angel hair was silvery white, and hanging down from the trees densely in just that one area. The voices were communicating with each other, not to her, but she felt somehow that she understood that they were interested in the vegetation. She also has a feeling of short beings in silver jumpsuits. When she got back home, she normally would have gone directly to her dad, her protector, and told him and asked him to come back with her and look. But she didn't do that. She didn't want either him or herself to go back to that place. John was only the second person she ever told this story to, the other being her 17-year-old son.

Section 25:
Radar cases

Once upon a time, ufologists and physical scientists thought that radar cases might end most of the discussion about the reality of UFOs. They didn't. Skeptics just debunked radar instead, or waited until people got cold on the case. After all, radar doesn't leave any traces permanently behind either. The skeptics have a powerful tool: just wait—the case will seem old, and, therefore, untrustworthy.

In the air near **Milwaukee, Wisconsin** – *October 1989, 2:00 A.M.*

An amateur pilot was flying five passengers in a private plane back from a hockey game. Milwaukee Air Traffic Control radioed that they were tracking an object directly in their path. Chicago said that they had it, too. No one on the plane saw a thing.

San Francisco, California – *sometime in 1950, time unstated*

A National Guard radar scope picked up a blip from an object clocked at 1800 mph. The scope seemed to be working perfectly both before and after the incident. "I was asked to forget about it."

Canadian Forces Station, Dana, Saskatchewan – *sometime in 1971, after midnight*

In a time period normally devoid of airborne activity, the radar picked up a blip going east to west. Its returns also indicated very rapid turns must be taking place. The straight line speed was guesstimated at greater than 2000 mph, maybe as high as 3000.

East of **Los Angeles, California** – *June or July 1966, 9:00 P.M.*

The station received reports from several outlying stations of radar returns and that an unidentified object was heading their way. Some personnel went outside and saw two disks come low over the base, making a whirring sound, turn in a circle and leave rapidly.

Hokkaido Island, Japan – *sometime in the 1950s, time unstated*

A man assigned to U.S. Army Security through Special Forces was involved with a radar installation on Hokkaido. There were incidents of unidentified craft being tracked on U.S. and (apparently) Soviet radars, and evading both militaries' airplanes. He says he listened to a tape where the two sides tried to cooperate in catching one of these things.

Anchorage, Alaska – *October or November 1965, late evening*

Radar operators (USAF) had several instances of unidentified returns. The objects would race in, stop dead still (radars multiply locked on), then shoot off at extreme speeds. "Of course we had to log everything. Our Commanding Officer would say: Well, who is going to turn in the report to the colonel?" John asked about velocity. "We couldn't track it... they'd just buzz right off the end of the dial."

Hickham Field, Honolulu, Hawaii – *sometime in 1952, after dark*

A plane was coming back in from a reconnaissance mission and the radar operator picked up several blips to their right. The copilot spotted five objects, roundish lights, over Diamond Head. They reported them to the traffic controller, who said that they had them, too. Suddenly, the objects broke a fast 90° turn upwards and disappeared in almost no time.

Over the **Atlantic** *(500 miles east of* **New York***) – 1964, date unknown, at night*

Crew on a radar picket ship were in the Atlantic when radar picked up a signal traveling in excess of Mach 38. The object was reasonably low, as a ship's lookout visually confirmed the return.

Over **Utah** *(in air) – sometime in 1967 or 1968, at night*

A commercial airliner was heading back to Chicago with only employees on board ("deadheading"). Ground control radioed the pilot that they were tracking an unknown in their vicinity. Several of the employees saw an object approach from the left side of the plane. It was a cigar shape and glowed all over its surface, changing multicolored hues, like a rainbow. It seemed about plane fuselage-sized and paced right off the wing. Suddenly it whizzed into the distance and was gone.

Clemington, New Jersey – *fall 1956, 8:00 P.M.*

Persons outside the base called the battery (an Army Nike site) and reported odd lights in the sky. They checked with their radar and also visually; both confirmed. The object, through binoculars, seemed to be a sphere of light (white). They informed headquarters in Philadelphia. The object seemed to be moving in a small circle about ten miles away. Personnel were sent out ultimately to try to drive out there and inspect it. Brass showed up to get in on the action. Jets were scrambled, but no one could make contact except by radar and ground visual. Photographs did not turn out. Finally, word came from Washington not to say anything about this for national security reasons.

Lockborne Air Force Base, Ohio – *late 1962 or early 1963, at night*

One night jets (F-101s) were scrambled in response to a report of an unknown nearby. The pilots got radar lock-ons, but could not tell what it was. The object flew over the base, and the pilots were given the okay to fire on it. Then the target took off so rapidly that they couldn't follow its departure. (The reporter here was the pilots' debriefer.). No more was ever spoken of the incident.

Parent, Quebec – *July or August 1953, 2 to 3:00 A.M.*

A Royal Canadian Air Force radar installation had unidentified returns three or four nights running. The returns showed not only extreme speed (1500 mph) but astonishing changes of direction (example, going from flat out north to south speed to flat out east to west speed within one ten-second turn of the scope's cycle). There was plenty of time to check the equipment and everything was operating properly. For a change, the personnel were not given a lecture about not talking about this to anyone.

Kensbau, Germany – *various times during 1957 and 1958*

A radar plotter in a central receiving facility for forces in West Germany several times saw the following phenomenon. An apparently solid object would show a track going across West Germany and zooming into East German space at 1800 mph and about 6000 feet altitude. Then the track would almost instantly reverse itself and zoom back out on the same path. Both sides would scramble aircraft in response to it.

Holloman Air Force Base, New Mexico – *sometime in the late 1960s, in the afternoon*

The radar operators at the base were picking up returns from five objects flying in formation. Photographers were called out to photograph the radar screens, and plotting board. The objects flew outside the restricted zone for awhile and four of them left the area. One continued on and penetrated the zone. The colonel said that the object was flying at a speed equal to a "YF12A topping out" [the YF12A is a version of the SR-71 spy plane].

Dow Air Force Base, Bangor, Maine – *sometime in 1963*

Several personnel on the base saw three spheres of pulsating light fly down over the runway of the base and pause about twenty feet off the ground. Their light was bright enough to light up the whole base. While they sat there, there was dead stillness everywhere. Then they took off straight up. 75th Air Defense Command sent two F-101 Voodoos to chase them. "Of course they couldn't touch them." Their tower had seen them, visually and on radar, and Westover in Massachusetts also had them on radar. Everyone was later interrogated. The reporter here was told that if he said anything about this incident he would be court-martialed.

Section 26:
Send in the clowns, er, planes

Everyone knows that there are no such things as unidentified flying objects, and that our government therefore takes no interest in them. And, even if there were such things, they are no threat to national security, and so our government takes no interest in them. And, please ignore those jets we just scrambled.

Oklahoma City, Oklahoma – *July or August 1978 or 1979, around dusk*

A man was listening to music in his home when his cousin squealed up outside in his pickup truck and yelled for him to come outside. There in the air over the bowling alley was a silent disk with lights blinking all around it. It hovered in the air at a 10 to 20° tilt and had puffs of cloud around it. They heard a loud hum then and it was gone. Thirty seconds later, Air Force jets were cutting the air above and hustling somewhere.

Somewhere on **Route 52, near South Carolina** – *October or November 1973, at night*

A husband and wife were driving to visit their son in South Carolina. She looked out the window and saw a green light in the sky which resolved into an elongated luminous object. Though a clear night, a mist developed around this thing and extended across a lot of the sky. Then the object diminished to a starlike point as they drove on. The wife said to her husband: "Gee, looks like all of a sudden it dropped a curtain or something." Upon reaching their son, who was stationed at an Air Force base, he said that maybe that's why they scrambled all those jets last night.

Middletown, Ohio – *sometime in the early 1950s, in the afternoon*

A streetful of people from the neighborhood were outside gawking at the sky. Above three pear-shaped UFOs, glowing white bright as burning magnesium were

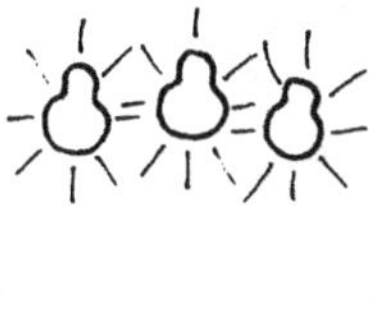

passing overhead. All this took place slowly and silently. Soon after they departed Air Force planes climbed into the scene going in their direction.

Maplewood, Oregon – *January or February 1964, 7:00 P.M.*

A young man saw a cream-colored light coming from the horizon while looking out his window. In his small spyglass it resolved into three such lights in a V-formation. He called his mother and she watched, too. The lights hovered overhead, and then turned red. The three lights moved symmetrically apart and then began to circle about. Then it/they (?) accelerated at extreme speed up and gone. Forty to forty-five seconds later, the air was alive with two Air Force jets.

Loring Air Force Base, Maine – *autumn 1975, 10:00 P.M.*

Two soldiers were in their barracks when they spotted some brilliant white objects, shaped round like plates, maneuvering in the sky. First there were four, then more up to a final count of about sixteen. They did smoothly controlled maneuvers (ex. figure eights) for several minutes over the base, but *the Air Force never responded* to them. "I was kind of surprised."

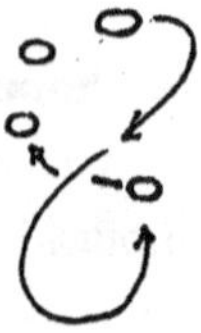

Southeast of **New Albany, Mississippi** – *December 10 or 11, 1952, 10:30 A.M.*

A rural postal worker saw an object out of the window of his vehicle. He stopped and got out. The conical-shaped device was moving slowly (with a faint buzz) toward an old Indian mound. The object was forty to fifty feet in diameter and taller than it was wide. It seemed to be made of silvery aluminum, and sported a set of exhausts around the bottom which spewed flames. After it went on, about thirty minutes later ("about the time it would take them to scramble from the Air Force base at Memphis") the air was full of P-51s.

Parma, Ohio – *spring 1951 or 1952, 11:30 A.M.*

A man walked outside his home and heard the sound of planes in the air. He looked up and saw two military planes (with propellers) chasing a flying disk. The object was "hamburger-shaped" (two large domes around a central layer) and colored pink or tan. The object then turned and left them behind.

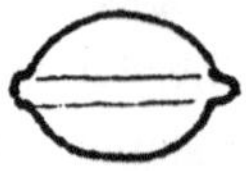

Waynesfield, Ohio – *fall 1957, about 9:00 P.M.*

A farmer and his wife saw what they thought was their neighbor's barn on fire. Then an object cleared the barn, looking very bright orange and "round as a silver dollar." It moved slowly to the west. Then it returned

and went to the east. It then veered north and left quickly. Shortly one large and two small planes came into the area and circled about for three hours.

Woodbridge, Ontario – *July 1957, at night*

A policeman received a report on his radio of something odd in the sky. Policemen began reporting in that it was a huge thing: "looks like an oil tanker. That big." It was sausage-shaped. The cops who hadn't seen it were laughing on the radio. The next evening it appeared again, and this time they reported it to the Air Force. Two planes were sent up and couldn't catch it. The next night the same thing happened. The planes would arrive, make a turn, and the object would then disappear.

Dennison, Ohio – *summer 1965, early afternoon*

The whole neighborhood was outside on a summer day, looking at the sky where a large disk object was hovering. Out of the large object emerged two small ones (too small for their shape to be determined). They flew around the larger for a while (several minutes) and then went back in. Two jets came from the direction of Columbus, and the large object rapidly departed after a 30-minute performance.

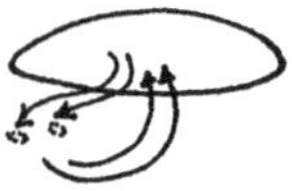

Vernonia, Oregon – *summer 1950, 3 to 4:00 P.M.*

The women were taking a break from giving one of them a permanent, when they noticed a shiny metallic ball hovering in the sky. It had the apparent diameter of a full moon. It hung there for twenty minutes when two jets came into view. "It began to play tag with those jets." It made right-angle turns and erratic maneuvers, and then shot up and disappeared.

Uniopolis, Ohio – *June 16, 1966, 6:30 P.M.*

A man was in his garage working on his car when his dog "kept raisin' all kinds of cain outside. I went out there and told her to shut up." The dog kept insistently scratching on the door and looking nervously to the south. Finally, he looked that way and saw a domed disk moving low across the field coming at the house. He ran in the house and got his wife to come out and watch with him. The object was a disk, small dome on top, and perhaps a couple dozen lights around the bottom perimeter. The color of the object was black. On the bottom was a light which could become a powerful beam. The object flew silently directly over the house. "We have an acre of yard and if it had set down, it would have covered the whole acre... and it was low enough you could have hit it with a slingshot." After it passed the house it went over the nearby woods, and the bottom light became a beam so bright that it was like being in a brilliantly illuminated room. Then planes (two or three?) arrived. "When it seen the planes, or whatever it sensed was coming, these lights around the side became one solid ring."

The light on the bottom went out, and then it made a zigzag run and was gone. The aircraft flew around the area for a few minutes and then flew back the way that they came.

Section 27: Just leave it to us. We're the government.

There have been many varied signals that we've been given by the government about UFOs over time. Sometimes it has been to actually take them seriously, but most of the time it's been: don't worry, be happy, daddy knows best. We've just seen a group of instances of jet scrambles (a very pragmatic evidence of government interest) and now here are a mixed bag of other government-related stories.

In the air over north **Texas** *– sometime in the early 1950s, around midnight*

On rare occasions a well-known (in some circles at least) person would walk up to John and talk about UFOs. This case was reported to him by H.T.E. Hertzberg, who was chief physical anthropologist at the USAF Aeromedical research laboratory at Wright-Patterson Air Force Base (1946-1972). In his job he worked with many of the test pilots and got to know them well. This is a case which one of these pilots related to him: After serving in Korea, this pilot returned to Keesler Air Force Base in Texas. He was training pilots and would fly students on great triangle routes (ex. to Chicago-Salt Lake-and back to Texas). They were on the last leg of this mission at 20,000 feet over Texas when the student spotted a light in the sky. The trainer ho-hummed and went back to sleep. The student woke him with the news that the light was moving. The trainer said: "Head for it." The object now came right at them and roared by. The trainer took over the stick and sort of a mock dogfight ensued. It was a saucer with a dome, glowing very brightly. It had a row of unlighted windows. The pilot continued the chase game until the disk emitted "a brilliant pencil of light" which came right into his cockpit. He thought: "this is no place for me," and dived the plane directly at the ground. The object had just demonstrated its utter technological superiority to him and he didn't want to sit around up there waiting for whatever it wanted to do next. When he flattened out at low level, he shut off his lights

and flew on into Keesler. They landed at 1:30 A.M., and he wrote his report and was let out from debriefing at 3:30 A.M. He slept at his home until 7:30 A.M. when the phone rang: it was the Pentagon. "We have just received your report of your dogfight with a flying saucer." Then ensued another two hours to explain every little detail to Washington, D.C. The pilot later (when at Wright-Patterson) looked for his case in Project Blue Book, but it wasn't there. Hertzberg said that the report was probably just kept in their Top Secret files at the Pentagon and never revealed.

Pertinent conversation: *1989, re: the USAF's news*

A father and son had a very good friend who was a career officer in the Strategic Air Command. The son had just seen a UFO when the SAC officer, stationed at that time in the Pentagon, came to visit them. The son couldn't help asking the officer if he knew anything about UFOs. "And he got real, real solemn, and he looked down at the floor, which I had never seen him do...so I kind of backed off and said: Oh, that's okay, if it's some kind of government stuff or something like that." But the officer shook his head and said simply: "No, I'll tell you. There's something up there."

Pertinent conversation: *1987*

A man was dating a young woman whose father was once a government employee at a rather high level in the intelligence community. He was now retired and "a rather grouchy fellow." The young man was very interested in UFOs and the girlfriend knew it. One day she told him that her father had been involved with UFO investigations, related to Project Blue Book. This very much fired up the young man's curiosity, but he knew that it was unlikely that he'd ever be able to quiz the older man about the subject. Nevertheless, he occasionally would ask his girlfriend how her father's health was, etc. So one day she told him that she'd done what she knew he wanted her to do, and asked her father, insistently, about UFOs. The old man wouldn't go into it, but gave her this serious response: "If the truth were known, it would destroy religion as we know it, and that was the central reason for any agency in power not to disclose the truth." [As an extractor of these reports, what interests me is not whether I believe the *reasoning* in a quote like that, but that I think that it is very interesting that people in those times and in those positions *had* those thoughts about UFOs].

Gulf of Oman, *near* **Iran** – *1978 or 1979, 11:00 P.M. to 2:30 A.M.*

The crew of the U.S.S. Nimitz spotted a glowing object about 1500 yards to starboard. It was a cigar-shaped UFO with two portholes just above the water's surface. Photography was attempted, and failed. The object was not picked up on ship's radar. Several members watched the object for several hours through binoculars. Commanding officers informed those who witnessed the object that they were not to talk about it.

Somewhere in rural **Mississippi** – *1968, at night*

A deputy sheriff was part of a police force which experienced a flap of nocturnal light UFOs during 1968. There were at least seventeen different occurrences. The lights would demonstrate extreme speed, hovering, fast maneuvers, and even separating into parts. They had radar returns on the objects from Jackson, Mississippi, and Memphis, Tennessee. The Air Force vectored interceptors into the area, always, of course, unsuccessful, as far as anyone could tell. "I think it was the Department of Defense Information Agency or something like that, some government agency came down later, took statements and tried to discredit as many witnesses as possible, including the police officers."

Plattsburg Air Force Base, New York – *summer 1978 or 1979, 4 to 6:00 P.M.*

A ground equipment mechanic at the base was also an amateur photographer. He heard something and went outside. Over toward the town was a large object, shaped like the Goodyear blimp but much larger (500 to 600 feet long; 300 feet thick). He got out his camera. The object was a grayish green, but shiny. It had different colored blinking lights encircling the perimeter. It moved slowly enough that he was able to get three 35 millimeter pictures. He tried for close-ups but the thing was too big for that. A friend with a private darkroom developed the pictures. The photographer had a friend at the base who was a lieutenant colonel, and he told him about the pictures. The colonel confiscated the pictures, plus all the unrelated ones elsewhere on the roll. "I asked him what it was, and he said none of my business. It was an experimental aircraft, and that's all you need to know... reimbursement for my roll of film? He wouldn't even give me that."

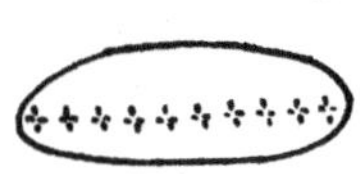

Fort Sill, Oklahoma – *summer 1968, in the morning*

The troops were marching early in the morning with a dense, low fog overhead, maybe 300 or 400 feet up. Just within the fog bank appeared this red light hanging there. Everyone was laughing about the silent object, and the march

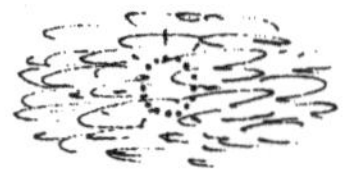

slowed down to a chaotic milling drill. Later that night a colonel came around to each barracks warning people that if they talked about the red light their leave passes would be cancelled.

During an in-air test for Air Materiel Command – *1952, 2:00 P.M.*

Flying at about 20,000 feet or less, a B-36 crew saw an object coming toward the plane. One member said: "Here it comes. Here the bastard comes, whatever it is." The crew chief replied: "Well, this isn't the first time."

The thing, a 20- to 25-foot diameter disk (apparently of metal with striations in it), parked just in front of the wing. It had a small dome, and was very shiny, and it sat there spinning counterclockwise. The two of them went forward this way at about 400 mph for one and a half to two minutes, during which time pictures were taken. Then the object angled up and shot away. Upon landing, everyone was debriefed and told that they basically didn't see what they thought they saw and that "you're all wet." A lieutenant colonel, who was pilot on the B-36, was hip to USAF attitudes and got everyone to just swallow it and shut up. "We all ended up back over at the club afterwards getting swacked, because no one believed it."

Utica, New York – *fall 1967, 8:00 P.M.*

A mother and daughter were in their home when they noticed three perpendicular red lights off toward the horizon; they thought briefly that these must be some previously unnoticed radio tower, until the lights pivoted and assumed a horizontal position. The object began to move and went directly behind their house (maybe only ten feet away and at ground level). It looked like a football, and the daughter thought that she saw a shadowy form moving behind one of the lighted areas. The mother took several pictures of it. The negatives never returned, and half of the pictures were not sent back. The few that arrived gradually frittered away through the years and none may still exist.

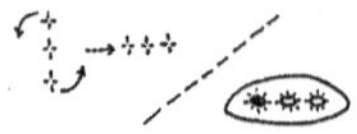

And now the fun part: "About the same time that we saw the big UFO, we had visitors of two gentlemen. They were in very dark outfits and hats, and they were dark-skinned, and they came and talked to my mother." The mother and daughter were puzzled that the men seemed to arrive without a car on a rainy day. "They told my mother not to say anything to anyone. And she was a very stubborn lady, and she said that if she wanted to tell somebody, she would. They somehow silenced her. They looked at me, at the time they said it." She said: "Then I won't say anything." And they were gone, and still no sign of any transportation that they used. Tommy Lee Jones and Will Smith?

Stroud, Ontario – *sometime in 1973, daytime*

A man was climbing down from his roof where he'd been doing some tarring, and as he reached the ground an odd wind rose up and he felt a rushing, blowing all around him. He looked back up over his house and

there was a silvery object looking like a cigar or a disk seen on edge. He went into his house and called the police. The next day ("to my surprise") his report was in the local newspaper. A few days after that, a man showed up at his door and identified himself as working for the Canadian government in the Emergency Measures Organization, something the witness had never heard of. The man took the witness out to his car where he had a large book filled with pictures of UFOs. There were:

> Kinds that can fly in the air and they can swoop right down, go in the water like a submarine and come up somewhere else. And just fly right into the air. I can't understand how such a thing could take place, but there is such a thing from outer space. And I looked in this book, it was such an exciting book, and finally I came across the one that I saw. And there were two kinds: one without windows in it, and there was one with windows all down the side, like a big spaceship. And he explained to me that there's such a kind as a mother ship which has a whole lot of UFOs inside them, and they explore all around the area where they go... and I thought, oh boy, that is really something.

All of the latter part of the above sounds like the witness was being hoaxed by some UFO buff with a fake identity, but I'll leave it to those who know better. The real point of the long quote is to show you how genuine the witness is. This was a common feature of John's interviewees.

Arizona desert highway – *an unstated year and time*

The witness was deliberately vague about this case, and was one of the few who wouldn't give John his name. He was driving between Phoenix

and Prescott when an object about the size and shape of an airplane fuselage that flew low (about 200 to 300 feet) over the road between him and an oncoming car. On the front was an extension of some sort like an antenna. Both cars stopped and talked. The other driver said he would stop at FBI offices in Phoenix and give a report, and the witness also did this when he got back to Phoenix, two or three days later.

> About three or four months later, I happened to be downtown, so I decided to go over to the FBI office, and the same gentleman (who took his report) was in the office. He denied ever having met me. He denied ever taking any kind of report from me or the (other) people I had sent there.

Jacksonville, Florida – *January or February 1965, at night*

One of NASA's space capsules had arrived at the base on its way to Cape Canaveral and was sitting under a shroud between runways with guards posted about. Several soldiers on the steps of the barracks noticed a group of five lights in the sky: one large with four small ones. The large light remained stationary while the array of four smaller ones approached the field, made a fast dip down across the area where the capsule was located, then lifted back up and returned to the larger, where they seemed to enter it. Sightings were occurring all up and down the coast at that time. A pilot friend suggested to the witness "you just don't talk about stuff like that." Well, it seems that if we're officially not interested in UFOs, *they* seem to be quite interested in what *we* do.

Pusan, Korea – *1954, at night from 8:30 P.M. and on*

The active phase of the Korean War was over, but troops were still there holding maneuvers. This incident occurred during a night exercise. The maneuvers were in a narrow valley and the forces were using live rounds. Observers on higher ground noticed a dark object which was hovering silently and keeping to shadows mainly, as if hiding. The object would get revealed briefly when overflights would drop occasional flares. The object would then rapidly flit to a darker area. The game of hide-and-seek went on for about forty minutes. The device was about the size of a compact car, but its exact shape was too difficult to see. "It moved as if it had somebody in it that knew what they were doing"… and, apparently, really wanted to know what *our* military was doing, as well.

Section 28:
Crashed disks

Yes, even persons alleging knowledge of Roswell, alien bodies, mysterious hangars, and desert discoveries showed up to talk with John at the exhibit. These tales were usually more secondhand than the case reports, as you might expect. But here they are, for what you would like to make of them.

Re: Roswell and Mack Brazel

An elderly couple came over to John (actually separately with five others in between) and told him of their experience with Mack Brazel. The gentleman was an air force man and had been assigned to a New Mexico base (not Roswell). He was married at the time, and there was no accommodation on base, so he and his wife rented an apartment in Tularosa. The landlord was Mack Brazel, who lived in the same building with his wife. This was after the 1947 incident (apparently by several years; the wife described him as perhaps in his sixties, and people had stopped calling him "Mack" and had begun calling him "Pop"). The Brazels were described as wonderful people, and well-loved in Tularosa, where he had been an exemplary sheriff for several years. Regarding the famous incident, Brazel was not at all reluctant to talk about it. The husband said that Brazel told him as follows:

> He was explaining about this unidentified flying object, or whatever it was...it was on his ranch. And he explained one thing about it that I can remember quite distinct. He had a piece of metal of some sort which he never seen before in his life. He got a hold of it and he wadded it up. When he wadded it up, it would wad up all right, but when he released it, it came back to its original form, just like a piece of spring steel. Apparently the metal was all taken away from him.

The gentlemen said that what got his interest back up about this was that he saw an *Unsolved Mysteries* show, which mentioned the Roswell book, and that he'd looked the book up to read about Mack Brazel for nostalgia reasons. John asked him whether what he just told him was from Brazel or from the television and book. He was emphatic:

> Oh yes, yes. From him. From him back at that time. No, that show, I just refreshed my memory a little bit about it...and I'm not sure that his name was even mentioned on that show. It may or may not have been. But I knew right away that that was (what was being) talked about up on his ranch.

The wife showed up later and her story has the same tone. Her mother and father had visited them in Tularosa, and Brazel took the father over to the ranch to show him the crash site. Her comments on the crash were:

> It was at the ranch where they saw this flying saucer that people call it. They said that they had people as far as England and all over coming there and looking at the remains of what they picked up. But Pop said that the government came in and they picked up every tiny piece that they could. And they took it off and they, from what I can remember, I think it was some place in Maryland that they took it back to. He said it was a very shiny metal and I can't remember how big it was. But he said it was over a large area of ground.

Well, folks, if you are Roswell aficionados you probably find that quite interesting. The only awkward moment in the tapes came when John made an interviewing error in mentioning "late forties" before the gentleman had a chance to give a date. This seemed to act as an unintentional "psychological bully" and he said maybe 1948 or 1949, when it's pretty obvious that the couple are really talking about the 1950s sometime when they met Brazel.

Re: Crashed spacecraft

A USAF physician became friends with an OSI agent, and the friendship grew close, so that when the agent told him this story (c. 1970s), he had great confidence in it: "he related a story to me which I am very, very sure was true."

> He was involved in a situation in the Air Force where apparently some sort of alien spacecraft had landed somewhere in the southwest, at some point in time, made some sort of crash landing. The beings on that spacecraft were not anything that he could identify from our planet. They did not appear like any human being he'd ever seen, but they were obviously not anything else.

> They obviously were living human beings and some of them were injured. Most of them were dead. They were taken by he and a number of other individuals to Wright-Patterson Air Force Base. They were put there for later evaluation, identification, examination by the Air Force and the military...I think he said that there were either four or six victims that were obviously not maimed badly, but some of them appeared to be dead.

The quotes are obviously intriguing. The main flaw is that this was one of the few people who refused to identify themselves to John. The guy was obviously in a battle between curiosity and secrecy, and said that he was trying to find out more about this incident himself, privately.

Re: Crashed spacecraft

A gentleman was telling John about an unusual cone-shaped UFO that he and his son had witnessed. When he finished he said that he had a friend who was a metallurgist and who worked (apparently) for the military in the San Antonio area many years ago. The gentleman had seen an article in the newspaper about crashed saucers just before visiting his old friend. That led to a conversation in which the friend told him:

> A thing that happened in New Mexico, about archaeologists who were doing some diggings and ran across a UFO with aliens. The metal that was retrieved from that site was taken...some of it was taken to, I believe, one of the airfields in San Antonio. (My) friend told me that the metal was brought in, they ran tests on it, and to this date I don't think they have found out what the metal was really composed of. The material from that site was taken to the place where he was working. And he tried to analyze the material. And after that, I understand, the material was gathered and shipped to Wright Airfield, along with the alien bodies that were found at the site.

Re: Roswell Air Force Base, one year post-crash

A man came up to John and introduced himself as an Air Force engineering technology officer, who had been assigned as a young man to Roswell in 1948. During an almost three-year stint at the base (1948-1950), not one person mentioned the crash incident. "They just completely ignored the fact that it had happened." He said that he would have never realized that there had been the big brouhaha a year earlier, had he not seen the later publicity of the eighties, etc.

Re: A mysterious hangar

A man related to John that during a period when he had been laid off from an auto plant, he was working odd jobs. One was as a night guard in a psychiatric hospital. His partner on duty was an older guy who said that he was ex-military (20-30 years) and retired, but decided to do some part-time work for his own reasons. He said that he'd been a colonel and had worked some odd assignments out of the Pentagon, including a tour at Wright-Patterson. The guy got to be a constant flow of reminiscence and technical information, filling up the late night hours. So, John's correspondent asked him one evening, as he was describing Wright-Patterson, "have you been in the hanger where the flying saucer is supposed to be at?" The emotional weather completely changed with him. "Who are you?", he asked. "How do you know about that hangar?"; and then he went silent on that subject and wouldn't talk about anything military for the rest of the night.

Re: An enigmatic structure

Well, we're really going in Vague Land here. A man had given John a reasonably interesting report about a delta-shaped object from 1957, when he very tentatively stumbled onwards with a mention of something that his nephew had told him about Wright-Patterson Air Force Base. "Well, I better not mention anything...I'd better not say anything...I'd rather not put that on tape." In between the hesitations all he would say was that there is an underground facility on the base "you can only see a hump in the ground... it's covered with green and all you see is ventilation pipes and that some people—I say people, I say some beings could be there."

Re: A mysterious hangar

A gentleman came to John and introduced himself as a deputy sheriff and a former pilot who has several friends who achieved fairly high-ranking status in the military. Two of these were lieutenant colonels who worked at Wright-Patterson sometime during the years when the UFO investigating project (Blue Book) was there. One of these, now retired, used to absolutely refuse to countenance the existence of UFOs, but now that he's retired "he will acknowledge it." The colonel was quoted as saying:

> Well, you know I always said that if I could catch one of those things on the ground, I could find out what it was. The sheriff asked him about the Wright-Patterson rumors: He said: "It would panic the people to know what has really gone on." He says, "Yes, there has been and there was at that time something in those

hangars which would have panicked the people had they known what was there." And he says: "You don't want to know what was there, either." That's as much as I could get out of him.

Re: Building, not Hangar, 17

A gentleman who worked in the emergency medical room at the base hospital at Wright-Patterson in the 1970s told John that something had come up where the press was interested in whether the base harbored alien bodies in some Hangar 17, and that the base had escorted some press to that structure to show them that nothing was there. The medical room worker wondered at this because there were (in 1947) five different buildings designated 17, all connected and all run by the T-3 engineering section of the base on the Wright Field side. He said that part of (or near?) this complex was the base hospital (in those days) and that the morgue was in the basement of one of these 17s. He said that the refrigeration units of that morgue were still in operation in the seventies. He said that even in the seventies med-techs like himself, on ambulance duty, were not allowed to go into those buildings without military police escort... even for a heart attack.

[As an aside: in 1946-8 Building 17 was a single structure, and it was Building 18 which precisely fits the med-tech's description—sounds more like Hangar 18, anyway. And, nearby in building 11/11A, were the offices of several T-2 intelligence community members, including Alfred Loedding, chief engineer for the first UFO project (Sign) and probable instigator of the famous pro-ET Estimate-of-the-Situation (shown with a model of a flying disk plane that he patented).]

Alfred Loedding

Re: Bodies?

As mentioned earlier in this monograph, John interviewed chief physical anthropologist of Wright-Patterson Aeromedical laboratory, Dr. H.T.E. Hertzberg. No creative genius is needed to imagine that if alien bodies had come to the base, then showing them to your physical anthropologist might be a smart move. John didn't pry into this, but the UFO community caught the drift of John's contact, and Hertzberg's address was let out. A UFO community member attempted to contact him (a few years post-interview) only to find that Dr. Hertzberg had passed on. John was asked if it was okay to release the interview to researchers, and he contacted Mrs. Hertzberg for permission. Now: I don't want anyone to get a wrong impression about this, so please note the facts. The earlier UFO researcher had inquired (of the then-deceased Dr. Hertzberg) about alien bodies, of course receiving no reply. John's inquiry merely asked for permission to release the interview. Mrs. Hertzberg responded to John: (1) informing him of her husband's passing; (actually at that very moment only totally incapacitated); (2) happily giving permission for the transcript; and (3) handwriting the following postscript (which one may make as much or as little as one wishes), "I do not know if Ed talked to anyone involved in examination of bodies, but if anything of the kind is on the tape, okay on that, too."

Perhaps just a very nice, cooperative lady with full awareness of the request, or perhaps a lady who knew that her husband knew something important and could have decided to finally speak of it.

Re: A later crash?

A person who had just told John of an interesting in-air military plane encounter said:

> I personally have a close friend who absolutely guaranteed me that what he was saying was God's truth. He was at a crash site where they have five bodies, which they took to a hangar and from there on he lost them. I think that it was Nevada—it was sandy…one of the western states.
>
> John asked of the year: "I believe that it was (after) the Vietnam war; reasonably sure. Five bodies; four feet tall, roughly; hairless; big eyes…(garbled)…no ears; had like a sheen to them, maybe a suit."

This person refused to give his name.

Re: A later crash?

A person told this story to John that he learned in detail from his employer on whose land the crash occurred. Around 1957 or 1958, near Horseheads, New York, some kind of object crashed into a hilltop in a heavily wooded area. Authorities (USAF) came and cordoned off the area, stopping all access. Barbed wire was used along with personnel. Heavy equipment arrived the very next day, and a road to the site had to be laid. When the military pulled out, the employer-owner went up to the site, and she found an area of about 200 square yards (one wonders whether she meant to say 200 yards on a side) where the soil had been removed and replaced with new soil.

Although the connection of this incident with UFOs could well be zero, it says something about military crash cleanup procedures.

Re: Allen Hynek on crashed disks in 1981

John even ended up running into Allen one time and taped his views on things. Here's Hynek on Roswell, etc.:

> I'd like to add to that that at the moment I do not believe any of the crashed saucer stories until some people will stand up and be counted. Now it has frequently happened at the end of a lecture that someone will come up and say that they knew the pilot that brought out the cadavers to Wright Field. Or that they... their aunt was the secretary in the office and papers passed through her hands, etc. And I say, well, this is excellent. I'd love to have more information about that. Would you be willing to give me a signed affidavit to that effect? Oh, no, no, no, I can't. Why not? Well, they are afraid of government reprisals, pension might be taken away or something. So the other day, I taped a TV pilot for a TV station, obviously, and it depends on whether the legal people at the network will let this go through or not, but I addressed President Reagan directly on that program, and said: 'Mr. President, would you be willing to grant presidential immunity to these people?' So, frankly, I don't think anything would happen if they did stand up and be counted, because it's been so many years and all that. But if they are afraid of it, okay. Let's see whether that would happen. If they got that sort of immunity, they'd have to be free. There would be no reason why they shouldn't make their statement. But until that happens, I will regard all these statements myself... I don't know how the rest of you, but myself will regard them solely as stories, interesting stories. But even if they are completely false, this says nothing whatsoever about the rest of the UFO phenomenon.
>
> Now this *Roswell Incident* book may turn out to be first class, but it's written in such a manner, it's not a scientific book in any sense of the word. It is a sensational book which makes money and I wish I made that much money on my book.
>
> ...(concerning) investigation of refuse [debris] and bodies and so on. It's very difficult to believe that this could remain a complete secret for 35 years.

Well, Allen, my friend, reasonable thoughts in 1981. As for now, twenty years later, it would be so good to sit and talk with you about Kevin Randle and Don Schmitt's research, and get your take on that and so many other things in our field's history that we never got to ask you about.

Section 29:

Pre-1947 reports

The modern UFO phenomenon is always dated from the "Summer of 47" wave in the United States, so anything prior to 1947 tends to be looked upon by UFO scholars as a purer or uncontaminated-by-press evidence that odd things really do go on in the sky. John collected a couple dozen or so of these stories scattered among the raft of modern UFOs. Here they are in date order.

Date: Summer of 1902, during the day
Place: South of London, Ontario
UFO type: A silvery, shiny cigar, narrower on one end than the other

Date: c. 1915, at night
Place: Southwest Virginia, in the mountains
UFO type: An erratically moving ball-of-light, which preceded a terrific thunderstorm

Date: July or August 1921, 4:00 P.M.
Place: Waldeck, Saskatchewan
UFO type: Light brown-colored round objects (3); apparent size = 1 foot diameter at arm's length (i.e., large)

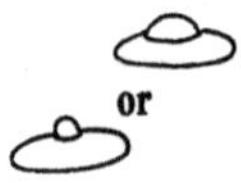

Date: 1926 or 1927, daytime
Place: East Liverpool, Ohio
UFO type: Shiny metallic disk with a dome

Date: 1926 or 1927
Place: Forest Hill Village (Toronto), Ontario
UFO type: A dirigible (or "airship") with smaller "planes" which emerged from opening in rear and later reentered. Dirigible made of shiny metal.

Date: 1930, daytime
Place: Vernonia, Oregon
UFO type: Object shaped like a hovercraft; ladder came down and two little men in shiny suits came out. Pointed a wand at child and caused unconsciousness.

Date: Fall of 1933, at night
Place: near Castor, Louisiana
UFO type: Silvery sphere (at first glance, witness thought it was Moon). Came down to railroad tracks, blew cap off, and blew down sage grass. About four to six feet diameter.

Date: Fall of 1935, 6:30 P.M.
Place: Oberlin, Ohio
UFO type: Cream-colored thin disks, like frisbees (2) going by car

Date: Summer of 1936 or 1937, 3 to 4:00 P.M.
Place: Carpathian Mountains, Poland
UFO type: Silvery rocket with cherry-red exhaust; longer than a bomber, going slowly, horizon-to-horizon, silent.

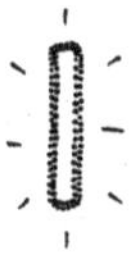

Date: 1936 and following, nighttimes
Place: Lake Cayuga, New York
UFO type: Several instances of columns of light (beautiful colors) appearing in bedroom, which would come and envelope the witness, and within which witness felt were kind, loving beings

Date: October 1938, 7:00 P.M.
Place: South of Alger, Ohio
UFO type: Round object with multicolored pulsating lights around it; sharp angle turn; conked out tractor engine

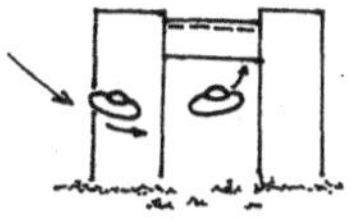

Date: 1940
Place: Kalispell, Montana
UFO type: Saucers with domes on top and flat bottoms; metallic; flew very low beneath bridge connecting grain elevators

Date: Fall of 1942
Place: Brookfield, North Carolina
UFO type: Silvery parachute-shaped domed object moving at high speed in a line

Date: Midsummer of 1942 or 1943, 2:30 P.M.
Place: Oshawa, Ontario
UFO type: Large group of people saw one large and five small objects high in sky engaging in very fast, erratic motions. Air Force officer said that nothing known could do what they were watching.

Date: Winter of 1942 or 1943, late at night
Place: near Fairmont, Minnesota
UFO type: A red-colored domed saucer which hovered near the ground and then just "went out."

Date: December 1942 or January 1943, at night
Place: Heath, Ohio
UFO type: Silvery domed disk with windows radiating greenish light, and shadows moving within; size of Volkswagen bug; hovered over power lines

Date: Summer of 1943, midday
Place: Adak, Alaska
UFO type: Spherical object colored like the Moon. P-38 sent up to investigate. He couldn't locate it (though they still saw it).

Date: 1943, daytime
Place: Afpla, Guam
UFO type: Small, round, navy blue craft, containing portholes around it (I believe he means a disk). Case involves paralysis, sound (a *buzz*), and a very odd follow-on story that evening involving a fire in the family house, and the entry of two mysterious beings in white suits who put out the fire by grabbing it up in their hands. The witness said that UFO activity was all over his village.

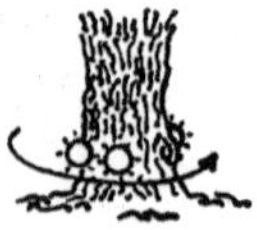

Date: Summer 1945, midnight
Place: Oquawka, Illinois
UFO type: Dull white balls-of-light near ground circling oak tree; size of basketballs
(sketched earlier)

Date: September or October 1945
Place: Malmstrom Air Force Base, Great Falls, Montana
UFO type: Large number of persons, including officers, saw cylinder-shaped object with flaming exhaust.

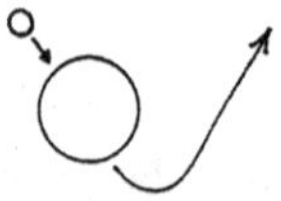

Date: March 1945
Place: Rhine river, Germany
UFO type: Yellow-orange sphere having apparent technological structure; 200 feet in diameter. Swooped down over tanks and infantry and back up and out high in sky. Silent.

Date: September or October 1945, 11:00 A.M.
Place: near Boswell, Oklahoma

UFO type: (This one deserves a little more telling.)

A 9-year-old girl was outside with her mother. The mother was nursing her baby brother on the porch while the girl played in the front yard. That morning, as often, she was climbing up in the chinaberry tree. She sort of blanked out, and the next thing she remembered was being suspended in the air above the tree.

> When I came to, I was not aware of anything other than there was something up there and I looked up to see it. And when I looked up to see it, and I saw it, it was like I woke up [fully]. It was like I had been asleep and I woke up and when I woke up I fell. I fell down through the branches of the outer edge of the tree and landed on the ground.

The girl was shaken but relatively unhurt. Her mother, unusually, was no longer on the porch. The girl ran into the house. Her mother was standing in the middle of the kitchen, and asked, "What's the matter? What did you see outside?" The girl replied: "I didn't see anything outside. What did you see?" The mother answered: "I didn't see anything either." And then the mother became very preoccupied about how the day had suddenly gotten so late that they had missed their lunch. And then, weirdly, didn't fix the late lunch at all, but instead everyone went to bed and slept the rest of the afternoon.

Later the mother and daughter recovered themselves enough to discuss the incident, and both saw a metallic ship coming with a curved upper area and a flat bottom. The mother then blanked. The daughter had her floating/falling experience, and watched the craft leave to the horizon, seemingly transforming into a pattern of individual dots before disappearing. And, another oddity, an older sister, another brother, and a grandmother all lived in the house and should have been around at that time. "No one knows where they were all afternoon." The mother claims that she did the following because of practical reasons, but shortly she moved out of that house and into a hotel in town, but it was more expensive. And the daughter never played in the chinaberry tree again.

Date: December 23 in the mid-1940s, in the evening
Place: Forchet, Saskatchewan
UFO type: A family and many others had gone (by sleighs) to a Christmas concert and were enjoying the event when a very handsome stranger, whom no one knew, came in. He looked a bit like representations of Jesus Christ. When the concert was over he was missing. Nearby outside, as they went to their sleighs, was a large ball-of-light with spikes of light, the bottom of which extended to the ground. Very brilliant.

Date: September 1946
Place: over Maryland, in air
UFO type: Shiny metal disk flying several miles from plane

Date: 1946
Place: Cross Lake, near Shreveport, Louisiana
UFO type: A strange area in the sky, which seemed to move and reflect light images from objects on the ground.

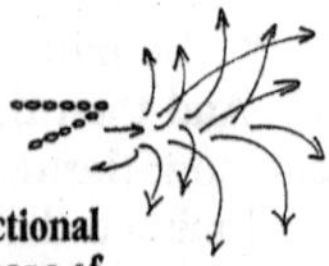

fictional shape of array

Date: 1946
Place: Santiago, Dominican Republic
UFO type: A fleet of twelve saucer-shaped objects, white in color, and flying in a formation which broke up and dispersed in many directions (actual shape of array not given).

Date: Summer 1946 or 1947
Place: Mackenzie Island, Ontario
UFO type: A round object shaped like a top which moved down river channel. Witness thinks it went into the water.

Date: 1946 or 1947
Place: Cross Lake, near Shreveport, Louisiana
UFO type: Nine round, bright objects in three groups of three moved across lake, and then up and into a kite-like large object which then disappeared rapidly.

Date: ? Since ancient times
Place: Near Kempton, Pennsylvania
UFO type: Indian and local legends say that on occasions a ball-of-fire will issue from a cave ("Dragon's Cave") and will travel to another cave of the same name to the south.

Section 30:
Echoes of the Classics

Every so often John would find that his correspondent would be talking not about some unknown case but about some very well-known case indeed. I'm not going to rehash these classic cases for you here. If you're interested, and don't know them already off the top of your head, just look them up: retellings of Mantell, Gorman, the Hills, etc., abound in our literature. What's below are the bits and pieces of what these people at the exhibit may have added to those cases.

Re: The Mantell crash of 1948

A person was on reserve duty and was in the tower at Scott Field when the air-to-ground conversation was taking place "between the pilot and the tower that subsequently ended in the pilot's death chasing a UFO or what he thought was a UFO." John asked: Do you have a feeling that this could have been explained by a high-flying weather balloon? "Well, not according to the conversation that I heard, it certainly couldn't have. Because he was talking about it moving in starts and stops, and laterally and so on. And then it would pull away from him abruptly and seemingly stop."

Re: Mantell

A last comment from John's interview with Dr. Hertzberg of Wright-Patterson, as has been mentioned earlier. He commented that he knew the chief investigator of the crash. [He doesn't mention "Al Loedding," but from my own research this is who he is talking about.] "The engineer sent down to investigate that whole affair, voiced to me his conviction that there had to be something there and that Mantell had been shot down." Hertzberg recounts Loedding's description of the incident this way:

> When Mantell... when he had told his flight, just go ahead and land because the UFO which had been just parked at about 400 feet over Godman Field, that had suddenly shot right up into the air when Mantell wanted to lead his flight in to land. Mantell had then left his flight, told them to go ahead and land. He immediately just

> shot up into the air, following this UFO, and suddenly apparently when he neared it, his airplane utterly disintegrated. Now that was a P-51 and that was a very solidly-built airplane. The news reports that were put out said that he had gone up into very high altitude, between seventeen and twenty thousand feet, and had probably passed out from lack of oxygen at that elevation, and had then spun in and crashed. Well, my friend, the engineer, who was a very high-ranking engineer on the field and who had studied the case very carefully, he simply said he could not believe that Mantell had passed out from lack of oxygen and had just simply crashed into the earth.

Re: The Gorman dogfight, 1948

A gentleman had served with Gorman after the incident and reported that Gorman believed that his plane had shown increased radioactivity due to the encounter.

> In 1951, when we were called back into active duty during the Korean conflict, the 146th Tactical Fighter Wing from California was called back along with fighter squadrons from Idaho, North Dakota, and Montana. And the gentleman... I don't recall the pilot's name at this time... but he was with the North Dakota Air National Guard and he was one of the gentlemen which Donald Keyhoe had interviewed and was talking to. He was flying the 51 that came back and when he arrived on the ground, the aircraft was radioactive. And that's all I can tell you.

Re: The Great Falls, Montana, UFO film, 1950

A woman was working at a radio station in Great Falls when Nick Mariana took his film. This is her memory:

> My husband was stationed at Great Falls Air Force Base. I was working at radio station KXLK at the time. We had a sportscaster who was—he happened to be at a baseball game in the afternoon, when UFOs came in over the baseball field. He took motion pictures of it. He brought the camera back to the radio station where I was working. The Air Force... and we had several people on the Air Force Base there who were working with the Blue Book group, came to the radio station and confiscated his camera and his film. A number of years later, when they were showing movies, like on TV and at the theaters, this man's film was shown. So I did

eventually get to see it. Anyhow, at that time in Great Falls, there had been a number of sightings.

Re: The Washington, D.C., *Merry-go-round* of 1952

A civilian, working for the military, had authority to go into the Air Traffic Control tower at the Washington airport, but when he got there on the day that the UFOs were all over D.C. airspace he was barred from admittance and no information was allowed out as to why. He only learned about the UFO flap much later.

A second conversation which John had, involved a pilot who (by coincidence) was returning to Andrews Air Force Base just at that time. Here is his bit of the story (a secondhand retelling):

> He was returning from some mission, some routine mission. He had a wing man and he was the squadron commander, had a radar observer, and he was making his initial approach to the runway when he was given a call by the tower, saying that there is some type of an optical phenomena that they wanted him to go over and check out. They vectored him into the spot and he got a visual on this thing, and his radar observer got a radar lock on. Now, he approached it and as he approached it... he approached it within, as I recall from the conversation, he approached it within 200 yards. But he couldn't approach it any closer than that, it would veer off immediately and he couldn't make a tight enough turn to keep onto it. As I recall the conversation, he told me that he was given instructions that if he could get it lined up between him and the Chesapeake Bay, he could shoot it down. Or fire at it. And so he was making an attempt to do that, but since he was on the return portion of his mission, he did not have much fuel left. And so he could only make a couple passes, a couple quick passes at it, before he had to break and come down and land. And when he did that, they had sent another pair of jet fighters up to take over where he left off.

Re: The beginnings of the first professional UFO group, CSI-Los Angeles One of the founding engineers told John this:

> What I wanted to share with you is that while I was at Douglas in the engineering department, we had many of the personnel, both Douglas, Air Force and Navy people that we worked with, who had different sightings of UFOs. All the way to the point of where

> the UFOs came directly over the Santa Monica plant and hovered over the plant in 1953. This set about a group which we—was an informal group within the engineering department, and our vice-president of engineering was chairing this organization but he was doing it without authorization of the top management at Douglas. This information started to expand itself to where people who had worked previously at Northrop as I had and people who worked at other companies, Lockheed, who had sightings, started contacting their technical people that they knew that were still in these other organizations.

Re: Ubatuba, Brazil UFO magnesium metal fall, 1957

John spoke with University of Arizona metallurgist, Dr. Walter Walker, who did analysis on the metal from the magnesium fall for APRO. This conversation resulted in an outstanding technical paper by Walker for the *Journal of UFO Studies*. Here are some of Dr. Walker's comments.

> Oh, well, what the story is and perhaps I should qualify this: this story first appeared over the byline of a society columnist Ibn Suad *[sic]* in the Rio de Janeiro paper. And he said these three pieces had been sent to him through the mail by somebody who recorded that they were down on the beach at Ubatuba, Sao Paulo Province, Brazil. They had seen this flying saucer shaped object come down. It was obviously in trouble. It got down near the beach, flew back up again and then exploded. And small pieces came out and fell all over the place, and these three pieces that were sent were three of the small pieces that came off the UFO.
>
> ...early in my career, early in the career of this material, I investigated the magnesium samples which were collected at Ubatuba Province, Brazil, in 1957. Now, this was a case where three observers observed a UFO apparently breaking up on the beach. They found three little pieces of whitish metal which found their way into the hands of Dr. Fontes who was APRO's South American investigator for South America at that time. One of the samples of the three was investigated by what was equivalent to the U.S. Bureau of Mines for Brazil and they found it was completely pure magnesium. Now this was impossible terrestrially to have completely pure magnesium. Any magnesium we make as humans by extracting from the ore is always going to have at

least trace element amounts of other elements in it. We cannot make anything that is absolutely pure and yet they reported it was absolutely pure. This was taken initially as being very good evidence of extraterrestrial reality. However, the sample which the Brazilians shot was either by them or subsequently burned up in an emission spectrograph test. None of it is left and we don't have the film or anything else now to verify what the Brazilians reported. The other two pieces were sent by Dr. Fontes to Tucson to APRO and I was given one of them to investigate. And my investigation, being a metallurgist, concerned what we call the stretcher, the way the atoms are put together in the magnesium sample. And my investigation found that this material was pure magnesium, that is commercially pure, at least, magnesium. It was not an alloy.

The magnesium in question was a cast magnesium, meaning that it had been cast... in other words, melted and poured and nothing else done to it. Whereas normal wrought objects of all types of metals are poured into what we call an ingot and then subsequently deformed and pounded on and everything. The structure is much different. This was a cast. The unique thing about this casting was that all the grains and all metals are composed of small crystals which are called grains... all the grains were aligned atomically in the same direction. That's what we call directional solidification in the casting field. Now this excited me at the time because at the time there was no interest in casting industry or in casting research of directionally solidified castings of any type. Since that time, directionally solidified castings have become rather prominent—or directional solidification, let me say, has become a very prominent method of making better castings. But in 1957, this wasn't so. So I felt that maybe this indicated that perhaps somebody extraterrestrially, if you will, had made these directional castings and at a time when we weren't doing it. Unfortunately, the biggest piece I'm talking about—or these two pieces, are about as big as the eraser on the end of a wooden pencil. And as another metallurgist that reviewed my paper remarked, and it's absolutely true, in ordinary cast magnesium which has all kinds of ordinary grains going every which way, there are small areas about that size which are directional. Just by happenstance. And these could very well be that. Which is true, he's absolutely true, I cannot prove the entire big casting, however big it was, was directional on the basis of these two small little pieces we had to work on. This in my mind points out the biggest problem that all physical evidence investigators have, and that is the collection of the original sample. Almost invariably, samples collected not by technically trained people. Which is not too bad a thing, except the chain of evidence becomes very weak, as the lawyers call it, back at the collection site and it always casts doubt on anything that the investigators do subsequently to that.

Well, unfortunately, over the years, thinking about it and thinking about it, another thing that crossed my mind is this could very well be a hoax. Unfortunately. Because at the time when these pieces were collected, they were certainly all over South America, anywhere there was a pipeline, they had what they called magnesium anodes attached to that pipeline which are commercially-pure magnesium castings in which the grains were every which way, but here and there in those grains there would be small pieces about the size of a pencil that would be directional. If my hoax hypothesis is true, it's one of the more sophisticated hoaxes I'd ever thought of, because you'd have to dig those small directional samples out of there and send those alone to Ibn Suad so he'd put it in the paper. And the whole point is you'd have to be a pretty sharp metallurgist to realize that that's what you should be showing. So, again, the hoax theory is probably no better than any other theory. This is just an unknown, in my opinion.

Re: Red Bluff, California, 1960

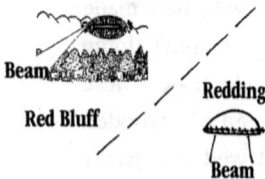

This was not a case from Red Bluff, but rather a UFO case from south of Redding, California, on the night that the famous Red Bluff case occurred, and that object was said by some observers to be heading in the direction of Redding. The witness wondered whether she and her fiancé had seen the same object. It's hard to reconstruct her description of the craft (ex. she uses the term "cylinder" in one place when it's obvious from the rest that she doesn't mean this), but I've given it a try in the inserted diagram.

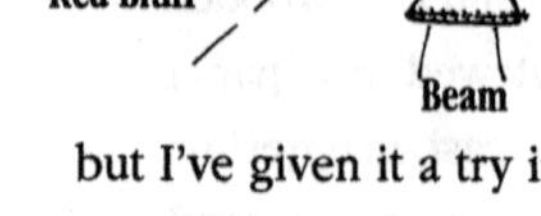

Re: Betty and Barney Hill, 1961

Some people showed up who had known Barney Hill, before and after the incident. He was their postal carrier and they had gotten to know him as a friend. When the article appeared that described his and Betty's experience, he wanted to explain.

> He came and he sat and had coffee with my mom and me. Because he was embarrassed about the article that was in the magazine. Not that he didn't believe that the facts were true, because he *did* believe they were true. But within his own mind he couldn't explain them, and he didn't want us... that's why he sat and talked—he didn't want us to think differently of him because he valued our friendship, because this had come out, in the magazine. And so he sat and he explained that this had come out through hypnosis, that he couldn't... he didn't know why it came out, you know. He didn't understand... he couldn't explain it. That's what I'm trying to say. He couldn't explain it, but that he believed it was a true thing that happened, even though he had no explanation for it. And that was it. It was just a matter of... he was very embarrassed.
>
> I know that everything that he related to the psychiatrist or the psychologist, whoever put him under hypnosis, he honestly believed it happened. To the extent that even when the things were revealed it embarrassed him but he wouldn't back down. I believed him to such an extent that it gives me a great deal of trouble trying to justify what I believe religiously and what Barney said. It is because of Barney that my husband is so interested in UFOs because, again, he was someone that we respected and someone that we knew and therefore we know he didn't lie.

Re: The Exeter incident, 1965

John met a man who was a writer-in-residence at Phillips Exeter Academy, and he became interested in the major police witness to the case. His comments are worth repeating in full.

> I met Officer Bertrand and we got to be friends and spent a lot of time talking, as you would in a little town. So I asked him about the incident and he described it pretty much as in that book. That somebody showed up in the station house, terrified, you know, all shook up and could hardly talk about it. And he said "Calm down,

calm down. We'll go have a look." And so he went back with him and he said he was just looking around, and there over the barn he saw this object. Described as he did in the book, ***Incident at Exeter***. And he said it moved around and kind of fluttered down, and he held his hand out and indicated with a movement like a leaf falling off a tree, just kind of fluttered in the air like that. And he said he thought he... he was going to pull out his gun and changed his mind... and he says they hid behind a fence. And he said within about ten minutes he was as scared as that other fellow. And he couldn't talk about it anymore coherently than the other fellow, at first. But he said finally he was able to give a good solid description of the thing, because as a police officer he is trained in situations of emotional upset and so forth to give good descriptions. Then he described it, the way the lights went around it or seemed to move, either turning or moving in some sequence so it would appear to be turning. And he made that kind of a distinction, you know, as a policeman would. Either it was rotating or it was sequencing. And so he got through with that and then he called down to the Air Force there in Portsmouth, where they have an Air Force base, and asked if they had anything up, or if there was any flight refueling or anything that night. He was an Air Force man, himself, and had been in in-flight refueling. And the fellow said, "No, we don't have a thing up in the air"; so he said, "Okay, great." And the next morning the Air Force released a statement that, sure enough, it was Air Force refueling operations going on. Not that he would have been confused by it, but... So he called his buddy back that next night. He says, "What the hell did you make this statement for?" And he says, "Well, that's the statement they told me to make, and if you say anything else, I'll just have to call you a damn liar." And he says, "Well, you know and I know there was nothing up there that you guys had." And he says, "I know that, but I'm not ever going to tell the story any different from this. I'll just say you were a liar, and that's what I'm going to have to do." And he says, "I don't know what you saw up there, but I'm going to say it was in-flight refueling." So then he said after that for months he was getting calls from astronomers, especially one guy in Arizona who was very interested in it and who wanted to know not only size and shape and movement but was particularly interested in this question of the lights and the way they seemed to move around, what colors and did he think it was rotating or in sequence. And he said that he really had... wouldn't be able to say anything like that. But he did point out again to me that he had been in the Air Force, he'd been in refueling, he was used to making reports under duress of what you've seen and with this kind of "allegedly this" and "allegedly that." But he seemed like a down-to-earth guy.

Re: The East Coast blackout, 1965

This is a simple observation by a husband and wife in Oshawa, Ontario, who looked out of their apartment window on the night of the famous East Coast blackout and witnessed between seven and twelve circular objects moving east to west in the sky. They initially moved very slowly, almost hovering for about ten minutes, and then raced away at extreme speed.

Re: Travis Walton case, 1975

Another simple observation of a young man riding with his parents on the night of the Travis Walton abduction in Heber, Arizona. The witness was heading north toward Flagstaff, and out of the back window of the car saw a brilliant starlike object move through the southern sky.

Re: Coyne Helicopter encounter, 1973

Two reporters thought that they had UFO experiences on the same evening as the Mansfield, Ohio, encounter, and in the same general area. The first was from Ashland, Ohio, and had at least seven witnesses. The person talking to John said that the object was the size of a small airplane and roughly cylindrical in shape. Its outline was a blur of green and red colors. They turned all the lights off in the house and when they looked again it was gone.

The second case was near Shelby, Ohio, around 10:00 P.M. or later and witnessed by a married couple driving home. They saw an object motionless in the sky with red, green, blue, and yellow lights. Its shape wasn't determinable. The red was extremely bright and the blue was *funny*. Several neighbors came out to watch this thing, too.

Re: Rendlesham, 1980

Two military men came to Rendlesham about one year after the UFO event. They heard stories and were curious. They claimed to check out the rotating lighthouse light idea as an explanation for the observation originally made by Colonel Halt, and, in their opinion, this idea was preposterous (especially since the density of trees in that area precludes much seeing of anything through the woods). "There's no way in hell that you can see that lighthouse." One of the men talked with hotel owners in Shadesham *[sic]*, and they said that they'd seen the UFO in flight that evening passing over their hotel on its way to Woodbridge (where the air base is).

Re: Underground bases (!)

An ex-soldier told this to John, regarding his experience in the military in 1949.

> Texas. Central Texas. The place is called Camp Hood. So we used to be sent to what they called Division Guard. We used to go and guard an area that was fenced. It was just a plateau. Why they sent us to guard a plateau was beyond me, at the time. So after we did this for a whole month, mind you, so one evening... well, it was morning, actually, about one o'clock in the morning, we see these lights come down from the sky, silent, bright lights, coming down, down, down, down. And all of a sudden, the end of the plateau opened up and we could see light coming out of there, out of the inside. And these other bright lights just come down inside the plateau. And the door closed.

Uh. You're not kidding me, are you, buddy?

Re: Marfa lights

John had a Marfa lights case reported: two people, husband and wife, driving up from Presidio, Texas, saw what looked like a passenger-train-of-lights out in the desert. Brighter lights were at both ends. They watched this for quite a long time. There were twelve to fifteen in the string, and basically white. They drove into Marfa the next morning and were congratulated by the gas station attendant for being another of the witnesses of the lights.

Re: Yakima lights

An older gentleman who'd seen lots of UFOs in the Pacific Northwest said that a relative used to take the calls for the police in the area, and she offered to give him a heads-up whenever they got a UFO call for the Yakima area.

> She did that many, many times. She'd send the police all over the area around Yakima, and she'd send them out by Selah, Washington, which was about a mile or two from Yakima, and she

said: "I'm sending some of them out to the firing range out there. They are out at the firing range *all* the time, the saucers." But you'd never hear anything about it.

Re: The Alan R. Smith photograph, 1965

The Alan R. Smith photo was a thing which had its moment of fame because it was a pretty, multicolored thing, and everyone likes UFO photos anyway. But it was controversial, and like most photos ended up in the "gray basket" of ufology. John met one of Alan R. Smith's teachers at a mall, who had seen the photo before it was sent to the newspaper, and in fact recommended that he do so. He said that he saw both the print and the negative.

Perhaps even stranger, John had *three* reports where witnesses said that they had later UFO experiences with craft shaped like Smith's:

1. Texas panhandle, near Oklahoma border. 1967 or 1968. An object looking like Smith's, and hovering.
2. Ashton, Ontario; early fall 1965. An object looking like Smith's, and hovering.
3. Kingston, Ontario; sometime in the seventies. An object looking like Smith's, hovering and rotating.

Re: The Waterbury, Connecticut, ellipse, 1988

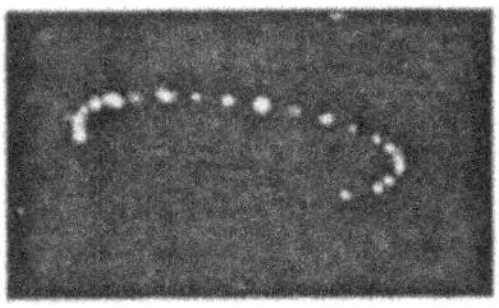

John had several people come to him and say that they had seen a circular array of multicolored lights in the sky, which resembled the famous, beautiful picture called the Waterbury Ellipse. These were:

1. Lake Cayuga, New York; 1989, summertime; four witnesses
2. Norton, Ontario; 1989, summertime; two witnesses
3. West Point, New York; 1986, fall; two witnesses (police)
4. Ossining, New York; 1985, summer; one witness
5. Verplanck, New York; 1984, summer; several witnesses
6. Santa Cruz, California; 1973, summer; two witnesses (but witnesses may think that they saw a disk rather than a circle)
7. Miraloma, California; 1958; two witnesses (again, this seems like a disk instead of an *empty* circle); but *all* of the Waterbury Ellipse-type sightings could have been dark disks, so this is still a possible congruent pattern.

Section 31: Langenberg, Saskatchewan: the Edwin Fuhr interview

Because Langenberg is such a well-known landing case, and because Edwin Fuhr showed up at John's exhibit (with well-known Canadian researcher, Chris Rutkowski) and engaged in a lengthy discussion, it seems appropriate to repeat all of that content at length here. The Langenberg event happened on September 1, 1974, and Mr. Fuhr will tell you the rest. "F" is Fuhr, "T" is Timmerman, and "CR" is Rutkowski. The year of this interview is 1991.

F: This was on a Sunday. And it was a cold dreary day. I was swathing at that time. I was cutting on the east end of the field, a fifteen acre field. It was all by itself in one corner. And I was swathing this crop east and west. Proceeding down to the center of the field towards where that object was. You couldn't see them from that distance but when I got close to, I noticed like there was something in the slough. I got off the swather. I walked towards the machines and there was one in front of me. And I never noticed the other three or four on the other side of me. I observed the first one and when I got close the machine like...

T: How close?

F: I was about fifteen feet away from it. It was about a foot off the ground when I noticed like the grass was moving under it. So I backed up. I got back onto the swather because I didn't trust myself, and when I got back on the swather I noticed there was four more on the left of me. And they was sitting like in a half moon position. Three big ones were sitting in the center and the smaller ones were on the end.

T: They were different dimensions?

F: Yeah, there were two small ones and three big ones. I'd say they were about 25 to 50 feet apart. They were gray metal color. You couldn't tell if there was windows in it or not because they were spinning at the time.

T: Spinning so fast you wouldn't have been able to tell?

F: Well, you could tell there was something on the outside like rivets of some kind but you couldn't tell if there was a window in them or not.

T: Were they very tall?

F: They were around four feet high.

T: Were they very wide?

F: Yeah, fairly wide.

CR: How wide was the big one?

F: The big one was about thirteen feet like in circumference.

T: By measuring the swirl in...

F: Yeah, the circle.

T: And the smaller ones?

F: The smaller ones were about, if I remember correctly, I think seven or eight. They weren't really that big.

T: Were the ones that were wider also taller? Or could you tell?

F: Well, I don't know. I didn't even take notice of that. I don't remember that. *[laughs]* But there's a few things on the machine. It's like the object or whatever it was, it had a lip on the outside. It was like it was hot at one time. It was about a foot to eighteen inches wide all the way around.

T: Around the lower edge.

F: The lower edge of the machine. But, I don't know, I can't remember too much but I only remember September 1, 1974, but if I keep talking about it, it comes back.

T: Were there any animal reactions?

F: Yeah, they had put the cattle through the fences all over. We had a pasture close by and none of the cattle were going through that field where they were sitting because the slough was about maybe 500 yards from the gate. There was a power line and there was water in the slough and there was grain all around it. They never landed in either the water or the grain but they were in that half moon position. When they took off, they took off in a step formation. One of them was in front of me. He took off first, and then the three in the center and then the one on the end. And they stopped over top of my head, I'd say maybe about a hundred feet up, and that's when I noticed on the bottom the machine that there was ports in the bottom of it. They looked like stovepipes for the direction of steering the machine or what, I don't know.

T: Remember how many you saw?

F: Five.

T: You saw five machines. How many stovepipes in each machine?

F: I think there was either four or five of them, I can't...

T: There were several.

F: There was several, yeah.

T: Were they small or large in comparison to the bottom?

F: Well, the stovepipe looked like about eight inches in diameter. The pipe.

T: Were they situated around the bottom in equidistant, around the edges, looked like they were regular spaced?

F: Yeah, but... you would tell they looked like they were in a four-corner position, like each corner and some in the center, and to me it looked like it was a way of guiding it. But those other, I can't remember too much of it. I'd have to go back and read all the history on it. There's a lot more.

CR: The next morning when you looked in the field, did you look and see all the markings? Were there any additional markings? There was a story that you found other markings.

F: Yeah, there as one back on Monday night. Next morning there was none there but Monday night, this was Tuesday morning when I noticed another circle in the field in the same spot, just from the front one where... was about 25 to 15 feet west of that spot and it had landed on the top of a rock.

CR: And it wasn't there before.

F: No. It wasn't there before.

CR: You said on top of a rock, so the markings were over top of the rocks, somehow?

F: Yeah. It had landed on top of a rock.

CR: One big rock or...

F: No, just part of a rock. The scientists, they dug the rock out and took them along back to where... I don't know which scientist it was, either a guy from New York or wherever he was. They took this... the rock wasn't very big. It was about I'd say maybe, oh, ten inches in circumference. It wasn't a very big rock.

T: But apparently the machine had come in contact with the rock.

F: Yeah. It had landed right on top of it.

T: Perhaps they saw what they thought was evidence of some scarring or marking or...

F: I don't know.

T: They didn't tell.

F: No, because they could have took the whole stone pile for... *[laughs]*.

CR: Were there a lot of rocks in the area?

F: Yea. It was a stone pile just west of the spot where they had landed. The only thing is... like the slough was still radioactive. It still is.

T: Who makes that determination?

F: Well, there's a fellow... told me he's got a geiger counter and he done some tests up there and he says it still is radioactive.

CR: As far as I know, it wasn't radioactive originally.

F: He's an electrician. He used to work in a radioactive place.

CR: And he took a counter ...

F: He took a test on it. He's got a geiger counter.

CR: When did he take the test?

F: This was a couple of years ago. I don't know if it's still radioactive or not.

CR: I have not heard of any radioactivity.

F: It was radioactive at the time.

T: It was?

F: Oh, it was. Because they had undercover... out with the geiger counters and it was radioactive.

CR: Because that effect has not been reported. I don't recall it.

F: That's kept quiet. I was there when they done the tests.

T: Did you see the needle on the geiger counter?

F: Yeah. It was in the red. And he wouldn't... there was two guys walking side by side and they were holding this geiger counter and I'd want to have a peek at it. They'd move it the other way but I was quicker than they thought *[laughs]* so I seen it.

T: Did they tell you not to go near the place?

F: I really didn't go into the place. I saw enough that time when it landed. My father, he was all afternoon in there. Sunday, from the time I had seen them. And Ron Moyer, a constable from Langenberg, he crawled around in there all day Monday.

T: Has anything ever happened to those two gentlemen?

F: No, my father passed away several years ago.

T: Remember how he died?

F: Of cancer.

T: Of what part of the body?

F: Pancreas. So, that following winter he had a lot of pain in his hands for some reason. And I still blamed it on that because it was, I'd say maybe 15 or 20 minutes when I had went to the house and he went back out because he read about that years ago in the papers and he never, ever seen a spot like that so he went out with the car and he spent all afternoon out there. And I was swathing the field and I stopped a couple of times and asked him what he was looking for. Oh, he said, they could have dropped anything. But I don't know, I looked all over. I couldn't find anything. But the only thing you could tell... they done tests. There was probe holes in the ground beside the three big machines.

T: Probe holes by whom?

F: By the aliens or whatever it was, but...

T: This was done before they were examined by scientists?

F: Yeah.

CR: Yes, they were there when they found them.

F: The holes were there. The size of holes like broom handles.

T: Beside each of the marks?

F: No, just by the three big machines.

T: Did they make much noise?

F: No. No noise at all.

T: How long do you suppose they were on the ground before you saw them depart?

F: Well, apparently some people in Langenberg had seen them the night before, because they saw this huge ball of fire in the north, and a fellow had picked up his father in Saskatoon hospital and they were coming home and his dad said: "The moon is kind of low in the north." We never thought nothing of it, but some fellows said in Langenberg the sky was all lit up. In the north. So what time they landed, I don't know.

T: They were already there when you arrived and they left shortly after you got there.

F: Uh-hum. (Yes) Well, I could say shortly but I can't say how long because I can't remember. There's about an hour, maybe an hour and a half that I was sitting there, because I was sitting there from 10:30 to 2:00.

CR: Did it seem like that long when you were sitting there?

F: Not really. Seemed to me like fifteen minutes. Because she'd been waiting dinner for me and I didn't show up until about 2:00.

CR: Has anyone ever suggested that you had some missing time and maybe there is more to what happened?

F: Some fellows, yeah. Said I should go under hypnosis. And I won't go under hypnosis.

T: Do you have some special reason for not doing that?

F: I got that from professionals. They told me not to.

T: Professional what?

F: Something like lawyers. They said that . . .

T: Something like lawyers . . . there's very few things like lawyers.

F: They said it's something to do with money.

T: Money?

CR: You want money from this?

F: I could have made a lot of money. I haven't made a nickel out of anything. Because there was people there—I'd say maybe from four to five thousand, maybe even more, because this kept up for one whole month. And the cars were bumper to bumper and my road is a mile and a quarter into my yard and it was bumper to bumper. In and out. They came at night. They came when it was raining cats and dogs. They come all the time. And some people who really couldn't believe it, who thought it was a hoax, and they told me I'd made it with a big air compressor. But the RCMP's undercover agents out there, they did all the checking.

CR: Were there any marks leading into the field besides your swather that you were on?

F: No. There wasn't any marks.

T: No indication that anybody had hauled them in there or something?

F: No. I know the scientist from Ottawa. He told me that he could tell what kind of oil used in the grain swather, but he took samples with a hair comb.

CR: Oh, really. Was this Peter Millman?

F: Yeah, I think so, because he wrote a letter to the RCMP later on, apologizing for the mistake he had made of taking soil samples with a hair comb, and grass samples. It was the oil he was checking on his own head and not on my grain swather. Because the scientist from the States, the samples he took, he never touched anything. He took it with all his instruments.

CR: Can you say something about the UFOs that you've seen recently since then?

F: Well, the ones I seen recently, they're about in the same form as the ones I've seen before, but I've seen... these were quite a ways away. I was about maybe a mile and a half away. The ones that were hovering over top of Langenberg, well, that playground, actually.

T: Do you remember what the date was?

F: Oh, gee...

CR: '89, sometime in '89.

T: Remember the time of the year?

F: It was midsummer.

T: How many did you see?

F: One. The only ones I seen are the lights, was one.

CR: It was just a light.

F: Just a light and you couldn't tell.

T: No object?

F: Yeah. I thought it was an airplane like the smaller planes with those big lights, landing lights. That's what it looked like. But it was proceeding west toward where the new elevators were setting that way. I just took it for granted it was a small plane. When I heard the kids had spied it, seen this UFO, so I don't know. I talked to some of the kids and they don't explain it too good.

T: Sometimes young people get excited about things they see inaccurately and they can't quite explain.

F: I think they were more scared. They were very close to the machine. They could have viewed it very easily. They shouldn't have run and waved at it. What I found out is, if you don't bother them that much, they won't bother you. But for the elapsed time, I can't explain that. Because I was only fifteen feet from the machine.

T: The elapsed time, again, you say was about how long?

F: About an hour and a half.

T: An hour and a half sitting there on your tractor.

F: On the swather. It was a swather, hydrostatic, because you couldn't move it. It was completely froze.

T: So the thing wouldn't operate.

F: No.

T: And you were there for that time and the object had not yet left.

F: No. They had left. To me it seemed like fifteen minutes but it was longer than fifteen minutes.

CR: Do you ever have any funny dreams about what happened?

F: No, not really. I don't try to think about it. Because I don't think they're down here to cause harm to anybody. I think they're more down here for experimental, the way it looks to me. The way they had landed, how can they tell the difference between water and grain? Or land, whatever. The fellows have told me, they said they're radio controlled. I says, well I don't know if anybody can pinpoint any landing machine radio controlled, unless it's controlled by a spaceship further up. How can you land without hitting the water? You know, it's so close and never hit the water. They were approximately three feet from the water and about three feet from the grain.

T: Is there anything that you'd like to ask us? Chris Rutkowski is his name. John Timmerman is mine.

F: What I'd like to know is what brings them down here?

T: You mean me?

F: No, the objects.

T: If we knew, we wouldn't need to be doing quite so much research.

F: Well, I should have brought all that information along because I've got letters there from all over the world. Lots of people think it's account of... well, like this war that broke out and all this stuff. Seems to me they're down here to control it. And I said if they wanted to control it, they could have controlled it from up there, wouldn't have to come down here.

T: These are just dreams on the part of the people who are guessing. We're all guessing.

F: They seem to be like professionals that wrote me these letters.

CR: There are people with alphabets after their names, PhDs, this, that and the other thing, who are just as crazy as anybody else.

T: Yes, so don't let that fool you.

CR: Just as crazy as you and me, right?

F: That's what they tell me. *[laughs]* You see, I didn't actually report this. A friend of mine reported it. He ended up in the hospital here, with an infection in his eye because he was out at this sighting on, was it Sunday? No, Monday. I don't remember. But he ended up in Yorkton and he told the nurses this and they went and reported to the television station, and the first thing they were out there and I couldn't figure how they got out there *[laughs]*.

CR: Why didn't you report it?

F: Well, the RCMP told him to keep it quiet because they were doing an investigation, and I never said anything because I never left the farm. I had undercover agents. I had dogs. I had everything out there. I had a hundred TV stations out there and CBC done a movie. They shot film, a length of film. Rain or shine. They were out there shooting film. And why I don't know. I still don't know.

CR: Tell you what. Just for our own sake, can you go back to the spot where one of the big ones was sitting and just fill up like a baggie or something like that with some dirt from there?

F: Well, you'd have to go to the RCMPs. They've got the . . .

CR: No, no. Right now.

F: Right now. Gee, that spot's been worked under. I wouldn't even know where the hell it is.

CR: Take a good guess.

F: I'd have to get a lineup of the center of the slough to whereabouts the three big ones were sitting, because that's where they took most of the samples from. The three big ones.

T: Well, the purpose of doing this now is . . .

CR: To see if there is any residual. If you said that fellow a few years ago had taken samples and said it was still radioactive, we might be able to detect any residual radioactivity.

T: We'd just like to verify his statement.

F: The only thing, he took it with a geiger counter. He walked all over the place. He didn't just walk to those spots.

T: Did he say it was everywhere?

F: He said the whole slough was like that.

CR: It wouldn't matter where it was taken from.

F: But if it still is, I don't know.

CR: If it was two years ago, it would be now.

F: Well, there was a guy from B.C. He loaded his station wagon up and he went into town to get a release from the RCMP. He had to come back out and unload it. They wouldn't accept it. They wouldn't let him go.

CR: Sounds very strange.

F: He was a fellow that was in research. Why he needed a station wagon full of it, I don't know.

CR: No, I don't know either. Maybe sell it. The uranium mines are north of here, a good 500 miles, right?

F: *Um-hum.* (Yes)

CR: Is there a river that flows this far south that might drain . . .

F: I don't know. Would it be an underground? Like there's underground lakes, would they be . . . , but they're quite a ways down.

CR: Uranium City, in the Northwest Territory, is just across the border from Saskatchewan. There are stories of the tailings from that contaminating the immediate area. Now it's possible that something could have been dumped, you know. And they were concerned about that or an underground stream or something. Possible, but unlikely, but a possibility. So it would still be nice to get a chunk of that soil.

F: I don't know.

CR: It would take just a baggie full, send it to us or myself or somebody. It takes just five minutes to take a check or overnight for a more thorough analysis.

F: Well, I'd have to go to the RCMP to get a release form.

CR: It's your soil, though.

F: They will not release any soil. It's all undercover. You cannot take any soil of any kind, anywhere, no.

CR: Well, it's your property, though.

F: You still can't . . . they've got permission.

T: You signed papers.

F: Yeah, I signed papers. Says no soil can be released unless they release it. They've got all the samples, if you want it.

T: Well, what about this fellow two years ago?

F: Well, I don't know if he took soil or what. He was just an electrician. He got a geiger counter and he wanted to see the spots where they had landed and I says, sure, I'll take you out there. And as soon as he got out of the van, he noticed like the tops of his hands and the back of his neck would get red, and I says well, what's that supposed to do? Well, he said he worked in a place where it was radioactive at one time.

T: I'd be very suspicious about that man.

F: So I don't know. He had a geiger counter and he went out and he said it's radioactive today.

T: I have a geiger counter, too, but that doesn't makes me a radiation scientist.

F: You can run out there and have a look at it, I don't know.

T: I don't have it with me.

CR: The only trouble with that . . . I find it odd that the RCMP would tell you that you can't give people soil from your own property.

F: You can't release it. It's under investigation.

CR: That's the Langenberg RCMP or the RCMP here?

F: No, it's Langenberg detachment, but in '74 there was a guy, he's retired, he was in the investigating, and there was nothing to be released without signing a piece of paper.

CR: Okay. If we were to get a letter from the RCMP, stating that it would be okay for you, you would do that for us?

F: Oh, I can do it for you, yes.

Section 32:
Pint-sized UFOs

The phenomenon seems to come in all sizes from mile-long monsters to baseballs. NPIC photo analyst and UFO-intrigued intelligence operative, Art Lundahl, once said (to Jim McDonald, I believe) that the UFOs which worried him would be the little ones, the ones that could hang right in the air in front of you, or in your fireplace, and you couldn't see them. Well, John didn't get any reports of quite that microscopic, obviously, but here are a few pipsqueak UFOs for your amusement.

Westbrook, Ontario – *midsummer 1955, daylight hours*

On a hot, humid morning, with flashes of sheet lightning in the distance, the witness was standing in front of his father's general store when a ball-of-lightning rose out of the graveyard. It rose to about five feet in height and then silently dodged its way through the headstones, out onto the road and *boom*. It disappeared. It was composed of beautiful bluish and reddish shades and moved without crackling nor any odor.

London, Ontario – *1968, near sunrise*

The witness heard a loud thunderbolt and looked out the window to see a ball-of-lightning enter the neighbors' house. It rolled down their hallway and burst a vase. Then it hopped onto a wire that two boys had strung between the houses (sort of a private telephone line). The ball moved across the wire, into the witness' house and sat on the top of the telephone. Multicolors swam in the ball for four to seven seconds, and then it just *went off* with a very light *pop* sound.

Maltin Airport (Toronto), Ontario – *1965*

Two persons who had just landed planes were in a parking lot cleaning snow off their windshields. A bright light just appeared between them about

ten feet from the witness. It hovered there for a few seconds and then "drove off into the wind." The object was a fiery white round ball about one foot in diameter. It never quaked or jiggled nor made any noise.

Banning, California – *November 28, 1988, after midnight*

A woman woke up and rolled over in bed to see a white ball of light overtop her dresser. It was about fifteen inches in diameter and slowly moved about six inches across the top. It was a dull graying white light with a soft glow. Before she could scream, she passed out.

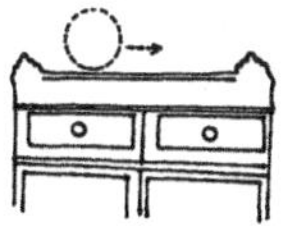

Groton, Connecticut – *multiple incidents, 1980s, in the afternoon*

"I don't know if this is interesting to you or not, but I have a blue ball that comes to the house. And it's a blue light. I call it my blue ball. And it's... to me it's a friend. It's very friendly. And also it has white streaks of light (in it)." John asked: when was the last time your blue ball came to see you? "Oh, yesterday... about 4:00. I was just drifting. Just sitting, drifting... you know, when you sit down and kind of daydream." [There is a partial phrase, unfortunately cut off by a question by John, which seems to indicate that her husband has seen this blue ball, too. If so, that, as they say, would "put a different light on it."]

Montezuma, New York – *spring or early summer, mid-1970s, 5:30 A.M.*

A man was driving to work when he saw a bright, luminous green light in his rear view mirror. It looked like it was on some flying object in that it seemed to be dropping down to come in to land. The witness stopped

the car to watch. The ground in the nearby field was covered with a low, three- to four-foot thick fog. The green ball was about three feet in diameter and came just above the fog. The ball split into two balls each one foot in diameter. These began to lower into the fog. Just at the fog's surface, each ball extended *silver wings* and then dropped below the mist.

Middleton, Ohio – *summer 1958, 9:30 P.M.*

A woman was on her front porch going to her door, when she noticed that she was being followed by a glowing object. It was a bright, cigar-shaped thing, eight inches in length and two inches in diameter. It glowed with very high energy and scared her. She ran into her house.

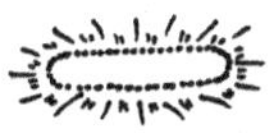

Spokane, Washington – *1958 or 1959, afternoon*

Two teenagers were in their home when they saw an object coming down out of the sky at their house. It drifted at first then accelerated toward

their window. They flinched and ducked, but the object pulled up and went over the house. It was a dull metal disk about two feet in diameter "like two silver hubcaps sandwiched together."

Near **San Jose, Puerto Rico** – *sometime in the late 1970s, 10:30 P.M.*

Two teenage boys were participating in a nighttime air crash simulation as volunteers for the Red Cross. They were walking through the bushes in the direction where someone was supposed to be playing hurt, when they saw a small, strange object about fifty yards away. They went over to it and found it to be an unsymmetrical aluminum-looking thing, about six feet high and seven feet wide, and spinning. You could see bolts in its structure, and it seemed flattish, but thick, with an odd dark opening in the bottom area. No noise; hovering. Its surface somewhere (all over?) was illuminated by something like short lightning flashes. They watched this for several minutes until it began to move slowly, then sped up and raced away.

Danville, Pennsylvania – *May 1989, at night*

On two different occasions, close in time, two lady friends saw this same phenomenon separately. It consisted of two lights or lighted objects. The larger of them was door-shaped and about six feet high. It hovered

perhaps ten to fifteen feet off the ground. The color was a dusty white. The second object looked just like an individual light and was stationed alongside. The first instance was close: "halfway between my place and the barn." She stood and watched a few minutes and then "just as if a switch was turned, it just went out."

North of **Nice, France** – *October 1975, 3:00 P.M.*

Some of the mini-UFOs have the feeling of robotic intrusions into our airspace by some technologists so distant that their machine is just going about its own simple business. This one has that feel to it. A husband and wife were at their home on the hillside of a very steep valley in southern France. Coming along the contours of the valley, flying at about 300 feet, which was the level of their home, was what appeared to be a metal box full of small round holes. It was black and 7x3x4 feet in its dimensions. There seemed to be a single light source inside the box which you could partially see through the holes.

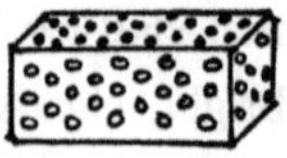

It moved silently and slowly, never changing pace, following the contours of the valley precisely all the way to the Alps.

Sterling Illinois – *summer 1970, around dinner time*

A 9-year-old boy was playing outside on a hot summer's day. Between his dad's car and the garage came an object that "looked like a little rocket." It was four feet long, and two feet in diameter and it had fins on it. It made a humming or hissing noise. But no exhaust. "It came right in front of me. Me, being a young boy, I grabbed onto

it (by the fins)." It was an off-white color and felt warm. The rocket didn't slow when he grabbed it and it tugged him along. His mom was calling him to dinner. "It pulled me and I kept holding on to it, and then I think it was the third time that my mom called me for dinner and I knew better. I let go of it and just watched it go into the distance." There's a 23rd century root for a fairy tale for you. What would have happened if he could have held on and mom wasn't so insistent about dinner? Where would that adventure have romantically led us?

Section 33: Really weird light

One of my favorite, albeit (unfortunately) rare, elements of the UFO phenomenon is the occurrence of effects with light beams and columns which seem impossible at first thought and then just extremely hard to do upon reflection (science and technology mental reflection, that is). The reason that this phenomenon interests me is that frontier physics can imagine ways to do it, but, if the reports are what they seem to be, it will take extremely advanced scientific understanding of light, space, dimensions and forces, etc., to exhibit this. Therefore, our visitors would be very much beyond us, indeed. The first couple of cases below are just mundane warm-ups for the so-called solid light reports that follow.

Muncy, Pennsylvania

Four persons were driving in a car late in the afternoon but on a bright day. The driver spotted an object in the sky, stopped the car and everyone got out to watch. The object, a domed disk twenty to thirty feet in diameter

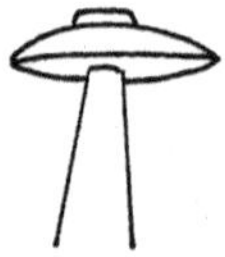

and about six feet thick, came over the trees at about fifty feet in altitude and crossed the road. From the bottom of the craft there was a white beam shining down. The beam was so thick and distinct that you could see it in its entirety all the way from craft to ground. The object drifted for several seconds then streaked away at enormous speed.

Commerce, Texas – *summer 1971 or 1972, at night*

A husband and wife were watching a drive-in movie, when they saw a bright object hovering only eight to ten feet above a pasture nearby.

The object was shaped like a truncated pear. In its side was a square window within which was auburn light. It was silent and emitted a beam from the bottom which came to a focused point in the air. It meandered a bit over the field, then slowly, then rapidly, accelerated away.

West Shreveport, Louisiana – *date unstated, at night*

A man's son came pounding on the door and yelling for his father to go outside and look at the UFO. He did. The shape of the object isn't described in the transcript. The witness keeps saying "the aircraft" but apparently means some elongated object (c. 1000 feet), moving relatively low over trees. As it went over silently, it emitted an intense pulsating light which remained the same diameter (c. eight feet) all the way down. As the beam struck the treetops, it seemed to make them move. The witness called the local Air Traffic Control, and they had no radar signal.

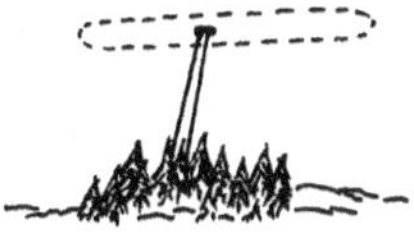

Near **Seattle, Washington** – *fall 1968 or 1969, 4:30 P.M.*

Three children were outside their house in the country, feeding their dogs in the kennel. The older sister saw a very bright spot of light over the hill. The dogs barked and the younger children got scared and ran inside. The light was intense white but you could not see an object from which it came. It blinked or flashed on and off "like taking a picture." For about four minutes she watched this disembodied light beam: "concentrated light, almost like a cone," with a seeming sawed-off top (the *end* in the sky from which it emerged). The thing, whatever it was, went over the railroad tracks, and was gone.

Between **Strasburg and Bolivar, Ohio** – *1979, 4:00 A.M.*

A man was driving to work. As he ascended a grade, there was a long beam of light residing stationary in the sky. He stopped and watched this for twenty to thirty minutes. Then he went on into work. He told his friend about it and they went back out and watched some more. The beam looked like a flashlight beam, if you could see the entire length of it. It originated high in the sky and got gradually wider (though not extremely so) as it descended to earth. But it never reached the ground and had a sharp cutoff end to the beam (still high in the sky).

South Zanesville, Ohio – *1982, 9:00 P.M.*

A man was watching television and glanced out the door. At that moment a beam of light shot down from the sky at a steep angle, and then the end of it just stopped in midair. It hovered, if that's the correct word, for a couple of minutes, allowing the witness to jump up and go look. The light beam then retreated back up the way it came. The description here is a bit confused, but it sounds like the beam went to a triangle-shaped object with different colored lights along the sides. The witness says that there were a bunch of UFO reports in the area on the radio the next day, and in the paper.

Sterling, Illinois – *September 1974, 9:00 P.M.*

Three persons were standing outside on the farm when they noticed that the tops of their silos were all lit up. A broad light source was shining over the top of them "but you couldn't really see where the source was coming from." This was despite the feeling that the source of the beam wasn't very high in the air. Suddenly the light source was directly above them. The world got totally quiet, not a sound anywhere. The rest of this commentary is interesting enough to quote at length.

> All of a sudden just in a flash the light was over us. It was so quick, you know, just like we were looking there and all of a sudden there it was, over us. And I don't think any of us moved, but I can remember looking at my husband and the other man and it was like you could see not exactly through them, but the light was a bluish white. You know, kind of, it was a bluish white, and you could almost see like not really their bones but the framework of the bones, because it was darker than what the rest of their body was. It was like they were . . . like an X-ray thing, almost. Not quite because it wasn't that clear. And I remember just standing there, thinking: "This is weird. Look, I can almost see through them." And then within a flash, just... we just... it... the light, like it... I'll tell you what the light was like when it left us. It was like it drew up from our feet, like the light come up.

John asked: Like an elevator?

> Yeah! Like an elevator. That's exactly right! Like an elevator. Yeah, because I could remember seeing their feet and like look through their legs and all of a sudden I couldn't, and slowly just the light come up and I couldn't see through their bodies anymore. And the light was gone. It just went, like that. And of course we were dumbfounded *[laughs]*, it was weird. It was so strange. Just unbelievable.

John asked, then, about missing time.

> That's funny, because we've talked about this, through the years

> later on, the more stuff you hear about UFOs and things. But, you know, I really don't remember. At that time I don't think we paid any attention to it. No, I really don't. I know the kids were in bed when we got in. *[laughs]* Our kids were all in bed at that time and they said they were going to wait for me to come, you know.

Hummm...

Bradenton, Florida – *1954 or 1955, 8:00 P.M.*

A husband and wife were out in their yard when they saw a set of lights hovering across a field on the other side of the river. It was at night and you could not see the shape of the object on which the lights were mounted. From this object came a cylinder of light, white in color which slowly extended to the ground "just like an elevator would be moving." The object and its "light elevator" sat there for about three or four minutes, then the column retracted and the object zoomed away.

Swift Current, Saskatchewan – *1965, 8-8:30 P.M.*

A pair of teenage girls was coming home from a church function, and were crossing a park. They heard a sound like a vacuum cleaner. They looked up and saw a simple dome-shaped object. But it was the light beam from the object which scared them.

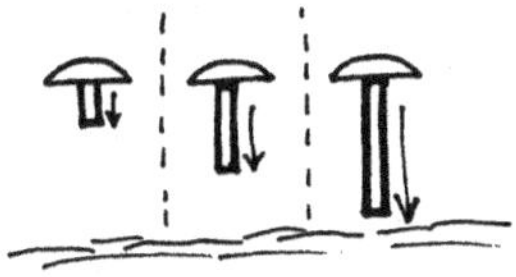

> It came down in stages. It didn't come straight down but it came in spurts. I don't know how to explain that, but it was like one, two, three, four, down, and then it would go back up. We were just stunned. I remember just being frightened and I can stand here feeling the feeling. Both of us ran to my place, which was a block and a half away, and we were just white. And our parents—we had lost two hours of time. I just get *[laughs]* shaky when I think about it.

Oshawa, Ontario – *March 1974, midnight*

Three persons were working on an ice rink (flooding it) when they noticed lights way up in the sky. They hung up there for a long time, and while doing so, a large red disk came very low over the house. The color was intensely *molten* in character. It was so big that it blotted out most of

the sky. The odd light phenomenon in this case was that just before the big disk appeared, there was a "streak of light" that quickly but gradually moved across the sky *uncurling* as it went, like a curlicue streamer. The huge object cruised silently overhead and then very rapidly was gone.

Elmira, New York - *October 1986*

I have no idea what this report indicates except that it is the exact opposite of a famous report in the UFO literature wherein a man can see what looks like a force field-like effect around a UFO when he puts on his Polaroid sunglasses. In this case a man is watching an oval object which seems to have a speckled *force field* effect around it ("like little twinkling marks and stars"), and then puts his polarized glasses on and the effect goes away. The object was perhaps 100 feet or larger in the long axis, and the speckling effect extended 50 feet further in all dimensions.

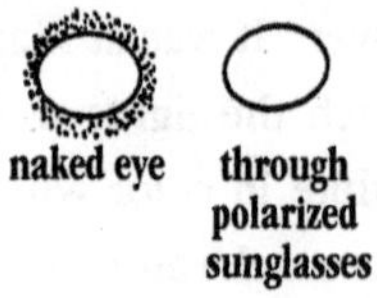

Ravenna, Nebraska - *June 9 or 10, 1956, in the night*

A woman was sound asleep when she was awakened by a noise which she thought was an airplane passing overhead. But she then realized that it didn't sound like an airplane, so what was it? She had a premonition of a *presence* coming. Then, into her room, a surge of light passed through—right through the roof as if these was nothing to impede it. It was intensely bright and it hurt the eyes to look at it. She put her hands over her eyes "and I could see the bones in my hands." The beam, or surge, passed slowly through the room in a few seconds and was gone. No one else in the house awakened and so did not experience the event. The only physical effect seemed to be that afterwards her wristwatches would no longer keep good time.

Section 34:
Now you see me

We've had several of these seemingly instant disappearance cases in the previous sections, but here is a cluster of them to drive home the point.

Gull Lake, Saskatchewan – *fall 1985, 4 to 5:00 P.M.*

A man was in a rural area when he spotted a circular orange-colored object, hovering very low (c. forty feet) over a field. The object was large (c. 100 feet in diameter) and very bright. The light was pulsating. It did this, soundlessly, for five or ten minutes, and disappeared suddenly in a puff of brownish smoke.

Yorkton, Saskatchewan – *July or August, mid-1960s, midnight*

A husband and wife were driving home when they saw a bright light ahead of them. It swung around behind them and followed at about 500 feet away and 100 feet in the air. It seemed like a ball of orange fire, perhaps 100 feet in diameter. This state of affairs continued silently for about two minutes, then it "just vanished; just like it went out, somebody just turned off the power. That was it."

Gales Ferry, Connecticut – *midsummer 1984, 7:45 P.M.*

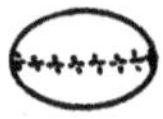

A husband and wife were driving home from the submarine base to their rural home. The wife spotted an elliptical object that was hovering over the nuclear plant in the vicinity. The husband (a naval officer) thought that it might be a blimp, but that explanation didn't last long. The object was hovering silently and had pulsating lights that were around the whole structure. It seemed very large. "Then suddenly, as we were looking at it, *zap!* And it was gone. It didn't go off slowly; it didn't go off as a plane would where you could follow it with your eye. It just completely disappeared."

Oshawa, Ontario – *March 1977, 12:45 A.M.*

A man had just dropped his fiancé at her house, and was driving home. He saw a huge, round, red object in the sky. It came toward his car at about 100 feet altitude. He stopped the car and it moved silently overhead and hovered over a lake. It was about thirty to forty feet in diameter. A smaller version of it emerged from the larger, and flew off somewhere. Then the large one simply turned off "like somebody turning off a light switch." When he reached home, he called his fiancé. She said that she'd watched the object and the emergence of the small one from her back door.

Houston, Texas – *1947-1948 (turn of the year), 5:00 P.M.*

A woman saw a slow-moving object cruising 500 or 600 feet overhead. It seemed to be about twenty feet in diameter and three or four feet thick: a disk-like shape. She called out to her neighbors after a few minutes and they saw the end of it. The object was silent and had a bank of lights (she's not a very good artist, but a drawing accompanying the case would seem to indicate panes of lights on the bottom). Then: "It was gone. It was so fast you couldn't believe it. I mean, it's like I'm looking at you, and they put a veil across between you and I, and you're gone. It was amazing."

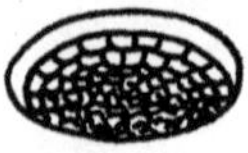

Kingston, Ontario – *September 1988, 4:30 P.M.*

A woman was in her home and saw an odd object across the road and apparently high in the sky. She called to her kids but they ignored her. It was a long bar or cane-like structure, colored white. It had the apparent dimension of two inches at arm's length. The thing moved very slowly and suddenly went from its stretched-out form to a little dot. Then it was gone. It's hard to tell what happened at the end of this case because the object could have rapidly rotated to point directly away from her. Unless this was a *performance* especially for her, this seems to beat the odds. Another interpretation is that what she saw was it shrinking out of our space.

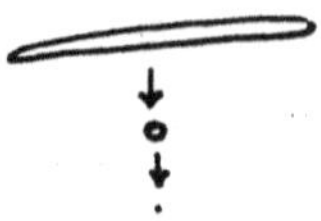

Swift Current, Saskatchewan – *sometime in 1974, noon*

Two men were surveying a road south of town when they saw an elongated silvery object in the sky. At each end of the object was a clearly delineated fiery red luminous cap. The object was 50 to 100 feet long, and low (about 100 to 150 feet up). It moved very slowly and crossed the road. Then it disappeared. John asked: How? "I would say it was like a light, because it didn't—as you see an airplane go in the distance and get smaller, but

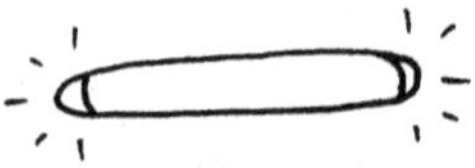

this thing just *disappeared*. It was still the same size as when we looked at it when it disappeared." John said: "It just wasn't there anymore." Witness: "Yeah."

Anaheim, California – *December 3, 1983, 6:35 P.M.*

A man, who had recently sent in a report on this sighting to CUFOS, showed up at the mall with his mother to repeat the story. He was out walking when he saw a metallic object hovering in the sky. It was about 100 feet distant and the same distance in altitude. It was a disk, with a luminous gold glow about it. Three tripod-like appendages extended from the bottom and on the top there were two small *fins* or *antennae*. After about ten minutes (during which he tried to take pictures which didn't turn out), "It just blinked out. It just went out like a light bulb."

Watch Hill Airport, Westerly, Rhode Island – *summer, late 1970s, daytime*

A husband and wife and several others were at a nearby beach, when they saw a circular vehicle in the sky over the ocean. It came closer and closer until it was directly overhead. The husband heard no sound; the wife, a faint one. It was a disk, rather flat and featureless on the bottom, but with lights around the perimeter, *windows* rotating in the upper story and a dome on the top. It moved just a little, slowly, and then suddenly disappeared. "Just disappeared off into the, you know, I tried to, we stood there for a while waiting to see if the object, you know, would come back." The object's disappearance obviously has flabbergasted the witness.

Cambridge, Ohio – *July 8, 1989, 11:20 P.M.*

A family was returning from a vacation and had just turned off the main highway on their way toward their house. They saw a glowing ball in the sky. It was hazy white and about the apparent size of the full Moon. Actually there were two such objects, one much dimmer than the other, and the dimmer one shortly faded away. They seemed to be getting closer to the remaining object as they drove along during the next ten minutes. Then, toward the bottom of the object a ring of light suddenly got extremely bright; and "just like a flash, it totally vanished, disappeared." After searching for it frantically, their daughter spotted what they felt was the same object far away to their right.

Chicago, Illinois – *fall 1954, no time stated (daytime)*

A woman heard a lot of airplane noise in the sky and went out to look. She saw (probably) four jets flying on each side of a large silver, circular *thing*. The array was very high and she could only keep track of the jets by their vapor trails but the circular object was huge. "You could see from the vapor trails that they were trying to corner it." The object was on its way, paced by the jets until "it just plain disappeared."

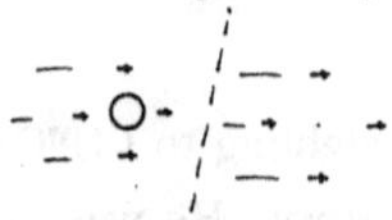

San Antonio, Texas – *1963, about dusk*

A bunch of kids came running in from outside to tell their moms that there was a UFO outside. They said: "That's fine, boys, go play. Have fun." Finally after a few minutes, and the boys excitedly racing in and out for binoculars, the women decided to go look. All sorts of people had come out to watch an enormous cigar-shaped object with flashing lights on either end, high in the sky. Jets were obviously trying to reach the object. The jets were pygmies in comparison to this thing. The huge cigar would pivot on its center axis, and lights would flash. Everyone was silently transfixed as this drama played out for forty minutes. Then the big object glowed: "It just glowed and it went—it disappeared. It was just gone." The next day the newspapers had a release from the Air Force explaining it away as a weather balloon. "It looked nothing like a weather balloon... and it made everybody angry." *Hmmm*, seems I've heard that before.

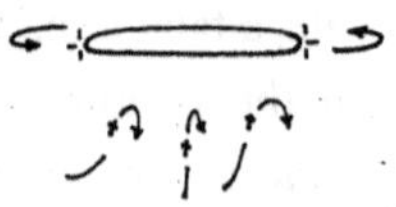

Between **Chihuahua and Durango, Mexico** – *Christmas 1983, at night*

Seven technical people (including a botanist, herpetologist, and two geologists) were exploring in Mexico near a town named Sabayo. They saw an extremely large object in the sky which was moving slowly in a north-to-south direction. It was football-shaped and the southern end would light up and glow a yellow-green color. The thing was estimated to be five to ten *miles* long. The object continued on its way for fifteen minutes, then suddenly glowed over its whole body and "then it blinked off. We were so astounded. Our mouths were just wide open." The object seemed to reappear well off toward the horizon and "did like a spiral over the curvature of the earth."

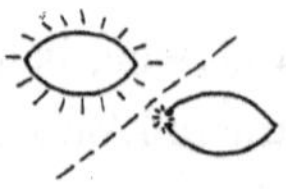

Bath, New York – *November 7, 1978, 7:00 P.M.*

A father and son were walking on a road when they saw an amber light passing over the valley, which simply went on. Continuing their walk, they came across what was apparently the same object hovering about fifty feet off the ground. It was shaped like a cone with the amber light coming

out the wide end. From its right side extended an arm at the end of which was a very bright white light. The object rotated so that they could see down the cone (all the light seemed to focus at a point). It then moved about 700 feet overhead. "The light went out... we couldn't even see the outline of the object. This object just seemed to disappear." Ten minutes later, the amber light showed up again and passed on down the valley.

Syracuse, New York – *January 1966, 11:30 P.M.*

A mother with her son was driving his girlfriend back to her home. The car stalled. They couldn't get it restarted. They looked down the road and there was a "classic flying saucer" hovering. It had lights around the bottom perimeter, and a row of windows at the base of the dome. The lights were red, green, and white. The girl was scared to death and stayed in the car. (She is the one who talked to John.) The mother and son got out. Everyone was *mesmerized.* There was a very high-pitched hum, and then it was just gone. "I did not see it shoot off anyplace. You assume they don't just disappear." When they got her to her home, they were about an hour later than they should have been. "I was not abducted, at least I have no memory of it."

Trans-Canada Highway – *July 1988 or 1989, 11:30 P.M.*

A Ukrainian Catholic priest was driving his car on the deserted highway when he saw what he thought was a van turning onto the road ahead. As he closed on it, he saw that, although roughly van-shaped, it had no normal lights, but rather arches of small *Christmas* lights running along its sides.

He tried to pass it but it moved into his same lane. Then, as he came to within inches of the object "all of a sudden the lights turned out and the object was gone." (Case was told to John by well-known ufologist, Chris Rutkowski, who took the original report.)

Pittsburg, Kansas – *July or August 1975, 9:00 P.M.*

A husband and wife were driving toward town when they saw what they first took to be a *falling star*. The *star*, however, stopped, changed to a horizontal trajectory, and came very much nearer, ahead and over the highway. It was a huge object (one gets the impression that she means a disk) and covered the whole width of the road. It had small inset panels which glowed more intensely than the object itself. The object seemed to coincidentally change its motion or direction every time that the wife said something to her husband about it. The time spent *chasing* the object was spent in an environment of "completely dead silence." Finally, the object picked up a little speed and "then it just blinked and it was gone... just one second it was there, the next second it wasn't. Like someone turned off a switch."

The aftermath of this experience is also exceptionally odd. I'll let her tell you:

> Another thing we noticed that night was rather out of the ordinary. This was on an open stretch with very few houses out here, and we noticed a lot of animal activity which really caught our attention... because the animals we saw, skunks and opossums and raccoons and dogs and cats and rabbits all over. Not ten or fifteen, I mean they'd be one here, then go a mile or so and one or two, and they were out running around like they were excited. We got home that night and our dog was excited. The landlady had some geese, and they were acting funny. They acted spooked like something was chasing them.

Greenville, Texas – *March 1965, 11:00 P.M.*

Well, since their spaceships are disappearing on them, left, right, and center, we might as well have a case where the ET astronaut disappears. A woman had just helped haul her somnambulant husband to bed, and he was snoring when he hit the pillow. She crawled in beside him, kissed him goodnight, and rolled over on her side. There standing in her hallway was a being.

> He had on a helmet type, clear type helmet. He did not look like one of these weird beings, he looked like we do, kind of I would say ruddy complexion. He had on a gray type spacesuit with zippers down the arms, zippers down the front, zippers down the legs, and he held a glass round—all I could think of was a crystal ball, in his hand. I had a feeling he wasn't going to hurt us. It was just—I don't know—like mental telepathy or something, because it was like he would say: "I'm not going to hurt you. I'm just here observing you."

Our galactic peeping Tom was not all that reassuring, however, and she was constantly reaching back and trying to get her happily snoring

husband to wake up (which he never did). When her daughter coughed in the other bedroom, the astronaut took his eyes from the glass ball and looked that way. That was too much, and maternal instincts took over, and she got up with "Don't hurt my children!" in her mind. She got as far as the door "and he disappeared. Just like that."

Section 35:
Magick-in-Space

We go from last section's question "where in the heck did that thing go?" to the even stranger thought "was that thing even here in our space at all?" As we go into weirder and weirder waters of the phenomenon, any conclusions that we draw, even the simple observations that we make, become more problematic. But here are a few puzzlers for your imagination.

Swift Current, Saskatchewan – *summer mid-1970s, 1:00 A.M.*

A woman got a phone call from her son (they lived on adjoining farms). They had an agreement between them that if either one saw a UFO, they would call the other. He had been awakened by a thunderstorm, and as he was rummaging about before getting back to sleep, he saw two bright lights rising from the ground over his fields. These fields were in the direction of his mother's farm. They were like disks with orange lights. They rose slowly, and he phoned. Although there were only two miles between one farm and the next, the father and mother could not see the objects, though the son watched them for two or three hours. "Well, they must have been either that he could see them with the way the light was, or... whatever; and we couldn't see them on the other side."

Oshawa, Ontario – *in the mid-1980s, at night*

Two men were driving down a back road and saw a luminous cylinder hanging in the sky above a group of trees off the road. They pulled over to watch. The thing hung there for five minutes, and then it was "just like it pulled a shield of darkness over itself and it completely disappeared."

California desert, near Edwards Air Force Base – *1980, 11:00 P.M.*

A man, who liked to enjoy the solitude of the desert, had parked his car, built a fire, and sat his young son in the backseat to go to sleep. He noticed a lot of peculiar animal activity about (birds and coyotes), and a large shadow, somewhat circular, moved overhead. He couldn't see *the ship*; it was just like a quivering "hole in the sky." It was as if space was quivering like liquid, like a "Star Trek cloaking device." It went on just to the top of a low hill. Then "it lost its cloak," and pivoted. It was a dark elongated object with lights (red and green to the right; red and orange to the left; the right side pulsing). When it stopped moving, it was startlingly crisp, like it was frozen; but during the turn there was a terrible grinding sound. He felt paralyzed and couldn't remember anything until he felt himself cold, fearful, hugging the car, and then in the car. The craft seemed a little further away, and it was rising and silently floating. The *cloak* returned, and the black hole-in-the-sky went away.

Oklahoma City, Oklahoma – *early spring 1978 or 1979, 8:00 A.M.*

A woman was driving along when she noticed something odd in the sky. She pulled her car to a stop and watched for a couple of puzzled minutes. There was no *object* in the sky, but, well, here are her words:

> This didn't appear to be a cloud. It didn't appear to be anything that I could have ever related to. It just appeared that the sky was moving—not the whole sky, just a piece of the sky was moving. It was kind of breaking apart in little particles and reassembling rapidly. It *wasn't* a cloud color—it really wasn't a color. It was almost as if some little piece of the sky had something overlaid on it that was moving.

Well, thank goodness, that we had such an intelligent and observant witness to describe this one.

Blairmore, Alberta – *summer 1976, 7:00 P.M.*

A husband, wife, and her friend came into the backyard and saw a small bright object seemingly sitting on a picket fence a little distance away. It was bullet-shaped (two foot high and eight inches in diameter), glowing with a pulsing orange light. It would make a very high-pitched shrill and glow very brightly, then dim down and make no sound at all. At its dimmest, the object would seem to completely go away. They watched this irregular pulsing go on for about two hours, until they finally got up the courage to get closer. They noticed a dog tied nearby—it didn't

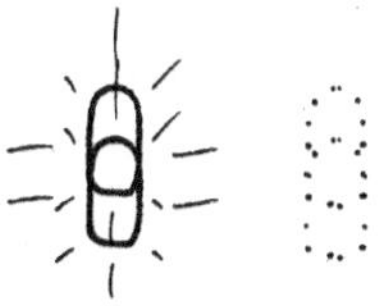

even seem to notice the object. They walked over to the object and "there was nothing there."

Hamburg, Pennsylvania – *October 1964, 8:00 P.M.*

A 19-year-old was driving to a dance, when his car radio began to act up. It seemed like he was picking up a really far away station. He then saw an odd starlike object and the radio began a weird Orson Welles-like broadcast, as if nuclear war had already begun.

> I get this feeling of unreality [I guess] and I looked down and I could see through the damn floor boards! I feel like I'm driving along but I can see through the damn car… The car looked like jelly. I felt like jelly. I get to the damn dance and I look at my watch and it's like a quarter after ten. It should have been a quarter after nine, and I felt like I was coming out of something.

As an extra-odd aftermath, about a month or so later, he was driving a girl home, when a big flash of light illuminated the car. The girl went into an unconscious state and the weird fluid experience took off again. He doesn't believe that there was lost time on that incident. This pair of occurrences started, in his mind, a series of *beyond reality* type experiences for the next five years; and he now thinks that he is psychic.

The "Iron Triangle," Korea – *spring 1951, at night*

There was a U.S. Army Infantry action going on and they had sent someone into a local village to warn the population that there was going to be an artillery barrage. When the barrage began, Army observation posts noticed an orange *jack-o-lantern* coming down the mountain into the valley. The object would somehow get itself right into the center of the artillery bursts, and not be affected. This activity persisted for 45 minutes or so, and then the object turned brilliant blue-green and approached the command post. A soldier received permission to fire his M-1 rifle with armor-piercing bullets at it. He did. And he hit it.

> The object went wild. The light was going on and off and it went off completely once. Briefly. And it was moving erratically from side to side, as though it might crash to the ground. Then a sound which we had heard no sound previously. The sound like—you've heard diesel locomotives revving up. That's the way this thing sounded. And then we were attacked, I guess you would call it. In any event, we were swept by some form of a ray that was

emitted in pulses in ways that you could visually see only when it was aimed directly at you. That is to say, like a searchlight sweeps around and the segments of light you would see it coming at you. Now, you would feel a burning, tingling sensation all over your body, as though something were penetrating you.

That one shot got it. Evidently their defenses were lowered briefly and when I connected... and then their defenses were thrown back up and after that nothing had an effect... We opened up with everything we had and after that nothing would affect it.

John asked: Did the bullets seem to go right through it?

No contact. But the first time, I did connect. And it was metallic because it was an armor-piercing projectile from an M-1 rifle and we did hear the metal-to-metal as it impacted... So the company commander, Lieutenant Evans hauled us into our bunkers. We didn't know what was going to happen. We were scared. We did this, these are underground dugouts where you have peepholes to look out... So I'm in my bunker with another man. We're peeping out at this thing. It hovered over us for a while, lit up the whole area with its light I'm telling you about, and then I saw it shoot off at a 45° angle. That quick, it was there and it was gone, that quick. And that was the end of it.

But, three days later, the entire company of men had to be evacuated by ambulance. They had to cut roads in there and haul them out. They were too weak to walk. And had dysentery. And then subsequently when the doctors did see them, they had an extremely high white cell blood count, which the doctors could not account for. Now let me inform you on this. In the military, especially in the Army, each day you file a report, company report. Now, we had a confab out that, what do we do about this? Do we file it in the report or not? And the consensus was no, because they'd lock every one of us up, think we were crazy. At that time, no such thing as UFOs had ever been heard of. We didn't know what it was. And I still don't know what it was. But I do know that since that time, I have periods of disorientation, memory loss, and I dropped from 180 pounds to 138 pounds... , after I got back to this country. And I've had great difficulty keeping my weight up. Indeed, I'm retired disabled today.

Section 36:
Magick shape

There are tales of transmorphing UFOs, another obviously impossible thing to do. John had these tales too. Optical illusions?

Lawton, Oklahoma – *late spring or early summer 1978, at dusk*

Two teenagers were driving in an area where a real estate development was being completed. They saw what they thought was the Goodyear blimp, but it was moving too fast. And it was orange. It continued to move about and the boys drove to their home in the finished area of the development. Shortly, both sisters and their father came out to watch. (The object had jetted away super fast, but by the time they went to their home, it had returned.) The father tried to take pictures of the object, but (apparently) they didn't come out. The object's size was hard to judge: 200 feet long? 50 feet long?

> The primary shape of this thing seemed to be a cigar, elongated shape. (But) when it would fly, it didn't seem like it was cigar-shaped. It would turn more into a ballish, saucerish-type thing. It would streak; the light would streak like a tracer.

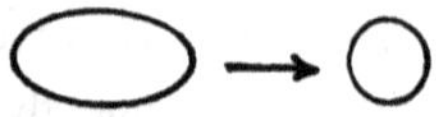

Finally the sky got dark, and the show seemed to end. Then jets came into the area, probably from the military base at Fort Sill.

San Diego, California – *late summer 1978, early evening*

Three women were seated at a dining room table, talking, when they saw a golden sphere in the sky out the window. They went out on the balcony to watch. The object most resembled a shiny brass balloon. It seemed huge (about as large in diameter as the mature trees it hovered over were tall). They called out a neighbor (a naval officer) and his wife to try to get some explanation. The object then shrunk nearly out of sight, but re-expanded into its beautiful ball form. Then it began to move horizontally and:

> ...within the blink of an eye, this golden sphere transformed into two beautiful spheres of color with a connecting blinking bridge.

> The color seemed to be either red or pink, and the other color seemed to be blue...we just watched this and it was like watching a Disneyland fireworks parade.

[I think what she means is that it was so beautiful a show you just stood silently and gaped at it.]

The naval officer was just as blown away and barely responded: "It's something...but I don't know what it is." It began a descent toward the ocean and "it just within a blink of the eye, it was gone." The next day on the morning radio there was a sighting of a golden sphere reported over the ocean off the coast of northern California.

Nah Tran, Viet Nam – *June 1968, 2:00 A.M.*

Three security guards at a missile post were standing about, off-shift, while the battleship New Jersey was firing just off the coast. Off to their left, the soldiers saw six or seven very large disk-shaped objects flying in a loose formation. Each disk had the apparent size of two joints of your thumb at arm's length. They were silent. They proceeded to the west and as they achieved a position nearby in front of the soldiers, they suddenly "became one large disk—became one unit."

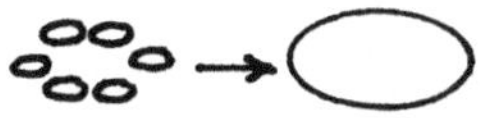

Eden, North Carolina – *1982, 9:00 P.M.*

Two women in their early twenties, cousins, were driving back to one of the parents' houses, when they saw a huge metallic object moving nearby at treetop level. It was "as big as the side of a house." It was shiny silvery and made a low humming sound. "When we first saw it, it looked almost liquid, like it was pouring out of something. Just silver liquid. And then it became round. Just a big round object." They drove on with the object slowly following, but by the time they tried to get others to come out, it had gone. "We were banging on the door, trying to get somebody to come out and see it, because we knew nobody was going to believe us." John asked if anyone they told the incident to believed them. "No. Nobody has ever believed us."

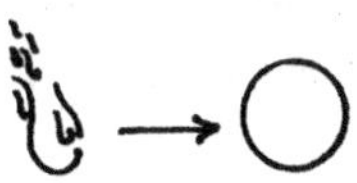

Shelby, Ohio – *July 20, 1952, at night*

The parents of a newborn had just returned home from the hospital and settled the other children to bed. The wife was relaxing on the back porch and saw a bright orange star in the sky. She called her husband and

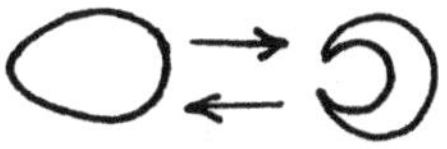

they watched. It dropped down and hung low over the field in the back of their house. It was an egg-shaped object. They walked closer. The object rotated, dipped down and back up very rapidly, and now took on the shape of a narrow crescent Moon. Then it repeated the act and was an egg again. Lastly, "it just seemed to evenly contract from all sides and it was gone. It moved so fast that you had no feeling of movement. It was just gone."

Algonquin Park, Ontario – *May 24, 1980, 6:30-7:00 P.M.*

Five persons were finishing a fishing trip and were standing on a sandbar when they saw what looked like a flying phone booth with poles mounted on it. It silently cruised across the water and seemed to land behind a small hill. A light came on behind the hill, and a white half moon appeared over it. The something rose from behind the hill into this half moon of light. It seemed to be a circular (disk-like) object with pulsating lights (orange, red, yellow) all around it. Then the "moon" went out and with it the object. One burst of light, then all darkness. All this without a sound.

Tyler, Texas – *September 1973, 5:00 A.M.*

At about 5:00 A.M. a truck driver was traveling a familiar route to work. A small "cub airplane" seemed to fly directly in front of another car on the road and nearly caused a wreck. [The truck driver is very sure that this was in the shape of a small plane.) The plane flew up over the side of the road and hovered above the trees, whereupon it changed into a long, cigar-shape; looking like an elongated balloon with lights. The truck driver stopped, got out of the truck to watch. The cigar moved off, then came right back at him in a round shape. It began to light up and display many multicolored lights. The lighted object was now overtop a nearby house. It made a low *loop-loop-loop* thumping sound, but no one in the house roused, and no cars had stopped on the road. Then a large, bright, square light seemed to descend and swing from the object. It seemed to approach the truck, go past it, and come back at him. This scared him so much he decided to jump back in the truck. But... "I thought I jumped into it, but when I come to myself I was standing holding the truck door. I got so nervous I think I passed out. Sometimes I think this thing picked me up. I had some marks on my hip, marks on my shoulder."

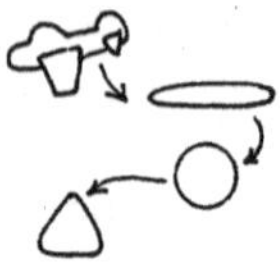

He remembers seeing the big machine ("larger than the house") turn from a round shape into a triangle, move backwards, and go out of sight.

Section 37:
Magickal miscellany

Other odd stuff happens. Here are ten more. They begin with a few cases of something that people interested in UFOs tend to take as an almost ho-hum given, but when you stop a moment to consider the implications, this element of the phenomenon (if real) has more astounding implications than any other. This is the allegation by witnesses that they just knew that a UFO was coming, and perhaps even heard that fact clearly stated in their consciousness. What on Earth would that portend? Probably nothing on Earth *at all.*

Oshawa, Ontario – *fall 1982, at night*

A husband and wife were asleep in their bedroom, when the wife awoke and saw an orange luminous object from her window. It was shaped like a half-ball, and seemed quite large. She heard nothing but had "just a great feeling." The object moved up and down, over and back, hovered, and finally left in a flash straight up. "Next night, I kept my husband awake to see it because I knew it would be back. I just felt that it was something living there." The husband watched it, and they watched it again the night after. "They knew I was watching."

> [One] other thing. Before we moved, I was always afraid of staying alone, always. And this one night I laid down in the living room to watch TV. Now, it could have been a dream. It was stupid. I woke up, the TV was off, and I was blind—I couldn't see. And somebody held my hand. I yelled for my husband; he wasn't in the house. And somebody held my hand and said: Don't be afraid, you'll be able to see in five minutes. I laid there for five minutes and somebody held my hand and when I could open my eyes and could see, there was nobody there but me. But I wasn't afraid. And I have never been afraid of being alone since. Now, was that a dream in my mind? Or was it real? I don't know.

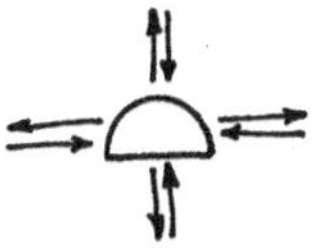

Mansfield, Ohio – *date not given, 4:00 P.M.*

A husband and wife were driving on the highway outside of town when they saw an isolated cloud with a contrail sticking out of it. The cloud seemed too low for a contrail to be formed with it, and they were puzzled and joked about who in the world would have turned *that* trick. Into the husband's mind came the message: "*We* are the ones who turned this one, and stick around and we'll show you some more." The contrail broke away and turned in the sky. Inside the trail, or self-generated cloud, was a saucer-shaped UFO. It came down, did a hard-angle turn, tipped up and climbed back out into the sky. At the greater height it jiggled erratically and "shook off the horseshoe-shaped cloud" generating around it [that's when they clearly saw the saucer shape]. Then it seemed to blend into the color of the sky, and disappeared.

Mansfield, Ohio *(different witnesses)* – *November 11, 1975, 9:10 P.M.*

A husband and wife were watching television (well, she was; he was snoring). A voice came into her head: "If you want to see flying saucers, go to your door." She ignored it. The voice persisted and she went to the door. Outside were six lights, side-by-side, coming toward the house. She woke her husband up, and he saw them. They got their neighbor out, and he saw them. The lights pivoted into a vertical stack. The neighbor rushed into his house to phone someone, and all the vertical stack went out. There was then only the humming sound coming from a dark presence which circled back over their house and over the field as it seemed to move away in the direction of Cleveland. There was a UFO report from Cleveland in the newspaper the next day, relating generally to the proper time frame.

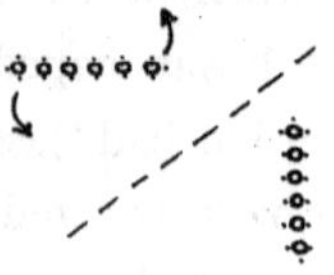

Kingston, Ontario – *May 1974, 2:00-4:00 A.M.*

A farm wife had gotten up to feed her baby (five days old). She placed him back in his crib and looked out the window of the back door. There, rising over a swampy area, was a fiery ball. She felt frozen by it. "It was staring at me and I was staring at it. And it was like it knew everything about me." Then, in silence, and at enormous speed it flew over the house. Finally she felt that she could move again. She went back to her bedroom and found that it was two to three hours later, and she had to go back and feed her son again. "It knew me and it had all pervaded me. And I was totally absorbed in it."

Cambridge, Ohio – *February 1989, 6:30 P.M.*

A woman was standing looking out her back door watching for a friend's car to come down the alley to pick her up. Instead she saw a light up in the sky, very bright and very blue. It was stationary. Then a white

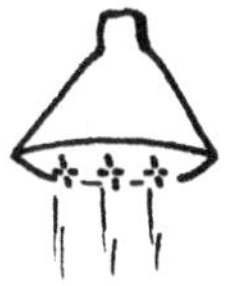

light appeared, and then a third light, and suddenly they all turned pink. These lights were sources like "stars", but they also were like beams, like bright rays coming down. They were lined up side-by-side in the sky, but the oddest part of this story is that they looked like they were emerging from some "funnel" in the sky. "It just looked like a plate with a funnel coming down." Her friend, a 75-year-old lady, arrived in her car, and was shown the object. She said: "Oh, it's a flying saucer. Come on, let's go eat."

Castlewood, Virginia – *year unstated, in the fall, 9:30-10:00 P.M.*

A 17- or 18-year-old was out gathering firewood, when a blink of light attracted his attention. There was an elongated object about the proportions of a finger, some distance away. It would blink in the colors of the spectrum (first one color, then adding a second, adding a third, until the whole spectrum was present). Then it would stay on (full spectrum) for a while. Finally, it tilted between 30 and 45° and seemed to stretch out like a colored rubber band, and then disappeared into a dot.

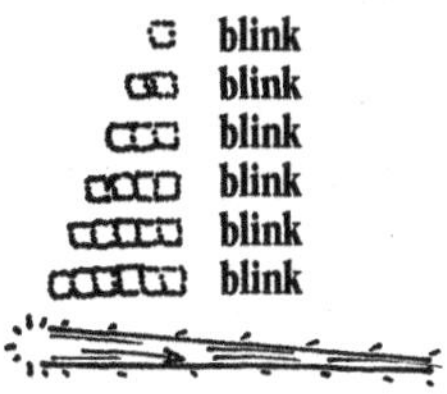

Yelapa, Mexico – *perhaps May 1984, in the evening*

Several people were sitting outside their hillside homes, when they saw bright lights in the sky. Most of these lights (they appeared on several nights) seemed distant or high, but one round, phosphorescent object came

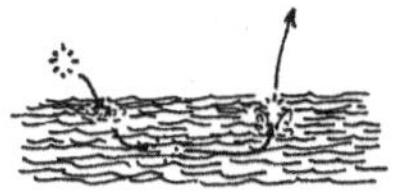

diving down toward the ocean. It entered the ocean making very little disturbance in the water. It kept going underwater the equivalent of about ten city blocks and then reemerged, shooting straight up into the air and away. There seemed to be some water churning when it emerged.

Dallas, Texas – *October 1976, 9:15 P.M.*

A woman was driving in her car with her 6-year-old daughter. She heard a very loud sound as she stopped at a stop sign. Looking out, she saw a large mass (about half the size of a basketball court) above the car. It was making sort of a roaring noise. The object was round, perhaps a ball, perhaps an ovoid disk, and silvery gray in color, with a mistiness about it. Around its perimeter was a smear of multispectral colors. It moved off and she had an urge to follow. As she followed, she began to feel it taking over control of her car (a tug on the wheel; the speedometer rising). She tromped on the brakes, and the car barely but grudgingly responded, and finally came to a halt. The object then was gone.

> It was hard to stop, but I stopped. And I turned around, and it scared me. I started crying. I went back to my mother's house and by the time I got there I was just real palish. I told her I saw something in the air, and she said: "Oh, that's crazy; come on in and sit down."

Later, on television, there were a dozen or more people who reported seeing something unusual in the sky. The strangest element of this case is probably this: "This is a very bad road that I was on. It's very bumpy, and if you were trying to go 75 mph [the speed she saw] on this road, it would be like up and down, up and down." But: "It was smooth, 75 mph on this particular road is not something that you would do safely, especially with a child in the car." John asked: Your wheels were apparently in contact with the road? "Yeah. Well, yeah, I would imagine so. I felt—it wasn't like a real bumpy ride, but I could feel contact—yes—just like I was being..." and she trailed off into silent thought.

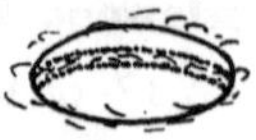

Boswell, Oklahoma – *September or October 1945, 11:00 A.M.*

This story has been told previously in the pre-1947 section, so you can read it there. But since it has a lot of magical aspects I thought that I'd just mention it again here. The case involves a child levitated in the air over a tree in which she'd been playing, missing time, very strange consequent behavior by both herself and her mother, and an odd pixilated disappearance of the UFO. All-in-all quite an Alice-in-Wonderland affair.

Windham, Nova Scotia – *summer 1982 or 1983, around 9:00 P.M.*

About twenty persons, adults and teenagers, were milling around at a camp alongside a lake. They saw a lighted object come up over the trees at the edge of the woods. It was a disk, humming, and lighted with about a dozen light sources. It hovered over the lake and slowly moved about two blocks-worth of distance as everyone gawked. Someone got out their camera and tried to take pictures of the object, but the flash refused to work. When the object moved, it moved with sharp-angled motions, no gradual curves. After several minutes, the object rose up, and at a fast (but

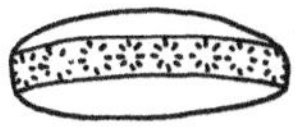

not incredible) rate of speed, it was gone. After it left, the useless camera, sitting on the table nearby, "took" two or three pictures with the flash going off. One suspects that someone, or the Universe itself, was smiling at that.

Section 38:
Entities from the edge

As our exploration of the phenomenology of the UFO Experience has grown odder and odder, we now go into very strange lands indeed. For the next five sections, we'll hear of things which will probably take you well beyond what you're prepared to believe about the world. And, perhaps, you'll be correct to shake your head and walk away from this stuff. Still, some of it seemed to have the same "gosh, I can't believe it myself, but..." feeling that much of the earlier witness/reporters had. So, on we go. This time: entities.

Decatur, Illinois – *sometime in the late 1960s, at night*

A pregnant woman had closed up all the windows in her house and locked the doors, and retired to bed. But she had a strange feeling that she was being watched. There, floating in the air, was a small being, who indeed seemed to be watching her. She stared at him, not very alarmed, and the being floated away and into the bathroom. When she examined that room, it was empty, but the formerly closed window was now open.

Lake Cayuga, New York – *around 1936 and after, at night*

We heard this story earlier (under pre-1947 sightings). This is another unalarmed woman in her bedroom, who sees (in this case) columns of light appear, come toward her, and envelope her. The light columns seem to be the vehicles whereby she is visited by loving beings of both genders.

Anaheim, California – *sometime in 1965, during the day*

A family was vacationing in Disneyland and was in one of the small shops ogling the stuff and deciding whether to buy anything. The wife heard someone say "hello." She ignored it. "Hello," again. And again. She straightened up and looked round: no one, except her family, the clerk, and a customer being checked out. The voice again: "I am speaking to you." She stood back up and whirled around. There was a person who hadn't been there before; very strong facial features and large pointed ears. She was being contacted telepathically, and was frightened. The man was very tall, and knew that he was scaring her. He told her not to be afraid, that he was "Velusian" and he was there on vacation. Her husband was still blissfully unaware of his wife's state, and was bending over looking in the display cases.

> By this time I was terrified because I had never encountered anything like this before and I am trying to get my husband up, you know, to try to...what am I doing, am I losing my mind? By the time I got him, he's going "What's wrong?" and I said, "This man here" and by the time I got him up this man had vanished. Out the door, vanished. Or just vanished.

Somewhere in a motel – *1978, near midnight*

A man was sitting in a motel room late at night watching television. He began to feel the approach of an evil presence. "Something bad. It scared me." Then the TV screen changed, and on it came a creature: "it was the ugliest thing that I have ever seen." Its eyes were shaped like diamonds; it seemed to have no nose. Some things like hands were moving at the screen as if it were trying to get past it and into this world. A glow surrounded the whole creature. Then it disappeared: "it went back inside." Coincident with the end of this event, the witness began to fall apart and had an emotional breakdown which put him in a hospital for about three months.

San Diego, California – *year not stated, in the evening*

A group of children was playing in the backyard with one of the children's parents seated nearby. There was a wooden playhouse in which three of the children had just run. When the fourth child was about to enter, he saw a small figure standing on the top of the playhouse. It was about three and a half feet tall.

> I called to our mother and stepfather and asked them to come over to see what we termed the "little man". And I recall very distinctly that my stepfather said in a very flat voice: "We can't come over right now." And it appeared even at the time, in our excitement, to be an unusual response from them, because they normally were so attentive to all of our desires. And we were a very close family and shared a lot of experiences together and I just felt it was unusual and still do think it was a little strange that this was their response. I recall remembering even at the time that this was occurring that perhaps my mother and stepfather were involved in an argument or something, because it just was not a normal response.

The children were all out, though, now, and trying to understand this weird experience.

> The appearance was more two-dimensional than three-dimensional, in the sense that it looked like a shadow sort of broadcast or against the night. And this small figure was very animated. It was jumping up and down and waving its arms rather wildly. I remember the elongated arms, the sort of ovoid shape to the head, and the very elongated fingers. Again, the motion of this apparition, whatever it might have been, was very animated and as I called the other children out to take a look at it, we were all poking at it with the playthings that we were carrying at the time...I waved this thing and poked at this apparition with seemingly no effect. Whether it went through the apparition, whether this was some sort of broadcast or projected apparition, I have absolutely no idea. But it appeared that our activities elicited absolutely no response from this entity.

The stepfather then said that it was time to come into the house, and the creature and the experience simply ended.

West Indianapolis, Indiana – *1977 and 1978, two strange evenings*

Whenever someone begins talking to John with phraseology like the following, you know you're in for a lulu: "This one is very different and it's sort of difficult to try and explain this to anybody and have them not think you are making it up; or you're from the loony bin."

John said something grandfatherly to him, so the witness went on. He was standing in his living room when he got a tingling all over his skin and the hair on the back of his neck standing up. "I could feel a charge in the air." He instinctively felt that he had to look behind him. Though frightened, he turned and saw a shoulder, upper arm, and part of the torso of some nonhuman creature. The rest of it wasn't there—or wasn't *fully* there, as it seemed to be emerging into his room along a line. This line did not seem to be physical (although there may have been a small colored glow to it), but rather just a geometrical delineation of a boundary between here and *there*. Almost immediately the creature disappeared back beyond the line. About a year and a half later it happened again, almost identically.

What did the creature look like? Well, the next time you see John rap him on the head, because he never asked. Maybe he didn't want to know what might be lurking just inside his closet, or coming up under the bed.

The southern end of **Guam** *– 1968, late at night*

A brother and sister were asleep, when the sister awoke to a noise outside. She then woke her brother. The noise was loud, but no one else woke (even another brother nearby refused to rouse when they tried to wake him). The sound turned higher in pitch, like whistles, and a bright light shone through the curtains. The sister was getting hysterical, saying that they were going to die. Then the sound grew softer. Their pet chickens were running around excitedly, and a small disk went over the house. The object seemed to land or a least stop right over the house. There were then three *zzzt* sounds, and a light so bright that it was like daylight. A ladder-like object descended, very shiny metal. Both the sister and brother fainted. The next morning both of them were in one bed covered with sweat. The parents wanted to know what had happened.

> And I said to her, "We've come to visit you like you've come to visit us. We mean no harm. Please do not be frightened. We see that you are frightened. We shall leave, but we shall return. When we return, please do not be frightened." And then they all went away. Mom was saying, "What are you saying! What is it? Get out of there!" So my dad took me to the kitchen and my mom took my sister to the bedroom and let her tell her story.

Hmm. Possession states now, too?

Afpla, Guam – *1943, in the day and evening*

We've heard this story earlier in the pre-1947 section, albeit briefly. The transcript makes it difficult to extract too much, but the case involves a small disk with portholes (in the day), and an apparently coincidental fire which burnt the witness' house that evening. Two beings in white suits (fireproof) with helmets with transparent faceplates came into the house, and somehow were able to gather up the fire in their hands and throw it outside, thereby saving the house and the family.

Seva, Puerto Rico – *sometime in the early 1960s, during the day*

A girl was going into puberty and was suffering from terrible cramps. She was on medication for them, but it didn't always help. She and her mother had lunch, and she went to take a little rest. When she laid down she suddenly felt paralyzed. She panicked and tried to scream, but couldn't. The mother seemed to think that she was asleep, but the girl was conscious of the mother right there, but ignoring her. Then she had an experience of an entity (which I'll tell you about later in Section 40). But this seemed to set up the following, one year later:

And that time I remember I had very sharp and strong menstrual cramps. And as a child I remember that this health condition, that every month my mother had to take me to the hospital for medication because of pain; it was so strong that I couldn't deal with that. So I remember every month she took me to the hospital. I remember that specific afternoon that I had the cramps and my mother is a dressmaker, and she was sitting on the bed with the sewing machine, and I was laying next to her because I felt so ill that I felt comfortable being close to her. And she told me that as soon as my father got home, they would be taking me to the hospital. And to please stay still and relax until he comes, because he was out doing something. So I remember that I got close to her and I started saying that I feel so bad and she said okay, stay there, let me go to the kitchen and let me prepare you a hot milk, with some pills, while we get to the hospital. And I say, all right. And I remember that she got up and she went to the kitchen and I stayed there like in the fetal position. And I could hear her, you know, doing the... warming the milk and all that.

While she was away, these two guys, similar to the first one but this time two guys, came in the bed. This time I don't feel that scary because I remember that he looks similar to the other guy that I got the experience a year before. And these two, they never talked to me, they only looked at me and they smile, they never talk to me. But this time one of them made this sign like "Don't talk, relax" and they come close to me. I remember that one of them sat me on the bed while the other one was like touching and examining my body. And at that point I feel like a needle going inside my spine and I tried to say "*Yi*" but I know I say "*Yi*" but nobody hears me. And the other one was like putting like... it was similar to a coin, a twenty-five-cent coin in my abdomen. He pushed that coin toward my abdomen, all right? And they very gently, they laid me down on the bed, all right? And after they laid me in bed, I just stand up out of the bed to look for my mother. And she was on her way to...with the milk and she said, "What happened?" And I say, "Oh, Momma, I don't know what. You know what happened to me?

But I was so excited telling what happened to me that I forget that I don't have the pain any longer. And the pain disappeared for the next eight months or nine months. My mother never have to take me back to the hospital. Maybe even close to a year, because I never had the pain again. And I made her look in my back and she say she didn't find anything.

Redding, California - *sometime in the late 1970s*

This is brief, but because it is of everybody's favorite entity, I have to include it. A woman was attending one of those business club speaker meetings, built around a breakfast or luncheon meal. This one was a little different in that it was the "Full Gospel Businessmen" meeting which always had a religious theme. Although the group was nondenominational, the day's talk was by a Catholic Charismatic. After his (doubtless) rousing presentation, the group (as was usual) prayed with and for the speaker. As they finished, the woman diverted her eyes to the ceiling, and directly over her head was a small angel. It was very white, had wings, and all-in-all was exactly like a proper angel image should be. She stayed so fixated on it for its approximately 30-second duration, that she never thought to draw anyone else's attention to it.

John asked her whether she also believed in UFOs. She said: "I believe that's all out there, too. I don't know for sure. My husband has seen things like that, but I think probably some of it is demonic. We've seen demonic spirts."

Unfortunately, John didn't ask her about *those*.

Section 39:
Something in the air

This section is about a variety of events which happened in the air, which have elements about them (or the whole experiences) which just don't seem comfortable to accept in any scenario one devises. A vast misperception, a simple tall tale, a universe where things don't always fit? Here are a variety of stories from police surveillance which shouldn't be to the time warps of the Bermuda Triangle.

Costa Mesa, California – *1981, sometime around 3:00 P.M.*

A man was driving in an urban area. He heard a helicopter and saw a disk in the sky. He stopped the car and got out to watch. At first he

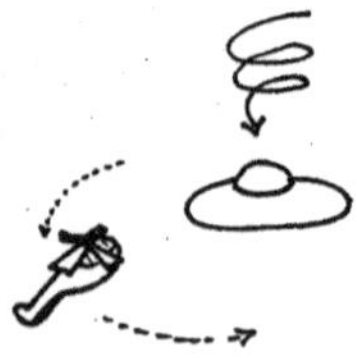

thought that the disk was just a piece of shiny metal falling from great height, as it seemed to be tumbling downward, end over end. As it fell, he began to realize that this was a domed disk with a helicopter circling about it as it fell. Then the disk stopped and righted itself a few hundred feet up. It hovered for about a minute and a half. As it hovered, the helicopter (a local police vehicle) circled around it, always pointing its nose toward the UFO. The UFO made no noise throughout this engagement. It began slowly to move off, then accelerated rapidly, leaving the helicopter behind.

How does a police helicopter know when there's going to be a falling UFO, leisurely observe it at close distance, and no public report of any of this is made? And why was this public street empty of all but the witness at 3:00 P.M.? Strange business.

Two cases at once:

Toronto, Ontario – *summer 1975, 11:00 P.M.; and*

Kanora, Saskatchewan – *May or June 1989, midnight*

In Toronto, the witnesses felt a rumble in the building and went up to the rooftop to take a look. There, coming overhead, was a huge triangular object. It was only about 100 feet overhead, and 1200 to 1300 feet long.

In Kanora, the witness was walking on a railroad track, heard no sound, but out of nowhere came an object. Just overhead was a huge triangular object. It came low over his head, and was gigantic, giving a "sense of awesome power."

In Toronto, the object moved slowly and silently. It was a long, sharp triangle. There were dim lights on the side and three round "engines" on the back.

In Kanora, the object moved slowly and silently. It was a long, sharp triangle. There were no lights on the side and there were engines on the back.

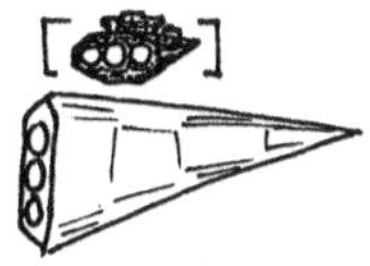

In Toronto, the witness described the craft exactly like the craft in the movie, *Star Wars*, but didn't say the words. In Kanora, the witness said: "A nephew of mine has a toy spacecraft from the *Star Wars* movie...and I realized that's exactly, more or less, what I had seen."

Now, how could that be?

Lenawee County, Michigan – *spring or summer 1968, at dusk*

A farmer was working in his milking parlor, and he came out to take a break. He looked up into the sky and was stunned to see a vast saucer-shaped object which covered a good portion of the sky. "Diameter-wise, it practically blacked out the sky from the west." Twenty-five percent or more of the entire sky. It was noiseless and black (it had shut out the setting sun and darkened the environment around him). This stunned him so much that he turned back into the milking shed to regain his composure. After a few seconds, he looked back out and there was nothing there.

A UFO covering a third of the sky?

Clairborn, Texas – *1977 sometime, 5:30 P.M.*

Witnesses were driving along and saw a plane in the air—standing still. They stopped the car and looked out. The plane was only about 600 feet up; seemingly frozen in the air. It had TWA markings on it. They observed it for thirty minutes, shrugged, and went on.

Duh?

West Palm Beach, Florida – *late 1960s, in daylight*

The witness was driving along and saw an object floating in the air. It was about 200 or 300 feet up. He pulled the car to a stop and got out. This witness is, by the way, a technical person working research and development for Pratt and Whitney. The object looked like an average-sized man moving slowly through the air. He looked like Superman. And he just kept going till he disappeared.

Near **Mt. Rainier, Washington** – *early 1950s, 5:00 A.M.*

Well, folks, here we are in Kenneth Arnold country, and at the time of George Adamski. So, what we don't need, in order to maintain our ufological sanity, are George Adamski-like spacecraft showing up. Oops.

> My mining partner and I, we saw three of them flying in formation about five o'clock in the morning. They were flying silently overhead. No noise whatsoever...We watched them; they flew overhead and kept right on going. I suppose up a couple thousand feet...They looked like they were about bell-shaped. Bell-shaped ones. Like AT&T bell-shape. The top was smaller and then the wide flange on the outside like that.

So...this same fellow gets interested in UFOs and:

Yakima, Washington – *early 1950s, 8:30 or 9:00 P.M.*

> So a few years later I watched TV at nighttime. I was still living in Yakima at the time, and about seven or eight people came over from Seattle to Yakima and were interviewed on the TV station—KIMA-TV in Yakima. And they were asked, "Why are you here?" And they said, "We're here to photograph the spaceship that comes down from Ellensburg, Washington, to Yakima, every night at nine o'clock. And we have all the photographic equipment with us." And they were interviewed for about a half hour.
>
> So about 8:30 we... I took my wife and my two children and we went out to a place where the people were all gathered out there, about a hundred and some people out there that night, including these photographic people with their cameras, moving picture cameras. And there, sure enough, at 9:00 came this bell-shaped flying object, low and no noise whatsoever, right over our heads. However, right alongside from the firing range which was about a mile away was a fighter plane and it was hedgehopping over the terrain so it wouldn't be seen. And all of the people saw it. And suddenly right overhead, the spaceship saw the fighter plane was closing in... it was about a mile away, but it was

> hedgehopping. And it just flew like a streak of white light toward Mr. Rainier and the fighter plane was left standing still. And that was the end of it for the night. But it came in at 9:00. You could set your clock by it.

And, you have to decide whether you want to set your model of what's going on with UFOs by this.

Wind River Reservation (near Lander, Wyoming) – *July 1973, at night*

While we're still reeling from TWA, Superman, and Adamski Bells, let's go to a Rainbow Family gathering. For those readers who missed the Sixties, the Rainbow Family is a loose association of people from all over who meet (with a lot of clever secrecy as to when and where) to engage in a continuing "Summer-of-Love (and drugs)" type blast. Don't ask me where the next one is, folks, you're on your own. In this instance, after a wild night (what else is there at a Rainbow gathering?) a bunch of people decided to go up onto the hill and recreate an Indian ceremony with some of the local native Americans' permission and help. They all sat in a circle and began to do their thing. The witness didn't join in but was back at a campfire with friends looking at them.

> We saw a—basically it looked like one of the stars had shifted, and was dropping straight at us. And the whole valley saw it. There was hundreds of people saw it. It came down at us, making no noise. It was falling in a long arc, coming from the southeast. As it got right over the valley, it did an instantaneous 90—it was falling one second, then it wasn't. And it laid—oh, it sounded like a string of firecrackers—a sonic boom, right through the valley. And went up and out to the southwest over the Wind River range. And you could see it accelerated to a fantastic speed and never made any noise beside the sonic booms but you could see it wavering through the atmosphere, it was going so fast. And then I'd say it only took three or four seconds at the most. It was going up and out but it went over the rim of the planet, it went so quick. You could see it where it left the atmosphere and started going straight.

A good, Earth-grazer fireball at just the wrong time to create a legend?

Bermuda Triangle – *winter, probably early 1970s*

This comment came from a very intelligent-sounding guy who worked in the Coast Guard from 1969 through 1973, the latter part of that at Cape Cod Coast Guard Station where "we were responsible for investigating all sightings from the beach out into the ocean. We took over where Blue Book stopped. (And) most of our information was sent off to Wright-Pat Air Force Foreign Technologies." To his knowledge, most of their Coast Guard reports were highly classified and ended up "in Washington."

Because their responsibilities covered things from the Canadian boarder to the tip of Long Island, some over-ocean anomalies that began in the northern area of the so-called Bermuda Triangle came to their attention. And in the case that he told to John, the Coast Guard was directly involved in an aircraft incident.

> On one particular flight, it was in the winter. We were ferrying aircraft. We had gone out to Bermuda. We were on our way into Miami International and there were three aircraft. Two of them landed two hours ahead of time, one landed two hours late. Flying through the Bermuda Triangle.

John asked if they stopped somewhere.

> No. No. There was absolutely no place to stop. We were over solid ocean and it was just one of those anomalies, one of those things that ends up getting filed under the Bermuda Triangle as an "Unknown." And a lot of that information the Coast Guard has, they've...I don't know if they've ever declassified any of the information on Bermuda Triangle or not. The only thing I could say to that is what we put down on the files as "Unknown."

Another claimed anomaly that we thought we had solved, thanks to Larry Kusche, maybe rearing its Fortean head again?

Section 40:
Consciousness in Wonderland

Maybe we humans don't understand consciousness, but it's all we've got. Each of the cases in this section suggests possibilities of powers and states of consciousness which most people would not credit.

Swift Current, Saskatchewan – *May 1967, at night*

A woman was looking out her basement window when a bright light illuminated the area. It was coming from a large object hovering across the road over a neighbor's house. The light source had three colors and was rotating, though you could not see the exact shape. She went upstairs and got the lady who lived in the upper level to watch it with her. Finally, after about twenty minutes, she decided that she should call her neighbors and tell them that there was a UFO over their house. She tried several times but the phone was always busy. The experience ended and she went to bed. The next morning she called the neighbor to tell her of the thing over their house. But the neighbor said that there was no way that the phone was busy. Rather, everyone in the house was sitting together, playing cards, and talking about UFOs.

So, why is this odd UFO experience in this section? Maybe it doesn't belong, but I am reminded of the apparent consciousness connection between the phenomenon and the mind, and here was a whole group of people thinking about the phenomenon when it appeared (although they didn't even know it). Coincidence may be a better explanation, plus another coincident phone oddity. Your choice. As the witness said: "Isn't that weird?"

Solvag, New York – *sometime in 1978, at night*

Twin girls walked up to John, one of whom had trouble before birth which had caused her health problems requiring ongoing surgeries over time. Both girls, though, were mentally sharp. When the girls saw the movie *Close Encounters*, the following occurred:

> I'd seen part of it as a child and I never really thought about it. When we saw the full thing, it made both of us very paranoid. We were very afraid to be alone. We turned the lights on and we turned the radio on very loud. And it's quite irrational. I get angry at myself for doing that.

This shock from the movie (we'll mention the part that did it later) brought up this memory from the twin with the surgeries.

> I was four years old at the time. It would be 1978. I was in the hospital for one of many operations I would have in the future. I was in my hospital bed and I had some feeling I had to fall asleep, so I did fall asleep. And when I woke up I was in a room of sorts, lying on a couch. And there were beings around me. They were around about five feet tall or a little less than that. Their heads were larger, quite noticeably large, but they weren't like ghost white pale. They were like more of a golden skin color. Strange as it seems, they had hair on their heads. Their eyes were large. They were almost like our eyes. They weren't all black—they had an iris and a pupil that were more of an oval shape. High set cheekbones. They were thin faced but they had a small nose. You could see it, that [dropped] out just a little bit. And mouth, they had very thin lips. Their bodies were very thin, wispy like. Their fingers were incredibly long, almost as if they had one too many joints in it. There were four fingers on their hands, I noticed.
>
> And it seems I was being examined. They were looking at me. They examined my face. They were looking, just peering at it. It was a surprise and curiosity. They sort of looked in my ears with something, I couldn't see it from where I was. I noticed there was among them...I could tell whether they were male or female. It wasn't the... it was like a feeling, you just knew that they were male or female, they...There was a commander who was in there and it was female because I remember she was one of the first things I saw looking directly in my face. She seemed curious. There was... see...they were looking at my hands. They looked..., only lifted my hand up and looking at the fingers. And the commander went and reached out one finger and touched my face, just felt it, you know, was feeling it. She was like running a finger down my nose, wondering why I looked like that.

> The way they were dressed, the clothing, there was like a... the commander wore a...it was like a turquoise blue outfit that was sort of form-fitting, not quite. It went down to the wrists and on the wrist there was like a...sort of like a pattern. There was like a stripe, a pattern of little dots, and then a stripe that looped up at the top. And there was a star set, a four-pointed star set in there in the loop. It was all silver. And I noticed from the shoulder draping down her back was like a swath of silver cloth. The rest of them were dressed in like gray, sort of like a jumpsuit with a jacket over it. Simple gray jacket that their [collars] just hung straight down about to their knees. I couldn't really see their feet because of the way I was standing. I saw...I noticed a...there was like a... The belt on the commander's waist had a symbol like a....it was a triangle and on each point of the triangle there was a circle. And set in the middle of the triangle was a stylized galaxy and there was another circle set in the center.
>
> All right, there was also one thing I noticed. There was a female. Her hair, there was hair in varying lengths and different colors. Hers was like a...it was deep like a burgundy, deep burgundy color, and it was very long. It was pulled back very close to their heads. The hairline was set back much more than ours. And [hung long] was gathered up at the back of the neck with a simple clasp or something. It hung straight down her back. What I noticed about her was her stomach. It was big. It was protruding like a woman pregnant, which I found quite odd because I didn't see anybody else like that. I wondered why, but I was too young.

The girls obviously had a wonderful sister-and-twin relationship, and the healthy twin had the same paranoiac reaction to the movie (hers is the first quote, earlier). She warned John that her sister has a very vivid imagination and "it's possible that she could be adding on." Her sister agreed:

> Sometimes I think of my [imagination/experience] and I could be making this all up. I just can't figure out why and I tried to think as rationally as like: "Am I imagining it? Could I be making this up?" There is a very strong possibility and I could be making the whole thing up, I don't know. It's just so vivid.

John asked in the end: what part of the movie triggered all this?

Oh, I remember that part. It was near the end when you see the very first alien come out of the mother ship. I see this thing, these huge eyes and they all have long hands and I just went berserk. I nearly screamed when I saw that thing.

Three Rivers, Ontario – *August or September 1964, in the evening*

A commercial diver was doing some underwater work near a bridge and somebody on the team made a mistake. As he was being hauled up, he became constricted both at the waist/chest and around his neck. It was as if he was being hung. Then his consciousness swung.

Somewhere in that point, I suddenly experienced being... how to describe it...flattened against like a window pane. And then I was suddenly inside of a room, in front of a person, huge person sitting in something. I couldn't see anything else and then suddenly I seen this person's face. I was so, so scared about this, that this face disappeared again, and at that same instant I was talking with this person. And I remember being shown around the craft. I was shown...I was asked what I wanted to see, what I wanted to see, so I asked to be shown the control room. Engine room, control engine room was out of the question, apparently, and so I was suddenly in this control room. I couldn't see anything. Then suddenly I could see figures like...uh...well, they didn't look like humans. They looked like androids, moving around and putting their hands up against the wall, which was all black. And then I must have been moving closer to those walls because I could...at one point I could see a difference of black shades. It all looked like charcoal but different shades of charcoal, like different shades of black... which were indicating some sort of control panels but very difficult to make out. There were no dials, no switches, nothing but straight lines, rectangular lines, horizontal lines of different shades of black, very faint.

And then suddenly I was out of this room and in another room which was brightly lit. A lot of humanlike...very humanlike people in there. They were...at first, were turning around and sort of staring at me and then going about whatever they were doing. And I remember, one person sticks in my mind, was a girl approximately between 20- and 25-years-old. Very long twisted blonde hair, and she stared longer at me than the rest of them

> *[laughs]*. And then from there I was in front of an older person, human, features were human, talked to me as we are talking here.
>
> And then something happened after that. I'm not very clear in my mind what happened. I remember traveling in this craft in a clear dome, seeing all the stars whizzing by. I suddenly found myself in the water. Someone had cut the rope, with a knife, I assume. And there were a lot of people standing on the deck, at that point. And they were pulling me up very carefully. They had taken off my helmet and they asked me to move my arms and whether I had broken anything or, you know. And I could move all my limbs and everything and I felt my back a bit sore. I couldn't really feel much of anything.

Very strange waters, indeed. It brings up the idea that deeply embedded in the human consciousness are structures which vividly vision-up images like *Close Encounters* when threatened with death (for Lord knows what reason). Or, maybe, Magonia is just always around us close to the skin.

Near the **Oregon-California border**; *sometime in the 1980s, at night*

Two women and their young sons were driving on the freeway, when they saw a bright light low near the hills. They decided to get off at an exit and watch it. They went down a side road and got out (the boys stayed inside).

> We watched this light. We found out it would move and when we would think to...so we started playing with it, because I have a vivid imagination, and was asking questions. And I would move this way for yes and this way for no. And then every once in... it was like it was playing. Because we were becoming slightly hysterical, giggling on the car.
>
> It would do figure eights every once in a while, and it would have different colors to it, but this lasted hours. We'd just sit here and freezing to death, it's cold up there by Mt. Shasta. But we couldn't get back in the car, because I was like we could feel the warmth, this love. Again, I feel like he was giggling with me every once in a while. Because it was like they knew we knew they were there. And so we stayed there for hours. It was almost dawn. And then we said this is crazy and we've got to get home. Cars are going by us and, God only knows, what they thought we were doing, sitting there. But it followed us all the way home. It stayed right with us all the way home.

And the aftermath:

> Well, after that something would wake me up, like at 3 or 4 in the morning and sometimes I'd fight it so hard. I'd keep trying to ignore it. Finally, when I stopped ignoring it, I'd start writing. And it wasn't that I heard words. I got thoughts. I'd write down the thoughts. And then I'd think, god, this is... this is too much. This is just my imagination. Until I'd get up the next morning and read it, and I know how I think. I know how I talk, and, my friends know me real well and they would read it and they're going: "No, it's not you." And this went on for a long time. And we've found out since then, because we are very open... I feel like if there's light forms under the ocean, there can be light forms up above. And they may know more than me and I'm willing to learn from any source. And it seems like they work a lot during the dream state. We notice when we go to sleep that they do a lot of work with it. And since then, there's just a real wonderful well-being. It's like I feel like... it's extra love and it does seem real silly and self-centered but I feel like there's one with me all the time. And they send down this amazing love and they just kind of watch over me.

And, a hypnosis-induced recall:

> It was very real. He walked me through the ship. At the time it was more real than it is now, when I went to meet with Roger. But we were sitting across from each other and he was asking me questions about what people were like on Earth. How it would be best for them to approach people on Earth. Because I think they are very concerned about how we react to them. Sometimes I think they work with us to get the feeling of how humans think. And what would be their best way to approach and communicate with us.

Somewhere in Iowa – *around Christmas, 1980, 8:30 P.M.*

A single woman was pregnant and worried about her future and whether she could go on with the pregnancy and have the child. She was trying to get into a state of prayer, asking God what she should do. Instead (at least of any "ordinary" way we conceive of a response from God), what happened was that a "glowing thing", an object, (otherwise undescribed), appeared to her and a voice came from it and said: "Yes, you should [have the baby]." Well, okay so far, but it continued: "One day you will know us." Since that experience, she went on with the pregnancy and birthed her son. And she feels that she has been visited two other times (details undescribed). Her husband (now) thinks that all this is crazy, and for the moment she thought, well, maybe the pregnancy *was* making her goofy. But two more visitations: no. She's become emotional about whoever these entities are, and more so about our own actions in our world.

> Somehow, we are screwing up in our world. I'm screwing up with my kid. They want us to go with them. They want us to be as one. That's how it is. And that's how it was then. They said they want us to be as one.

John asked if she would go away with them.

> If they ever ask me, yes, I will. And so will my son. My husband decides not to go. Hey, hell with him. I will, forever. I appreciate these people that we never knew they were there. Maybe they have some significance. Maybe they know how to better our planet. We're certainly screwing it up. If they've got a better plan, let's hear it. I'm open. I'm willing.

I suppose that almost all of us (that actually do much thinking) agree with her that we are environmentally and socially screwing up our world. What does the constant underlying burden of that awareness do to our consciousness? And what can "other beings" have to do with it? There are a large number of hypotheses.

Seva, Puerto Rico – *in the early 1960s, in the afternoon*

This is the precursor experience of the young girl, just entering puberty, whose story we heard earlier in Section 38. It is placed here because it may have more to say about consciousness and perception than the latter experience. Like it or not, I've split them. So, ready or not, here it is:

When she was eleven or twelve, she had an experience when lying down for a siesta after lunch. As soon as she placed her head on her pillow, she felt strange, as if she couldn't move. She was panicked and tried to scream out for her mother (nearby) to help her, but her mother thought she was sleeping. Then:

> And I saw this guy enter into my bedroom. It was not something like a ghost, so to speak, because I could see him clearly. And he was wearing like some type of spacesuit, very similar to the one like the astronauts, except he has no helmet at all. And he has long hair. And I was very scared, when I looked at him. He was

fair-skinned, blue eyes and beautiful long hair. Long hair. And he looked at me and he tried to smile at me but I was so scared that I wasn't smiling. And I still was crying, you know, inside me I was crying "Help me! Help me!", you know. "Somebody is in the bedroom." And he showed me the wall. It was a cement wall, my bedroom, and he showed me the wall and I looked through the wall. And it was very interesting because I realized that I could see through all the walls.

And I saw the cars coming and going, the neighbor's house and all that. And I felt maybe I'm dreaming it all. I thought to myself, "I'm dreaming. It's just a dream." And I saw all the movement that was going on at the time. And I was able to hear. My hearing was developing in such a way that I could hear miles away, everything that was going on. And I could even see the car that was going to come maybe three minutes after. And for me at first I was scared but later it was for me like a game, you know, that I could feel this, it was something that I enjoyed doing it, hearing whatever is going on three or four miles away. And looking at everything. And he just moved the finger and everything stopped. And when that happens, I look at him and he turned his back and disappeared. And then I was able to move again. And I say, "Wow! What a dream!" And then immediately I talked to my mother. She was doing some chores in the house, and I say, "Mama, what time is it?" And she say, "Why?" I say, "How long was I asleep?" She say, "Maybe two or three minutes." So it couldn't be. You know, for me it was a long time, and I told her, "Do you see me sleeping?" She say, "Yes, you got your eyes closed. I didn't bother you. I saw you fall asleep." I said, "No, I did not fall asleep."

And another thing that I did not mention was that when I was looking through the wall, I just moved my head and see what happens, not only in front of me but in the side. And I saw my aunt that lived nearby come into my house. She did not come in the front door, but she came through all the porch. And I saw her talking to my mother in the kitchen for a few seconds but I was able to understand what they were saying. And I remember when she left the same way she came, and I told my mother: "Don't tell me anything, all right? I'm going to tell you what I saw and you tell me that was true or if it was a dream." And she looked at me like

> I was out of this, or crazy. I say, "Now, Mommy, I want to know... to be sure that was dream or that was true." So I told her my aunt came here, and I told her, answer yes or no, and she say yes. She was wearing this dress? Yes. She came this way? Yes. She told you this? And you answer her back, this? She say, "Yes. How you know that?" "Because I saw that." "How come? You were in the bedroom, sleeping." And then I shared the experience with my mother. She said that I was dreaming. And I say how come I was dreaming, if you say yes, that everything that happened was true? And I was not there. We leave that alone. We never talk about that experience, and a year later I got another experience.

Which was the one where the entities seemed to come and remove the problems with her menstrual cramping that we told earlier. This one, however: Dreams? Psychic dreams? Enhanced sensory perceptions? *Impossible* seeing through walls and at-a-distance? A delusional story? What?

On the other hand...

Around **Snoqualmie, Washington** – *c. 1983 and afterwards, nights*

A young man had an experience (see earlier) wherein a voice on the television told him to go out and look for a UFO. Since then he feels that he's seen several (disks and "Vs"). On one occasion with a V-shaped object, the lights suddenly went off and two beings emerged. They wore street clothes, spoke English, and looked exactly like us. They wanted to talk. About?: "Photochemistry and stuff," and "exotic propulsion devices and stuff." And not to approach crafts too closely because you could get burned by "radiation poisoning and stuff" and "it messes up your nerves and stuff." Where'd these people come from? "This planet" [not, thank God, followed by the phrase "and stuff"]. And from a time warp from the distant past.

Milwaukee, Wisconsin – *fall or winter 1977, about 3:00 A.M.*

A husband and wife had been having a very odd sequence of evenings where they were awakened each night around the same time. It was caused by nightmares that the wife was having—more or less repetitive dreams. The husband:

> She claims she was upset by dreams and that they were in color, she dreamt in color, and she felt like somebody, like Orientals, were attacking her all the time. I did not have this, I just woke up. I did not do anything but read and try and get back to sleep after several hours.

Then one evening something different happened. The wife:

> Probably the precipitating event was a dream and an experience with a dream that I had had earlier in the week. In fact for several nights, I can remember dreaming extensively. And I do always dream in technicolor like a Cecil B. DeMille epic. But this particular night, I remember working very hard in my sleep. I remember feeling very exhausted, that I was dreaming many, many diverse situations, ramifications of situations, and they all had to do with disaster. For example, I was dreaming that there was an atomic disaster and I was dreaming how people in this country might cope with such a situation. And then other components were added. How would people cope if then food was taken away. How would people cope if then a flood came. And it went on and on like this.
>
> And I can remember very consciously feeling, no, I'm just not going to do this anymore. I'm not going to work this hard. And waking up very quickly, coming up to the levels of consciousness. And as I did this, I was aware that there was an entity of some kind and I got the impression it was somewhat of an oriental entity, that's probably the closest I can describe it, even though that was only impression, who was demanding that I respond to these situations that he was outlining. As I became more conscious, the demands became cajoling... oh, why don't you try? You could do that. And as I was fully awake, I realized that the entity realized that I was awake and it quickly withdrew. I felt that this, whatever it was, had not selected me out for anything other than perhaps I could dream and perhaps was doing the same thing in my area with a hundred other people. I was in no way unique, or the only subject of this investigation, because that's what I felt it was. I also felt that whatever it was viewed me and us as a race or people as we would view rats in a maze. There was no concern. There certainly was no humanity on the part of the entity towards us. After this, I programmed myself to awake instantly if I felt this occurring again and I woke continually throughout the rest of the summer and fall, and it stopped about the first part of January 1978.

After that "battle" that the wife had with whatever was tormenting her that evening, the husband roused and had his own different experience.

The husband:

One night after this happened, I came down the stairs and before I descended the stairs my brain or head felt like a million tingling needles came into it. And as I walked down the stairs, at the very bottom was a complete light of cylinder, or a cylinder of light roughly three to four feet in diameter from floor to ceiling. I've checked several hundreds of times but I've never been able to duplicate that phenomena of seeing any kind of lights through the curtains or headlights of cars or any other rational explanation. This light disappeared after about twenty or thirty seconds, as I walked slowly down the stairs with this tingling head.

I then, at my wife's request... she was so upset after a while... I concentrated very heavily one night almost into a trance, if you want to call it that. And I really was able to mentally to perceive many small spaceships out, I don't know where. I could not describe them to you. I could just see them in my mind and by concentrating very heavily and utilizing electrical energy, I was able to blow up one of them. I could see it in my mind, blown up. And with that, someone communicated with me somehow, and we made kind of a pact that if I would leave them alone, they would leave me alone. And that's the way it's been since. Until that happened, I was very disturbed with headaches, lack of memory, couldn't solve problems on calculators, highly mathematical problems. I teach marketing and do a lot of quantitative things and I had a very bad time. And I took naps and lost my energy. After this pact was made, I seemed to be okay and I wouldn't have anything else to do with it. I refused to even discuss it. I did make some notes on it and when I went to get the notes a year or so later one time, to show them to one of my children, a lot of them had been... just somehow they were just unreadable. They were just smeared and yet when I wrote them, I know they were written in good ballpoint pen and readable. So that's all I can tell you. I don't know any more.

Attacked by predatory dream merchants demanding emotional responses? Mentally blowing up their spaceships and panicking them into leaving you alone? How far do you want to stretch your universe?

Columbus, Ohio – *year and times unspecified*

So now that you're all terrorized by the last case, I'll let you reduce the stress by relating a little "good clean UFO fun."

For most of you this one will probably seem like trivia, but I rather like it. Part of that is because I, like Budd Hopkins and Tom Deuley, grew up in West Virginia, and we all secretly know (as did Gray Barker) that the ol' home state is the center of the weird universe.

This story involves four guys who decided that the best way to get inside information was to get it off a Ouija board. They were playing around with this thing, and asked it how they could get into contact with a flying saucer. The board told them, of course, go to West Virginia.

The directions were elaborate and the social pressure probably high, so the adventurers decided to go for it. Across the mighty state of Ohio they fearlessly trekked and into the Mountain State of Mothman, Indrid Cold, and the Braxton County Monster. Into the hills on a certain road, through a farmer's gate at a certain time, over the hill to a certain white barn...and then.

There was the barn, just as the board had led them. And there, behind that barn, was an eerie glow. And they ran and jumped into their car and raced back to Ohio as fast as they could go. Can't blame them too much, though. We hillbillies don't cotton to uppity strangers from the big city.

But still, one wonders a little: did anything speak to them through that Ouija board, and lead them onward toward their barn and their mysterious glow? As a good Irish Catholic boy, I recommend that you all leave the Ouija board alone and let whatever's behind there sleep in peace.

Section 41:
Grounded in unreality

I don't think that we can top the stuff in the last section for concentrated weirdness, so let's come (figuratively at least) out of the Consciousness Fairyland and "back down to Earth." Yet, these "feet flat on the ground" reports seem equally strange when you think about them. But, after all we've gone through, you're probably suspecting that it's a mighty queer universe that's providing all this entertainment, I'd imagine. So, off into the woods we go.

Lancaster, Ohio – *fall 1966 or 1967, at dusk*

A family was driving in their car outside of town. They came upon a field where there was a landed flying saucer. It was a thin disk about thirty to forty feet in diameter, and was perched on legs which extended from the bottom. Around the perimeter revolved a ring of small lights. "And there was an Army 'copter beside...camouflage type... they was sitting there keeping an eye on the object." Their mother refused to stop the car and drove on. But...a UFO parked in a field with a U.S. Army helicopter parked twenty yards away watching it? What universe did *that* event drop out of?

Near **Medford, Oregon** – *winter 1985, at night*

A husband and wife were driving back home from visiting friends on a very familiar road. They were planning on stopping at a certain store in a small town between. Suddenly the road looked strange, and they realized that they hadn't passed the town or the store they were looking for. "I know where that town is and I couldn't find it. It wasn't there." *Oops.*

Near **Grand Island, Nebraska** – *around 1970, in the evening*

A wife was driving her sleeping husband outside of town but on a relatively unfamiliar road. To her right the land dropped off into a little valley and a side road went down into it. Stretched across the valley below was a curtain of red light. You could not see any landmarks or objects on the other side of the curtain. Another car had gotten off the road and was driving toward the curtain. It drove right through it and disappeared. "Boy. That was really a strange feeling because I would have liked to have seen where that car went." Yes, darling, so would have we.

Sundown, Manitoba – *sometime in 1977, 4:00 A.M.*

A gentleman was driving to work at his regular time and on the usual highway he traveled. This morning, however, he encountered the abnormal. Ahead and above the road came a shimmering disk of light. It passed over his car and went away behind. As he was contemplating this, three "creatures", or somethings, appeared on the road directly in his path. They were shaped like featureless bowling pins. He slammed on the brakes. Too late: he plowed right through them. But...there was no impact. In his rearview mirror he saw them apparently "deflating" in the road. He drove to the nearest police detachment, and they went back to investigate. They found only his own skid marks.

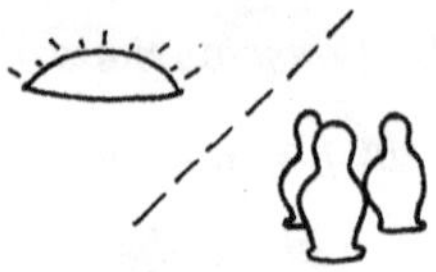

Forchet, Saskatchewan – *December in the mid 1940s, in the evening*

We heard this young lady's case earlier (in the pre-1947 section). The salient details are: a mysterious stranger showed up at a Christmas concert in a town where basically everyone knew everyone else. There was no evidence of how he got there or how he left. He was taciturn, never saying anything, but always smiling gently. He looked like Jesus Christ, and the girl telling the story obviously got an instant crush on him (should I say Him?). After the concert this person disappeared, but in the pasture next to the school was a huge brilliant Christmas star-type UFO with solid light-like points extending sharply off it. The bottom one's point touching the ground. *Hmm.* Jesus Christ attends a Christmas concert in Saskatchewan, and the concert goers are greeted with a grounded Christmas Star UFO as they leave? What's this all about?

Rialto, California – *fall 1960 or 1961, at night*

Okay. We're headed for weirdsville now. This is a complicated story but I'll do my best to unravel the sequence. A young man and his wife-to-be were returning to her house from the movies. They saw "some greenish-type objects" rise from the ground and zoom off to the west. He dropped her off and drove to his home. When he got there, the police were inside. Whatever it was, it concerned his brother, and his brother refused to talk about it. All that they could discover was that the brother had some kind of encounter.

Although the brother wouldn't talk until some USAF officers came out from Norton Air Force Base two days later, I'll say what he told them now, because it keeps the events in a more understandable storyline. Unfortunately, the UFO-related details were still not known by John's reporter, but one detail of interest did come out. The brother was returning home from the bowling alley when he had this UFO encounter, whatever it was. The travel time would normally be about three hours. Instead, he showed up at a friend's house (same distance) in a couple of "minutes". Why he went there he doesn't know, nor, obviously, how.

The next day the ultra-weirdness occurred. John's reporter got a friend and went to the location where the brother had said the encounter occurred. And...

> We parked the car, got out and went to a railroad track bridge. We went down to the tracks and as we came down to the tracks, we noticed that the... it was... the tracks were between two rows of eucalyptus trees. They ran east and west. And on the north side, all the branches of the eucalyptus trees seemed to be bare. It was a circular area of grass that looked like it had been whipped down and squashed and there was four cylinder-type-like landing pods outside of that circle. We heard birds chirping, the breeze was blowing. Before we went into the circle. When we went into this circle, there was no breeze, there was no birds. My buddy and I talked to each other without moving our lips, because I was away from him and it was almost like we were doing this mentally. When we stepped back out of the circle where the grass was mashed down, I again noticed the breeze and the birds and I turned to my buddy and asked him if he had experienced the same kind of feeling that I had.

The two friends got frightened, got in their car, and got out of there.

> We left the area, went back to my house, and we discussed what we had both felt while we were there. And it's... it's ... I don't know. It's an undescribable feeling. I mean I can still feel it today as I'm telling you this. I can feel it come through me. It's weird *[laughs]*.

Nervous laughter at the Doorway to Magonia?

Furnace Creek, California – *in the early 1970s, 2:30-3:00 A.M.*

I call this case "Don't Make the Ball Mad." Two young men in their twenties were walking back to the small house that they roomed in while working on the staff of a desert hotel. Their shift had ended at 2:30 A.M. They saw a cactus-like shape off the left side of the road, but nothing should have been there. Then there was a green flash, but no noise. Then it flashed again. And once more. This was getting freaky, when a red ball of light appeared about fifteen feet behind them. It floated at about head height and was the size of a beach ball. They ran.

The Ball followed. One man fell, cut his knee and scrambled up to follow the other into their house where they slammed and locked the door. The Ball stopped at the boundary of their yard and waited. It pulsed. When it grew large it would be transparent and faint. When it shrank it would get to the size of a grapefruit and blaze so brightly that the mountainside behind it lit up. The red light was so strong that it made all the dust in the inside air sparkle, adding to the eeriness.

Macho behavior gradually began to emerge as one guy said: "Why don't you go out and try to communicate with them? This is the chance of a lifetime." The other guy replied: "Why don't you? You're bigger than me." But actually what was going on in his mind was the impression that the Ball was impatient at them for not coming out, and was getting angry.

After four or five minutes of waiting, the Ball backed away. Across the road it began creating a vortex at the base of the hill.

> The rocks started rising into the air... They'd shake from side to side. There were hundreds of them [the largest about the size of melons]. They started going around in a circle, like it had complete control over them... Then the thing went way up in the air and it looked kind of like a tornado and it was all red... The only noise you could hear was this *clickety-clack*, *clickety-clack* when the rocks hit together.

Then the light blinked out, and everything crashed down the mountainside and onto the road. The Ball blinked back on again at the top of the mountain and meandered away. One guy spent a sleepless night peeking out from the covers. The other spent it staring out the window. The next day they both quit their jobs. Well, I suppose an encounter with Hell's Tornado is as good an excuse for unemployment as any.

Newark, Ohio – *sometime around the year 1981, 3:00 or 4:00 A.M. (and others)*

This is a case where there were traces left on the ground but their description is difficult to understand. I'll give you my best guess. Otherwise, the details of the case seem pretty clearly stated, although royally mind-boggling. A husband and wife were sleeping in their farmhouse when their dogs sent up a terrific row. They could hear some people talking outside their window, in some nonunderstandable "foreign" language. They didn't get up to investigate. The next morning they saw traces sort of like footprints outside. There were three sets of them of what seemed to be bipedal walkers, creating elongated (about twelve inches) "scratch mark" prints as they went. The prints were very "perfect" in form and stride, and went all the way to the fence line and through it.

And then...the couple began to have a "visitor" at night for about the whole next month. It was a "perfectly round white circle of light." Not a ball. It was about an inch and a half in diameter. The circle:

> Would start here and go clear around that wall. And it bugged me so much, it about drove me crazy. I put the blinds, the curtains, so that this light could not come in. But it did anyways, believe it. At night when the lights was out, you could see it. It would come in and go clear around this room and sometimes stay there. This happened probably about a month straight. I suppose this happened. It about drove me crazy. Because no matter where I put them curtains and how I pulled them, we still had that light going around that room. It moved around as though someone was looking the whole room over. It sort of moved slow. Clear around the room. Sometimes it even, well would stop, say in the middle of the room or past the middle, it would stop there and it would stay there for maybe hours. Yeah, just like a circle of energy light. I don't know what created it or how it come from, but...

John then asked how well they slept. "Not too well, believe it." Yes, we believe that for certain.

Bethel, Alaska – *the Friday before Labor Day, 1976, and following*

On an early morning, the witness heard a very high-pitched whine, and looked out onto the tundra where a small (two to three feet in diameter) white beach ball seemed moving in the air close to the ground. After awhile it tilted so that you could see that it was a disk with a rotating "platinum-shiny" area in the middle. Then the object arced upwards, then back down and seemed to just disappear into the ground. As soon as it entered the ground, the sound stopped. On inspection there was no sign of any ground markings.

Following this incident by about a month, the same witness had a little dog on the porch facing this area. She went inside for a couple of minutes and the dog wandered off. The witness immediately began to search for her, following tracks in the fresh snow.

> It was snowing. And her little track went out there and she just disappeared... she weighed maybe five pounds max. So possibly some owl or something could have... but there wasn't, you know, any other disturbance in the snow.

Since these events, the witness feels that she has had a few very unusual light-projecting experiences which result in vivid dreams or out-of-body experiences. The content of these experiences is difficult to describe. Here are some of her words:

Now, this is what really gets weird. [Uh, oh. We're in for it, now.] I know this sounds crazy, but I call these my red light experiences. I have no explanation.

> I am a nocturnal person. I stay up and I like to be by myself in evenings and I like to read and have time to myself, when everybody else has gone to bed. And I had been up reading and it was probably somewhere around 1:00. And I was getting tired, so I have his little ritual and I would always do when my kids were younger. I would turn out the lights and we always had, even to this day, had little night-lights in the house, like in the hallway and the kids could see to get to the bathroom and so forth. I would go back to their bedrooms and make sure, you know, they were tucked in and kiss them goodnight while they were sleeping and so forth. And then I always came in, because, not wanting to wake my husband up, I'd get undressed in the dark. Well, it was kind of odd because as I was going down the hallway, now this is difficult to explain, it was like I could see a red light. But it's not a red light that's outside, but it was like it was coming from within me. You know, when you look at the sun, and there's a bright light, and then you close your eyes and you can still see that. This was that kind of a deal, only it was red.

I had had no bright light that was on. I mean I had been kind of walking around for a little bit in the dark and getting ready for bed. And it kept growing and getting larger and larger and larger, so where everything... I mean, it was a very deep, deep red... until it was like it filled the whole room. And I was in the bedroom and I was getting undressed, and I'm saying: "This is weird. What is this?" I mean, there's this red light, but it's like it was coming from

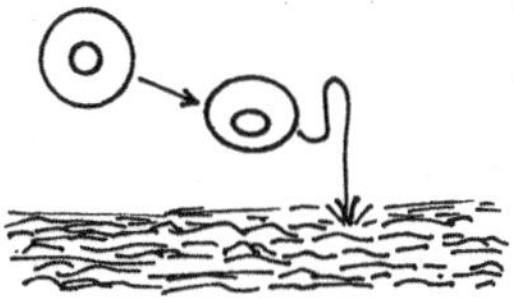

within me. And so I was... not like I was scared or anything, but I was... not confused, but wondering: "What is this weird thing that is happening? That I'm seeing. It's red." So I went ahead and got into bed and I thought about... my husband was asleep, and I thought about waking him up. And I didn't. But I had this feeling. It's like "let it go and see what happens." So that's what I did. I just laid there. After I laid down, even a minute or whatever, the next thing I knew... and this is kind of like an out-of-body experience... I really don't know what to call it, it was really weird.

I had the feeling of movement, and there were these enormously huge objects that were like suspended in space, that were all around me. And they were very bright shining. They were all different kinds of geometrical shapes and forms. I can't begin to explain to you what they looked like. They were just beautiful; I've never in my life seen anything like it before. But they were immense. And I have a feeling like it was an invisible corridor that I was moving down. I remember saying to myself at the time: I wonder what it is that they want?

So, dear lady, do we.

And, I guess in the spirit of disclosure I have to admit: I don't care how wild it is, I can't help liking this case a lot. So, perhaps ensuring my own ultimate certifiability, I say thank you for glimpses into a hopeful expanded Universe. Even if it doesn't turn out to be real. Or, after all this, what does that mean anyway?

The coast near **Stockton, California** – *February or March 1974*

Last report for this section. Let's come back down from the Clouds of Oz and relax with a little good ol' fashioned incredible conspiracy. In the seventies the witness was a member of the 12th Coast Guard district, was an officer, and in charge of training personnel to operate craft in difficult sailing conditions. He was in his office one day and was approached by people from the federal government: "These two gentlemen came from Washington in their street clothes, and they were not joking." They said that they were interested in a cave along the coast out of which ran a subterranean river into the ocean. The water issuing from the cave was rapid (about 25 knots), and the sailing would be tricky. Therefore, since he was the sailing trainer, he was the man for the job. He was to pick a locally trained crew, take light sailing craft (motorized), and go into the cave to explore. But why?

> Because they were having a great deal of UFO activity coming in and out of that cave. Much of the UFO activity in the western area out there was coming—they felt was connected with this cave. Coming from subterranean sources of some sort.

What was his response to this outlandish request and explanation?

> This really changed my attitude on UFOs. I knew exactly they were real. I knew the government knew it. I knew they were ordering me to go after them, but at the same time I said, "What are you going to do if I don't?" They said, "Well, there's not really a whole lot that we can do to you. Because we're not sure what's going on and we just would like you to help us find out. And I refused to go.

Ladies and gentlemen, what do we do with stories like this?

Section 42:
Love it or leave it

So, after all our journeying into the Ufological Unknown there are still a few reports that I think are worthwhile to share. They are (sort of) "what's left." Each of them has something very odd, probably incredible, and possibly having nothing (really) to do with UFOs—but maybe not. You'll be your own judge. Love them or leave them. As usual, we'll start softly and get weirder.

Fulton, New York – *summer 1967, predawn*

A boy was sleeping in his home when he was awakened for no reason that he recalls. There at the foot of his bed were two (possibly three) figures. They weren't like normal physical beings, seeming rather to be mere outlines of creatures. They never moved. As he stared at these outlines, the air above him became filled with "leaves" of electricity, which began falling downward on him and the bed. Ultimately, as this went on, he fell back asleep. John asked him why he didn't believe that this was just a dream? He said that the next morning he and his friends got together to play in the field behind his house and discovered a fifteen- to twenty-foot diameter circle of depressed and slightly browned grass.

The desert near **Tucson, Arizona** – *in the 1980s, daytime*

(A secondhand story, but with odd elements) The person who reported this to John knew the individual involved as a friend for twenty years. The individual was a school teacher and a photographer. He liked rambling about in the desert and taking pictures of ghost towns, Indian ruins, etc. One day he met his friend for lunch and showed him a picture from his last outing. In the shot there was what looked like an alien creature, standing about eight feet away. The photographer said that he had been hiking down around Ruby, Arizona, in some canyon. He heard an odd sound—something *swished* the air—but nothing more. Then twenty minutes or so later, he saw movement in the rocks. A small creature appeared, four to four and a half feet tall, in a dull, silver-metal skintight suit. He got off one picture, and the creature began scurrying away. The man chased after, but was outrun.

Back in Tucson, he developed the film, and the one picture was just fine (for a change in ufology). He showed it to his friend, but was worried about the implications for his life (publicity, etc.) if he made it public. He decided to go to visit a relative in San Diego, and discuss it. When he returned, he told his friend that his brother had recommended selling it to the *National Enquirer* for big bucks. His friend tried to talk him off that. The photographer was worried about any public course of action. Shortly, he took another trip to his brother's. The friend has never seen him since, and has had no contact of any kind.

The house went into disrepair, yard cluttered, mail piled up. Finally, it was sold. The picture has never appeared anywhere in print.

Near **Akron, Ohio** – *sometime in 1967, in the afternoon*

In a rural area outside of town, a lady was sitting and carving walnut wood into forks and spoons for serving salads. She cut herself, rather badly. One of the tendons on her left hand was showing through the cut, and her neighbor wanted to take her to the hospital. This is a tough lady, however, and she said, no, that her husband was coming home soon and she could wait until then to go. So she crudely stopped the bleeding, put ice cubes on her hand near the cut, and lay back on the davenport in her living room. In a few minutes, a beam of very pure white light ("It was just like what they call the laser beam now.") came from outside, across her front porch, into her living room, and onto her hand. The beam played along the two-inch cut from her left thumb to her wrist, and, in an hour, when her husband got home, the tendons had retreated and no longer could be seen. Although the beam was gone, the cut continued to rapidly heal, and by morning all you could see was a small scar. "No, by morning you couldn't even tell it had been there."

That was the *good* hand story. Next the *Bad Hand.*

Near **Warren, Manitoba** – *dated unstated*

As Chris Rutkowski said when he told John this story: "This one stretches the imagination considerably." Amen, past the breaking point, perhaps.

Some young males (we're in trouble, already) were driving in their truck in an isolated area, and were passing alongside a swamp. Out of the swamp ascended a classic domed-disk UFO. It rose slowly, but disappeared at high speed. On the surface of the swamp water beneath it, there seemed to be a yellow, foam-like substance in a roughly circular pattern. They decided to go home, get their wader boots, and come back. Which they did, taking only about fifteen minutes to do so. The foam was gone, but they waded in anyway. Near the center of where they guessed the UFO had been they found a sealed plastic bag. Inside you could see what looked like a mummified hand (four fingers and a thumb).

For some reason, this brought to mind the legend of the Monkey's Paw, sort of a talisman of evil or bad fortune. They took the bag back to their truck and decided to go home. The truck started but then, with "terrible gasping noises" stalled and would not go. Their radio began going on and off. They immediately accused the Monkey's Paw of these difficulties, and threw the bag away. Upon which, the truck started up without problems, and they drove off, one presumes rapidly, with a world-class case of the heebie-jeebies.

I guess those ufonauts were dumb enough to take the Monkey's Paw on board, but didn't want to become another Roswell, so they jettisoned it in a Canadian swamp... a reasonable hypothesis, don't you think?

Carolina, Puerto Rico – *October 1974, at night*

Folks, this reporter was obviously a real character. His story is over-the-top enough on its own, but I wanted you to know that his transcript is unusual in that he's obviously enjoying telling his tall tale (perhaps too much so).

This is a story of a guy who had a neighbor, who, although a big, strong individual, was easy to spook. So the fellow telling John this tale was fond of rattling him. The neighbor had been reading a newspaper story about Close Encounters, and so this fellow began ragging him that UFO people were going to come down and take him away. He stood in front of him in the middle of the street, arms and eyes raised, and shouted at the sky: "Hey You! If you really *do* exist, come down and show to this guy that you really do exist." All of which made the neighbor mad and him happy.

That evening, as he was watching television, a small light entered the room and began cavorting ("joking") about. Our human joker wasn't amused: "Hell. The goddamn dead people, the spirits are fooling tonight." He turned the television off and left the room. It was dark in his house (except for the joking light). When he got to his room, the whole room was lit up. Then he saw "two little guys" at his room's doorway. "Bigheaded guys; midget-type boys." No ears, slit mouth, point-for-a-nose. Eyes? "Round, like very white with a dot. They remind me of Humpty Dumpty." They spoke to him via a pink "microphone" with a pulsing light. They had uniforms and a front buckle which contained little lights.

The conversation was ironic in that the beings were berating him (the joker) for not wanting to go with them on a UFO trip. He argued that he was not interested—saw all about space already when he was in school. Then, diabolically, to get them off his back, he showed them his friend's house from the window and said: "Go to my neighbor's house. He's the one who wants to go." Meanwhile, our brave joker had been trying to wake up his wife and son, and both of them were sleeping soundly. The beings approached closer, and one passed a hand over him, and he began seeing "something like a movie" about things in his world. They asked him about specific items, one of which was a real-time view of his neighbor and wife in bed. They asked him to go with them again, and he was adamant. They finally left. His wife promptly woke up, asked what-the-heck was wrong with him and pointed out that it was 5:00 A.M. He thought it should be about midnight or 1:00 A.M.

The next morning he saw his neighbor coming angrily over to his house with obvious malintent. He informed him that the joker had "sent him some ugly things that scared the hell out of him."

Three months later he was visited by children and his granddaughter. At 3:00 A.M. the little girl came into his room, woke him, and told him that little people had come and she was to tell him that they're all full up there right now and that they'll have to give him a trip later.

I guess a joke can get way out of hand.

Landers, California – *summer 1987 or 1988, at night*

John began the interview with: "A gentleman who would rather not be identified"... uh, oh; and the location where this occurred? "It's called Giant Rock" ... uh, oh, squared. "And there was a lot of confusion around in the area." As Mr. Spock would say: that much, at least, is certain.

Our witness was out in the desert with at least two adult friends and at least two children. "I saw some lights in the distance but didn't think anything about them." He and one of the boys had wandered off down a ravine. "We were warned that there were people out there that weren't too nice. We were kind of just watching because you never know what kind of nuts are out in the desert." *Hmm.*

Jeeps came in their general vicinity; they ducked down behind rocks. The jeeps kept circling the big rock. And left. Apparently. "It was pretty scary having all those jeeps around. You don't know if they're the government, you don't know who they are. They could be a bunch of nuts out there, shooting at people or whatever." Somewhere in this episode of dodging jeeps, the boy leaves and our witness is left alone. Maybe.

> So the next thing I know, I start walking around and it's kind of...you know, fuzzy, but I do remember kind of feeling a shift especially in the air. There was a shift in the air pressure. That I do know, for a fact. So after that was the occurrence. Something came around. I couldn't explain it. It was like footsteps. I could hear them. I knew it was small and it was kind of, it wasn't all physical, and that's about it. It started walking towards me. I know there was more than one of them. And I could hear them more than I could see them. More like, it was in sand, so I was hearing this *tchh-tchh* like that. And I couldn't quite get away.
>
> Well, something hit me in the arm and it was rather painful and so I started to run but it felt like it was in slow motion, like I couldn't quite run. And the next thing I remember I was walking back up. My hand was still burning, my left hand. And I went up to my friend and I said: "My hand's burning." And so it kept burning and burning and burning. And suddenly it star...there was, I don't know how to explain it, it was like a pressure inside, it felt like something was in there, I don't know how to even explain it, but it was like a ball. And it went up my arm and went up further and then went into the heart area. It felt like...and just exploded. And I was in extreme pain during this whole time. After the explosion, I turned totally green, glowed green.

Revenge of the Little Green Men? Well, this whole business was rather unpleasant for everyone, especially our story's hero, who was in convulsions with burns on his hands, knees, feet, and especially fingertips. Until the ball of fire (or whatever it was) exited his body (backwards out his left arm and hand as it had arrived), his "friends" weren't overly supportive.

> Because I went into convulsions and everything. It was rather painful and my friend thought I was demon-possessed *[laughs]*. The other one was going: "Oh my God, leave him here!" You know, and so...we went to Denny's.

Denny's is a national restaurant chain, so it all worked out in the end. The witness went on to inform John that one of his friends has a friend whose father works for the CIA, and he told her not to go out there. "Which makes me think that they probably know who we are, but I'm not sure. And I don't want to find out." Also:

> He told her that there are some things that they're doing out there, that people shouldn't go out there, if they're not prepared. All I know is one thing, that whatever is out there shouldn't be played with. You shouldn't go out there.

John asked: Have you gone back? "Many times."

The Upper Peninsula of Michigan, *near* **Calumet** – *1954 or 1955, daytime*

A young girl, age ten or eleven, was walking home from the store when a huge balloon-like UFO with jagged thorn-like edges came at her from the

local school ground. It glowed and flashed with red and blue light. The UFO "tried to grab me. I was running into the house whiter than a sheet. I couldn't get over it for three or four days." The UFO was bad enough, but she might have gotten over that. After all:

> In Upper Michigan, you see them every once in a while. They go dive into the lake. The oar boats see them dive into the lake and come out of the lake. In Lake Superior.

[Actually, folks, this is a very commonly heard comment by lakeside Michiganders.] The problem is that the UFO, or a least some persons associated with it, won't leave her alone. They continue to bother her. The problem comes in the form of persons, who "look like you and I… whenever I'm alone, they try to bother me."

She feels that somehow related to all this she's become psychic, able to have premonitions of volcanos, earthquakes, air disasters: "You name it. I know about three or four days before." And, as a last insight, this: "They live in North Dakota, one of the Badlands in North Dakota, inside of a mountain. UFOs. And they come out at certain times, and they do it at night."

John asked how she knew this. "A lady told me on a bus."

John: Really? How'd she know?

"She's from one of the places from there."

John: Why do you believe her?

"Because of certain things she said, you know, I understand those things. (And) because as soon as she got off the bus, she disappeared, *phuuu*, like that."

Near **Ashland, Oregon** – *1967 and/or 1968*

In the sixties there was a little fad called "dream-sharing." Inspired by the cultural practices of the Senoi people of Malaysia (who share dream memories in the mornings as a family and community-building element of their culture), some Americans tried to do the same. One such family is the subject of this story.

One morning the mother reported an unusual, even unique, dream. A flying saucer landed in the backyard and the extraterrestrials wanted to take the family with them. She was upset not because of abduction but because she had on a terrible nightgown with a hole in it, and insisted on changing. The father thought this dream interesting because he apparently had the same one. He said that a flying saucer landed in the backyard; he was all for going, but she wanted to stop and change clothes. The daughter then said:

> Wait a minute, you guys. In my dream we're going somewhere and I couldn't go with you, because I didn't have the right equipment. It was these flying saucer people, and they wouldn't take me, but they did take my cat.

None of the three family members could remember anything else from their shared dream, but it was an interesting experience and stuck in their heads. But then the kicker came, that put the whole thing over-the-rainbow. The husband was ill and he did not last for more than a year. He went into the hospital finally and passed away in 1968. On the night he died, a small child, a girl living next door, awoke and stared out the window. In the morning she told her mother that their neighbor had died. But how do you know that, her mother inquired. "Because I saw a flying saucer land in their yard."

Try to wrap your head around *that* one, folks. Because this story seemed to intersect UFOs, dreams, and death, I wrote Ken Ring, probably the world's leading authority on near-death experiences and author of an interesting book, *The Omega Project*, on these peculiar matters. Ken, who by-the-way is retired from NDEs and thoroughly enjoying life in San Francisco, was as flummoxed as I was to the possible meaning of such an event. So he preferred to believe that it didn't happen, and maybe most of the rest of us might, too.

Natchez, Mississippi – *summer 1958, prior to midnight*

This is a very strange case which was reported to John by the son of the editor of the local paper, and a prominent citizen at the time. Because of the availability of the editor's news item (given to John), and the straightforward nature of both it and the son's language about a follow-up to the story, I'm going to rest my pen and let them tell you about it in their own words. The editor's story:

At 11:20 last night my wife and I were watching the Jack Paar show. Suddenly she pointed across the living room. "What's that!" she said. I looked and saw a housefly buzzing past my nose. "A fly," I said, waving it off. She was on her feet by then and peering through the window. "No, this! Come quick!" What we both saw at that window I will never forget as long as I live.

A wide swath of orange light split the sky just above the horizon. Unlike a streak of lightning this phenomenon seemed to cut a gulch in the sky. In its great wide path it moved, slower than lightning, from left to right as far as the sky was wide. There are only fields behind our house, we are on a hill, and the view is completely unobstructed. Then this unholy light started from either end of the sky and joined in the middle.

My wife then ran to the front door to look at the other part of the sky. What we saw there made the sky light at the back seem like child's play. What we saw was our neighbor's house—twenty yards away—completely covered, top, sides, and bottom, in about a 12-foot cloud of orange light. The texture of this cloud was rough. It hung around the house for ten or fifteen seconds. It also played tricks with our depth perception, too, for the neighbor's house suddenly seemed not twenty yards away but ten, or less. It was as if the whole house wrapped in a thick cloud of orange smoke was set down just outside our front door. The cloud of light left, but we have no recollection of its leaving.

We then rushed to the back door again and a line of clothes in the backyard was brilliantly illuminated with white light. It disappeared after about ten seconds.

To paint the emotional overtones one feels at the sight of such an awful sight is close to impossible. If you can imagine the Red Sea opening up, you might come close. We thought of H-bombs of course. We thought of the end of the world.

By midnight it was over. I am just glad I had a witness.

As the son grew up, his parents told him the rest of the story, which (perhaps) the editor/father didn't dare include.

The follow-up is that in the house, there was a young girl living there. I think she was my age, three or four years old at the time. I was born in 1954. Shortly thereafter, I don't know how long a time, I think it was just a matter of perhaps hours or the

> next morning, apparently the young girl woke up and she started saying the word "baby" over and over, like: "ba-by, ba-by, ba-by, ba-by" and she couldn't stop. The girl became hysterical, still unable to stop. The parents didn't know what to do. They either called for an ambulance or they took the girl to the hospital. From then on, we don't know, but my parents found out the girl died. That same day. From this. Died. And they didn't tell me this for years because I apparently was friends with her and you know at three or four it would have been too traumatizing. Not really could have understood it at all. But later, the family—my parents would talk about this every so often, and they would mention it. Then I would get involved, asking questions. Then they finally said: "Well, you know, she did die." And that's all I know. My mother said she kept saying the word "baby" over and over and over and over.

Whatever this was all about, it's the place where ufological fun stops and we need to remember that we're grownups, and that life and death and real people are serious matters. One can only hope that the two halves of this story are only coincidentally connected.

Paxson, Alaska – *sometime in 1976, on a gloomy day*

A former Alaskan state trooper was telling John about how he and his coworker would try to catch up to a mysterious L-shaped array of three lights using snowmobiles. They never could do it. When he finished that report, he added the following, seperate incident, almost as an afterthought:

"This is something totally different... I don't know what to make of it, but I was on an emergency run in my patrol car." He was doing 80 mph; even on the dry snow his auto had good traction, and the road was empty. Suddenly a pulsing globe of light came directly at the vehicle. He jerked the wheel slightly, but the light swerved away at the last moment. Then it came at him again, again barely missing. And then again. And again, always in his driving lane. Thoroughly boggled, he pulled over into the empty left lane and drove on. Just then he roared around a curve and there was a moose in the road... in the right lane. And they missed the inevitable collision. "If I would have stayed where I should have been, I would have hit him. Dead center. I would have hit that moose and if you hit one it will kill you." And so what was that light?

> It was just kind of a—the way I describe it is it looked like it

> was alive. It didn't look like just a light shining. It looked like it was a pulsing, breathing type thing... Again, you know those long Alaskan nights, sometimes you imagine things, so I don't know... All I know is there's something out there that I don't know.

Amen.

So, with the state trooper's retelling of his little "Guardian Angel" light, that ends the phenomenology of John's cases. Hope that you enjoyed them as much as I did reading the transcripts. There are a few miscellaneous things left to be said in the next section, and then we're done, and can hope that someone else gets the energy and enthusiasm to do something like John did in the future, so that we can enjoy this sort of stuff again someday.

Section 43: Anticlimax

There are just a few other things from the conversations which I judge to be worth passing along: a little about USAF investigations, strange rumors, impacts on witnesses, odd behavior, why some things don't happen, and a few words from Allen Hynek and John.

Re: Wright-Patterson and Blue Book

A person who worked in both Area A (intelligence) and Area B (engineering tech) at Wright-Patterson told John that he had reasons to occasionally be with the Project Blue Book folks. This was in the last years of the Project in the late sixties. He was a computer guy involved with data analysis (often of uncorrelated aerial targets, once identifying a secret SR71 flight, for instance). He said that at Project Blue Book they had a set of UFO files which were basically "open to the public" (in the sense that someone outside the USAF might get special permission to see them) but that "the rest of the records were over in the 'FTD Book'," meaning that the really sensitive stuff was *not* at Blue Book. John asked him if there was more at FTD's central building than at Blue Book. "Oh, a great deal...orders of magnitudes." He then went on to describe FTD as a mainly underground facility with powerful computing capability.

Another person spoke to John about the early fifties, when he was serving (USAF) in the Lubbock, Texas, area. At that time, UFO officers, if they could, had to use special cameras to photograph a UFO sighting. If they succeeded, then they had to personally take the next flight to Dayton with the camera.

These two comments are two more data-bits which give the lie to the statements that the Air Force, and the government, didn't take UFOs seriously.

Re: MIBs

We've seen a case or two of mysterious questioners earlier. The name "Men-in-Black" is unfortunate because it gives one an excuse to place this in the goofy urban legend class of things. What we're really concerned with is the occasional entry of government into citizens' lives and consequent meddling with reports and information. Here's one more instance.

A husband and wife were playing around with a new video camera when by chance they spotted a UFO and were able to film it. They reported this to the government. At 6:00 A.M. the next morning government people arrived and confiscated the film. "Tell no one of this, and we'll return the film. We just want to study it." A week went by and the couple called for an update on their film, and no one would admit knowing what they were talking about, visiting the house, the film, nor anything. The film has never been returned.

Again, the government has no interest in UFOs.

Re: Government games

A son told John of this story that his dad told him. He was working at Edwards Air Force Base (1958) on bombers. He and five other people were asked to report to a building on the base. They were led in and shown what appeared to be parts of a spacecraft or flying machine spread out, and the remains of "men—something that could be men." The group was then led out of the area with the wreck and bodies, given paper and pencil and told to write down everything that they thought that they had seen. They were dismissed without explanation. What psychological game was USAF intelligence up to here?

Re: UFO Coverup Live

Pushing credibility far over the edge, John received this comment from an ex-serviceman who worked in military intelligence and had a Top Secret clearance. It regards the notorious Falcon/Condor secret-leaking business that was reported in the television documentary of the case name above: aliens living in U.S. bases and liking strawberry ice cream, that sort of thing. This gentleman was interested in UFOs and asked people of high rank at Fort Davis, Massachusetts, about the secret-leaking "birds." He was told that the information leaked was true. *Hmm.* I suppose that anything's possible. However, some of this sounds suspiciously like more government games, perhaps testing loyalties, trustworthiness, or even spy traps with a tasty baited hook.

Re: UFOs and emotions

We've read of emotional responses all over the map: from thrills and joys to terrors and paranoia. UFOs in other words "play close to the fire." In 1974, in New London, Connecticut, a young man spotted a silent, low UFO with a large number of lights, over a telephone pole. He was very frightened and ran in to tell his friends. As it turned out, they were in the backyard and had seen it, too. Everyone was excited but one person actually snapped. He became paranoid: "Well, you never know when they're watching you; they could be in your TV, you know." This person was ultimately hospitalized, and released on medication. The point here is: this is not just fooling around—not just *har-har-har* games for entertainment, and not something that the "government" should be fooling around with, either.

Re: UFOs and personal beliefs

For some people UFOs are just a fascinating diversion, but others seem driven to incorporate them deeply into their view of the universe or their religion. A woman told John of her experience with her brother. He claimed to have had an encounter with an alien whereupon he received telepathic communications. Whatever this was all about, it precipitated a nervous breakdown. His life restabilized, happily, but his sister became interested in UFOs herself, as she had her own UFO sighting with two girlfriends. When she visited her brother she wanted to talk about it, but he'd have none of it. He said: "Don't believe it; it didn't happen. It was there [his case, now] and it was real, but I don't want to discuss it further. I think it's of the Devil." He has now become very religious (probably meaning far-right dogmatic) and "doesn't want anything to do with this."

Once again: the subject plays close to the fire. Many of you know that the notoriously un-Christ-like Christian Evangelist, Pat Robertson, has stated that anyone having anything to do with UFOs (even sighting one) should be stoned (no kidding). On the other end of the spectrum, Billy Graham thought that they might be Angels, and Louis Farrakhan believes that Elijah Muhammad resides in a mothership over Mexico ready to blast Farrakhan's enemies when the time arises. World-class drug addict, Terence McKenna, believed that UFOs were:

> ...within us. It is the Soul of us... the Collective Unconscious, the Overmind... The UFO is an idea intended to confound science because science has begun to threaten the existence of the human species as well as the ecosystem of the planet.

Note that although you probably don't buy into the theologies of these guys, they are all (in their own way) very intelligent people. Yet look where UFOs have led them.

Re: Strange and deliberate ignorance

A gentleman who was a licensed private detective was working as part of the security force (actually a paramilitary team which hired out on jobs to protect company property during times of labor disputes). In this case the company was Boise Cascade and the area was about twenty miles south of De Ridder, Louisiana. Personally, he had been assigned to work in the town rather than out on the company property, but he got a change of assignment and went out there. This part of the job was analogous to military perimeter guard duty, complete with walkie-talkies and guard dogs. His first evening out there the following happened.

He and his partner (someone who had been doing this for a while) spotted something that looked like a "truck" with a lot of lights on it, but moving along the top of the tree line. It moved slowly, changed directions, and seemed to move the tops of the trees aside as it went. It was about two and a half times as big as a passenger van. Their vicious attack dog absolutely refused to go into the area. The new guy immediately called it in as a security breach. The other guy told him not to, and to back off. He said: don't go down there. The new guy was totally flummoxed. How could they not be calling this in? Two company vans with men arrived shortly due to his call. The veteran guy looked at one of the drivers and said: "I told him not to call it in. I told him not to say a word. I knew what it was and I wasn't going down there with him." Shortly afterwards, this veteran guy quit; said he was terrified.

What in the world is this all about?

Re: What are we dealing with?

We've seen cases where the event seemed to be random and we've seen cases where the event seemed to be staged. We've seen cases where the event seemed to be nasty, and we've seen cases where the event seemed almost caring. And, in many of these cases, the overt, gross, activities of the UFO don't need a lot of interpretation (i.e., there seems a minimum of subjectivity in the report). In this following case, the observation is pretty simple—you can (subjectively) make of it whatever you want. But I include it here because it's cute, and allows a point to be suggested.

A young man was driving in the evening on the interstate at the edge of Indianapolis, Indiana. He saw two spherical objects, the lead one going slower and the rear one trying to catch up. Which it did. They hovered together for about thirty seconds and began to move slowly. They reached a point where they were over a high school football game. And: they stopped.

To watch? They stayed there above the game for quite some time before moving off at high speed.

Now, did these UFOs really stop and watch the high school football game for awhile? It would be a very *human* thing to do—taking a break from the duties of the evening, or just having a little fun. The point is that sometimes the UFOs seem not to be particularly on the job. One wonders? Are we dealing with many different technologies, cultures, things? Are there many different agendas? Are attitudes "up there—out there—and beyond there" across the whole spectrum? Are there free-wheelers and rigid agents acting as parts of a machine? If there is more than one thing going on, it explains our diversity better on one level, and makes the mystery more difficult on another.

Re: Who are you going to trust?

Veterans of the ufological trade know that you can't trust the government on this, and the American public largely feels the same way about the government and large corporations and organizations, about everything, for that matter. We're living in a sad age in this respect. John felt that his trust in the reality of the UFO phenomenon was magnified greatly by standing there face-to-face with a real person telling their story. You get the same sense reading transcript-after-transcript. So, it ends up that who we trust are individual people, but not necessarily any one individual person. It's a paradox. That paradox also may have played itself out in a slightly different twist in the following case. A ufologist's nightmare? The *good* case by the *bad* witness?

Oshawa, Ontario – *August 27, 1988, 10:00 P.M.*

The witness was coming into work when a disk-shaped object rose over the GM parking lot. It was noiseless and self-luminous (glowing white). It hovered momentarily and then began gyrating in the air. "Gyrating" here means that the outer perimeter of the disk began to spin while the inner section remained stationary. The craft then blitzed away so rapidly that it left an after-image streak on his eyes as it left.

Well, fine so far: another fairly well-spoken witness giving a solid, conservative, and detailed sighting. Now the gentleman begins to speculate:

> It was coming from the area where there is a power line, leading from Pickering Nuclear Power Station to General Motors. I believe that they were just passing through and getting energy.

Well, okay, not a terrible idea, fine.

> But I think you might be interested in (knowing that) I think I was made to see that...because it hovered over the lights in the parking lot. So if I would have gone to tell somebody about it, they would think I was crazy or just seeing things. But I know that what I seen was real.

John wasn't sure how to follow that statement up, so he asked if the witness talked to anyone about the case. "With First Aid. I had to go there and get a sedative because I was all shook up." Okay. We're still with you on this. Then this: "And about a week later I found a *National Enquirer* and the owner died of a massive heart attack one week later. My story wasn't in the *Enquirer* but President Reagan's story of the UFOs over California when he was governor in 1974 was in that *Enquirer*." *Wha-aa?* John is boggled by this shift in what had been a perfectly normal UFO report, but gamely hung in there.

> My story was never verified by police or military people. But the next night there was an airplane from the Oshawa airport, flying in the same vicinity about the same time when I was coming in to work. And I don't know what he was looking for, but I believe that this UFO is directly related to General Motors Corporation. A huge multinational corporation, one of the richest in the world. And I believe these people are working at GM, extraterrestrials. And they got in there through Hughes Corporation and the CIA. And the CIA has a great deal of influence in Canada because they want to infiltrate the government and the local authorities through General Motors and to insure that their investment in Canada is stable. And I believe we have a little colony in this area of the country and I'm taking a chance telling you and I should warn you that my telephone is tapped, too. *[laughs]* If you were to go to ask my superiors anything, they would say I was drinking or something. That might just prove that (maybe one or two of them are flying around in those UFOs?).

John then ended the interview on the pretense that his tape recorder was malfunctioning. Well...*hmm*...what in the world have we got here? The whole front end of the interview was solid, reasonable, good ol' disk ufology. The back end of the interview rocketed out into Conspiracy Theory Land. One hypothesis: the whole thing is bunk. A skeptic naturally wants to immediately believe that. Another hypothesis: the case is good and the guy is probably also correct about GM harboring extraterrestrials (and I am just a naive academic ivory-tower inhabitant for not crediting the possibility). Okay, fine, but I think that there's another possibility. We have thousands and thousands of UFO cases. Some of them are bound to occur to people already immersed in conspiratorial paranoia, or substance abuse or mental disorder, or just loose story tellers: i.e., the good case with the bad witness. Almost certainly the famous Florida Scoutmaster case of 1952 was such a situation. So what do we do? Who do we trust? I believe that we look for corroboration, physical evidence, patterns, and we do *not* simply throw the case away.

Re: Taking a picture of a UFO

We've heard several cases involving filming UFOs in these files, and either something malfunctions, or the film is confiscated, or (what you'd really expect if you meditate on it) you can't really *prove* anything from it anyway. Still, skeptics gripe about there not being more pictures. One gentleman told John this:

> I get a kick out of the debunkers saying about people having pictures of it. I know myself at the time, I would have never took the time to take my eyes off of it, to look on the seat to get a camera, to take the picture of it. Because it's...you're so entranced by seeing the object, your mind like takes a break. I mean, it's just like the visual stimulation just completely occupies your mind. You don't have time for the rational, saying "Oh, I should have took a picture."

John, CUFOS' photography expert, replied:

> And this is one of the reasons we have difficulty finding good photography of these objects. Quite often people say they had a camera hanging around their neck or they had it on the seat beside them or just inside the house, and it never occurred to them to go get the thing until it was all over.

Thanks for making that comment.

Re: Well, I've never seen one!

After telling John of his case story, one guy, an Hispanic fellow and an ex-G.I. said: "People say, well how do you see them when I don't? Because you're not looking for them. You're looking for quarters and dimes on the street." Though a bit oversimplified our ex-soldier has a point. Many people's lifestyle, location, and behavior will make it highly unlikely that they'd even be in a situation to see a UFO. Looking down, not up. In a bright city, not the country. In their houses not outside. Asleep or in the bar somewhere, not looking at the sky past midnight.

Re: Our godfather

Allen Hynek gets the second-to-last words. We've already heard him from 1981 on Roswell, now these are a potpourri of other topics from the same era.

On the UFO phenomenon:

> It's characterized by the constant flow of reports from 130 countries. And what is most important is that we have many cases from highly responsible people. You finally get to the point where you say that something strange is going on, and I can't keep calling all these people liars. (And) if there are independent witnesses, you have quite a job proving that they all hallucinated.

Amen, Allen.

On the movie *Close Encounters*:

> We were all afraid that people were coming out and looking up at the sky, not having looked up in the sky much before, and see a twinkling star and say, *ah-ha*, a UFO. We sort of braced ourselves for that but that didn't happen. What did happen was the movie sort of made it more acceptable to talk about UFOs. Usually, you know you had your mouth washed out with soap if you used that dirty word UFOs, but here people were talking about it. So we began to get oldies but goodies.

On Pascagoula:

> I was down there in Pascagoula within 48 hours after it happened and examined and worked with Charlie Hixon and Calvin Parker. Calvin Parker afterward had a nervous breakdown but since then he's married and living a normal life. Charlie is...it has profoundly affected Charlie's life. He asked me, "Why me? Why did I get it...get picked?" And I pointed out that somebody's got to win the Irish Sweepstakes, you know. It doesn't necessarily mean you are somebody very special. A very good writer has written a very excellent account of that but they can't find a publisher. What happened later on? I maintain a telephone conversation with Charlie about every six months or so. Nothing drastic has happened.

On the Andreasson case:

I wrote the forward of that book. I wrote it only because of the credibility of the investigator. Ray Fowler over the years has been very dedicated and sincere. In fact, I was the one who first got that case. Betty Andreasson sent the letter to me and it kicked around in my desk for a long while, because I thought it was absolutely preposterous. It didn't make any sense. And then I was about to throw the letter in the wastebasket and then thought hold on. Ray Fowler is in that area. Maybe he would like to take a look at this. After hours and hours of hypnosis and so forth out came the book, *The Andreasson Affair*. I frankly don't know what to think of it myself. I still...it's an aspect of the phenomena that I don't like. I wish it didn't have it. Yet in science, you don't throw something out because you just don't like it. You have to accept that it's there. And it's not an isolated case. There are many of these so-called "psychological" cases.

Allen was asked if Betty's religiosity put him off the case.

No. Just because Betty Andreasson is highly religious herself shouldn't really have any bearing on it. It certainly would be logical for her to put the religious interpretation, but whether it would rule out whether something really happened or not, I don't think it would. Her interpretation would be highly colored by her religious beliefs.

On Erich von Daniken:

Certainly there are stories all through history of strange things having been seen in the sky. But I mentioned a little while ago the fast buck artists and I think Erich von Daniken is one of them. He'll probably try to sue me. But I'll quote Carl Sagan of *Cosmos* fame, who was asked on the Johnny Carson show once what he thought of the book, *Chariots of the Gods*. He said it's a unique book. It contains a higher percentage of illogical statements per page of any book this century.

On personally seeing UFOs:

Never had a close encounter. I don't know if I should be happy about it or sad. I suppose if I had a close encounter it might ruin my objectivity. But I have on two occasions seen something which certainly satisfies the definition of UFO. Obviously flying,

> obviously an object, and to this day in both cases the object has remained unidentified. But it doesn't mean that this was little green men from outer space.

To me, Allen's first remark on the cascade of UFO reports by solid, responsible people (and often multiple, independent witnesses) is the important one. To those of us who have made a commitment to really read many cases and taste the whole flow of UFO history, this is what builds up and becomes overwhelmingly evidential. Unfortunately, almost no one is willing to do this. Even the majority of people allegedly interested in UFOs know next to nothing about UFO history, nor have any depth anywhere in dealing with the phenomenon. So, it's a hard sell. To convince, one has to make a real commitment. To make a real commitment, one almost has to be convinced. Reading John's case files was one way to become convinced. Hundreds of cases of profound puzzlement—obviously unidentifiable, obviously flying, obviously objects. Were they all the result of lies and hallucinations? Allen certainly didn't think so, not even most of them—and neither do I. But how does one get anyone else to see it that way? One method is to get a friendly old UFO warrior to go around the countryside for almost a decade collecting grassroots UFOs, a saintly angel to transcribe all the tapes into readable hard copy, a foolish retired science professor to extract them and write a monograph, another saintly angel to type it all up, and the Fund for UFO Research to fund and print it. Then it's your job (which, if you've gotten to this page, you've done well).

And now, the respected position of the *Last Word* to our friendly old UFO warrior himself, John Timmerman.

> I've been doing this for about ten years and listening to people tell these cases. To begin with, I didn't use the tape to do that. I would take notes and hope that I'd remember the details, but I found that I was losing the flavor of reality that comes across when you have people speak in their own words. Saying their own things, but with the same emotional impact.

God bless you, John, for a job very well done.

Section 44:
Sighting locations

Alphabetic listing of sightings by cities, towns, and locations

Section 45:
The CUFOS UFO Exhibit

Locations the exhibit was displayed, listed by date and location.

	LOCATION	CITY	STATE	MONTH	DATES	YEAR
	The Original CUFOS UFO Photo Exhibit appeared in the following locations:					
01	Prestonwood Mall	Dallas	Texas	May	19 – 23	1980
02	Conestoga Mall	Grand Island	Nebraska	September	12 – 14	1980
03	Woodfield Shopping Ctr.	Schaumberg	Illinois	January	22 – 25	1981
04	Northridge Shopping Ctr.	Milwaukee	Wisconsin	March	18 – 21	1981
05	Assn Spiritual Developmt.	Horseshoe Bend	Arkansas	May	3 weeks	1981
06	American Mall	Lima	Ohio	June	20 – 21	1981
07	Public Library	Fort Wayne	Indiana	August	21	1981
	The First Free-Standing Exhibit design appeared at the following locations:					
08	CUFOS Scientific Conf.	Chicago	Illinois	September	25 – 27	1981
09	Northland Mall	Columbus	Ohio	May	30 – 31	1982
10	Dutchess Mall	Fishkill	New York	January	13 – 15	1983
11	East Towne Mall	Madison	Wisconsin	April	23 – 24	1983
12	Park Plaza Mall	Oshkosh	Wisconsin	April 30	to May 1	1983
13	Crystal Point Mall	Crystal Lake	Illinois	July	8 – 10	1983
14	Roanoke-Salem Plaza	Roanoke	Virginia	August	5 – 22	1983
15	Long Ridge Mall	Rochester	New York	August	26 – 27	1983
16	Southcenter Shopping Ctr	Seattle	Washington	October	6 – 9	1983
17	Trexler Mall	Trexlertown	Pennsylvania	October	28 – 30	1983
18	Shoppers Square	Reno	Nevada	May	4 – 6	1983
	The new display on Plexiglas panels appeared at the following locations:					
19	City Shopping Center	Orange	California	August 31	to Sept. 2	1984
20	Southcenter Shopping Ctr	Seattle	Washington	October	5 – 7	1984
21	Mesconi Convenion Ctr.	San Francisco	California	April	18 – 21	1985
22	Sangamon County Fair	New Berlin	Illinois	July	3 – 7	1985
23	Severna Park Mall	Severna Park	Maryland	October	18 – 19	1985
24	Southcenter Shopping Ctr	Seattle	Washington	April	4 – 6	1986
25	Midtown Plaza	Rochester	New York	June	12 – 14	1986
26	McAlister Square	Greenville	S. Carolina	Oct. 31	to Nov. 2	1986
27	Eden Mall	Eden	N. Carolina	January	16 – 18	1987
28	American University	Washington	Dist. Columbia	June	27 – 28	1987
29	Adrian Mall	Adrian	Michigan	July	9 – 12	1987
30	Amherst Center	Amherst	Nova Scotia,Canada	January	11 – 16	1988
31	Highland Square	New Glasgow	Nova Scotia, Canada	January	18 – 23	1988
32	Fundy Trail	Truro	Nova Scotia, Canada	January	25 – 30	1988
33	West End	Halifax	Nova Scotia, Canada	February	1 – 6	1988
34	County Fair	New Minos	Nova Scotia, Canada	February	8 – 13	1988
35	Highland Square	Moncton	New Brunswick, Canada	February	15 – 20	1988
36	Loch Lomond	St. John	New Brunswick, Canada	February	22 – 27	1988

37	Fredericton Mall	Fredericton	New Brunswick, Canada	Feb. 29	to Mar. 8	1988
38	Orillia Square Mall	Orillia	Ontario, Canada	March	14 – 16	1988
39	Senzar, Inc, Sheraton Airport Motel	Burlingame	California	April	16 – 17	1988
40	Arnot Mall	Horseheads	New York	June	15 – 18	1988
41	Ted Tufty Dodge	Sioux Falls	South Dakota	July	14 – 16	1988
42	Decatur Celebration	Decatur	Illinois	August	4 – 6	1988
43	Thruway Mall	Cheektowaga	New York	August	19 – 21	1988
44	National UFO Conf.	Cleveland	Ohio	September	17	1988
45	Richland Mall	Mansfield	Ohio	September	23 – 25	1988
46	UFO Conference	North Haven	Connecticut	October	8 – 9	1988
47	Carolina Mall	Concord	N Carolina	January	5 – 8	1989
48	Pierre Bossier Mall	Bossier City	Louisiana	January	27 – 29	1989
49	New Town Mall	New Philadelphia	Ohio	March	3 – 5	1989
50	Security Square Mall	Baltimore	Maryland	April	7 – 9	1989
51	New London Mall	New London	Connecticut	April	21 – 23	1989
52	Penn-Can Mall	Clay	New York	May	19 – 21	1989
53	Franklin Mall	Franklin	Ohio	June	2 – 4	1989
54	River Valley Mall	Lancaster	Ohio	June	9 – 11	1989
55	Pavilion Mall	Tukwila	Washington	June	16 – 18	1989
56	Indian Mound Mall	Heath	Ohio	July	21 – 23	1989
57	Lebanon Valley Mall	Lebanon	Pennsylvania	August	25 – 27	1989
58	Agana Shopping Ctr	Agana	Guam	September	2 – 4	1989
59	Station Mall	Altoona	Pennsylvania	September	15 – 17	1989
60	Indiana Mall	Indiana	Pennsylvania	September	28 – 30	1989
61	Lycoming Mall	Muncy	Pennsylvania	October	6 – 8	1989
62	The Pier Shopping Ctr	St. Petersburg	Florida	October	27 – 29	1989
63	Greenpoint Mall	Houston	Texas	October	27 – 29	1989
64	Mt Shasta Mall	Redding	California	November	10 – 12	1989
65	Rogue Valley Mall	Medford	Oregon	January	12 – 15	1990
66	Woodland Mall	Bowling Green	Ohio	January	19 – 20	1990
67	Neil Armstrong Museum	Wapakoneta	Ohio	January	21	1990
68	Town East Mall	Mesquite	Texas	April	5 – 7	1990
69	Cross Roads Mall	Greenville	Texas	April	20 – 22	1990
70	Tupelo Mall	Tupelo	Mississippi	May	6 – 8	1990
71	Penn-Can Mall	Clay	New York	May	19 – 21	1990
72	Cornell University	Ithaca	New York	June	8 – 9	1990
73	Plaza Las Americas	San Juan	Puerto Rico	August	13 – 18	1990
74	Kingston Centre	Kingston, Ontario	Canada	September	4 – 8	1990
75	Oshawa Centre	Oshawa, Ontario	Canada	September	11 – 15	1990
76	Market Place East	Philadelphia	Pennsylvania	October	25 – 27	1990
77	Wright State University	Celina	Ohio	February 20 – 22, March 1		1991
78	American Mall	Lima	Ohio	April	1 – 6	1991
79	South Side Savings Bank	Lima	Ohio	April	1 – 6	1991
80	North Park Mall	Oklahoma City	Oklahoma	April	18 – 20	1991
81	Sherwood Village	Regina, Saskatchewan	Canada	May 30 &	June 1	1991
82	Parkland Mall	Yorkton, Saskatchewan	Canada	June	3 – 8	1991
83	Swift Current Mall	Swift Current, Saskatchewan	Canada	June	10 – 15	1991
84	Fort Saskatchewan Mall	Fort Saskatchewan, Alberta	Canada	June	26 – 29	1991
85	Arnot Mall	Horseheads	New York	July	16 – 21	1991
86	El Con Mall	Tucson	Arizona	September	6 – 8	1991
87	Central City Mall	San Bernardino	California	September	19 – 22	1991
88	Omega Conference	North Haven	Connecticut	October	12 – 13	1991
89	Park Central Mall	Phoenix	Arizona	October	18 – 20	1991

90	Camillus Plaza	New York	New York	October	25 – 27	1991
91	The Sands Pavilion	Atlantic City	New Jersey	February	1 – 2	1992
92	Northland Mall	Sterling	Illinois	September	11 – 13	1992

A duplicate exhibit of the first Plexiglas 9-section unit was constructed in 1988. Later, both units were expanded to 10-section units to include panel numbers 19 and 20. In 1992, one unit was sold and placed on display at the International UFO Museum and Research Center at 400 North Main Street in Roswell, New Mexico 88202. In 1993, the second unit was sold to the town of St. Paul, Alberta, Canada, and placed on display in a special UFO museum and a new library there.

Section 46:

Bibliography

Recommended reading and contact information

There is a lot of bad information and poor scholarship out there on the UFO phenomenon, but is "the Truth out there" anywhere? When you have an unsolved mystery, it is difficult to say, but in my experience in this field there are some reading materials which are much more responsible and well grounded than others. I could not name all of them, but here are a few of the best.

1. Clark, Jerome. *The UFO Encyclopedia* (2nd ed. 2 Vol.) Omnigraphics: Detroit. 1988. This is the UFO reference masterwork. If you could only own one UFO library piece, this should be it.
2. CUFOS (Center for UFO Studies). *The International UFO Reporter.* 1976-present. The best edited and scholarly UFO magazine. See below (at end of Bibliography) for CUFOS' address.
3. CUFOS (Center for UFO Studies). *The Journal of UFO Studies.* 1989-2003. The field's only academic-quality research journal. Again, see CUFOS' address below if interested in back issues.
4. Emmons, Charles. *At the Threshold.* Wild Flower Press: Mill Spring, North Carolina. 1997. Wonderful, intelligent treatment of UFOs and their researchers vis-a-vis the sociology of science.
5. Fawcett, Lawrence and Barry Greenwood. *Clear Intent.* Prentice-Hall: Englewood Cliffs, New Jersey. 1984. Still the best book on the government document releases.
6. Haines, Richard (ed.). *UFOs and the Behavioral Scientist.* Scarecrow Press: Metuchen, New Jersey. 1979. Dick has written many good additions to our literature. This is a nice mix of scholars, wide-ranging in views and interests.
7. Hall, Richard H. *The UFO Evidence, II.* Scarecrow Press: Lanham, Maryland. 2001. Dick Hall in many ways is UFO history. Here he presents a Casebook (sort of a super-Timmerman Files) for the field.

8. Hynek, Allen. *The Hynek UFO Report*. Barnes & Noble: New York. 1997. This is Allen's version of the UFO casebook, originally written in 1977. Still interesting on phenomena and government activities.

9. Hynek, Allen. *The UFO Experience*. Henry Regnery: Chicago. 1972. The closest thing that ufology has to a textbook. It lays the groundwork for definitions, case types, approaches, and science.

10. Jacobs, David. *The UFO Controversy in America*. Indiana University. Bloomington, Indiana. 1975. It is a tribute to Dave's scholarly ability that this history is still as accurate and useful today as it was thirty years ago.

11. Jacobs, David (ed.) *UFOs and Abductions*. Kansas University Press: Lawrence, Kansas. 2000. Another rare example of a scholarly collection of writings, emphasizing abductions, but including history and sociology.

12. Keyhoe, Donald. *Flying Saucers are Real*. Fawcett Publications: New York. 1950. Still the best way (along with #13 and #16) of recapturing the true feeling of the phenomenon and the military at the "beginnings."

13. Keyhoe, Donald. *Flying Saucers from Outer Space*. Henry Holt: New York. 1953. An important historical book: a unique insight into the Pentagon and military responses to the rise of the phenomenon.

14. Randle, Kevin and Donald Schmitt. *UFO Crash at Roswell*. Avon: New York. 1991. The climactic book on the Roswell crash has not been written yet, but until it is, this presentation is the best overview.

15. Ring, Kenneth. *The Omega Project*. William Morrow: New York. 1992. Ken is the world's scholarly expert on Near Death Experiences. Here he creatively searches for links in consciousness phenomena which might lead to new ideas about some close encounters.

16. Ruppelt, Edward. *The Report on Unidentified Flying Objects*. Doubleday: Garden City, New York. 1956. The open-minded head of the USAF's Project Blue Book gives us a revealing inside story of it and the Pentagon in the 1952 era.

17. Sagan, Carl and Thornton Page (eds.). *UFOs: a Scientific Debate.* Cornell University: Ithaca, New York. 1972. Papers of the famous AAAS Symposium of 1969, featuring William Hartmann, Allen Hynek, Robert Hall, and, especially, James McDonald.

18. Vallee, Jacques. *Anatomy of A Phenomenon.* Henry Regnery: Chicago. 1965. One of Vallee's two masterworks (see also #19). This volume was so good even the Air Force put it (briefly) on their recommended reading list.

19. Vallee, Jacques and Janine. *Challenge to Science.* Henry Regnery: Chicago. 1966. Sort of "volume two" to the above. Cases, patterns, history, scientific method, technological hypotheses, solid intellectual stuff.

20. Vallee, Jacques. *Passport to Magonia.* Henry Regnery: Chicago. 1969. This is the UFO book which attempts to forge the link between UFO phenomena, folklore, and Forteana. [If you want to read where some of this inspiration came from originally, try: W. Y. Evans-Wentz, *The Fairy Faith in Celtic Countries.* Citadel Press: New York. 1990. (Original was published in 1911). This "case report" of fairy world phenomena will indicate why Jacques and others think that there is a larger mystery to be probed here.]

The J. Allen Hynek Center for UFO Studies

CUFOS

P.O. Box 31335
Chicago, IL 60631
(773) 271-3611

www.cufos.org

The Fund for UFO Research, Inc.

FUFOR

P.O. Box 7501
Alexandria, VA 22307
(703) 548-0405

www.ufoscience.org

Michael D. Swords
Author's biography

Michael Swords was born in E. St. Louis, Illinois, but spent most of his life growing up in West Virginia. He graduated from the University of Notre Dame in Chemistry, Iowa State University in Biochemistry, and Case Western Reserve University in the History of Science and Technology. Dr. Swords then taught Natural Sciences and Environmental Studies for thirty years at Western Michigan University. He is now retired.

He has been interested in anomalous phenomena for as long as he can remember, and witnessed a domed-disk sighting along with his brother (and several other people) in West Virginia in 1959. He has spent 20 years of scholarship and service with the Center for UFO Studies, writing over a hundred articles on the general area of mysterious phenomena, and editing the peer-reviewed *Journal of UFO Studies*. He has known, and liked, John Timmerman for all that time with the Center, and is delighted to help bring John's work to the public.

www.ingramcontent.com/pod-product-compliance
Lightning Source LLC
Chambersburg PA
CBHW052033090426
42739CB00010B/1896
* 9 7 8 1 9 3 3 6 6 5 5 3 5 *